Emperors of the Turf

Also by Jamie Reid

Easy Money

Emperors of the Turf

A colourful and entertaining picture
of the international flat-racing industry

JAMIE REID

MACMILLAN
LONDON

This book is dedicated to the memory of my grandmother, Marie Tanner, and her bookmaker, Charles Allen.

He had never been to a racetrack before . . . and it was interesting and exciting. There was the crowd, and the little windows, and the smell of horses, of women, and of money – most of all the money, which seemed to have a clean, outdoor smell to it, like a crap game in an open field.

Walter Tevis, *The Hustler*

The breeding of thoroughbreds, the marketing of thoroughbreds and the racing of thoroughbreds are not for the faint or weak of heart. We have a highly competitive industry . . . but it also has its moments, both emotionally and economically, which are unsurpassed in any other sport.

James E. 'Ted' Bassett III, President of Breeders Cup Ltd and President of the Keeneland Association 1970–86

Copyright © Jamie Reid 1989

First published 1989 by
MACMILLAN LONDON LIMITED
4 Little Essex Street London WC2R 3LF
and Basingstoke

Associated companies in Auckland, Delhi, Dublin, Gaborone, Hamburg, Harare, Hong Kong, Johannesburg, Kuala Lumpur, Lagos, Manzini, Melbourne, Mexico City, Nairobi, New York, Singapore and Tokyo

A CIP catalogue record for this book is available from the British Library.

ISBN 0–333–47125–3

Typeset by Wearside Tradespools, Fulwell, Sunderland
Printed and bound by WBC Ltd, Bristol & Maesteg

Contents

List of Illustrations

Introduction

When I was a teenager I used to spend as much time as I could hanging out in a deliciously seedy betting office, which was situated roughly equidistant between a record shop and a cinema in a quiet back street in the not generally riotous town of Tunbridge Wells. The betting office was presided over by a cheery little man who regularly wore a check three-piece suit and a spotted bow-tie. He looked exactly like William Hartnell or Sydney Tafler in a post-war Ealing movie. His wife was a luscious and sexy brunette, some years younger than himself, who persisted in wearing stiletto heels and beehive hair right on into the late 1960s.

I found the atmosphere in this family-run shop completely intoxicating. It was a combination of things. The cigarette smoke, which wasn't drearily disapproved of in those days. The nasal tones of the Exchange Telegraph commentator. The cut-out pages of the *Sporting Life* pasted around the walls and announcing the details of Lester's latest classic winner or Scobie's Brighton treble. The occasional glimpses of large numbers of crumpled five- and ten-pound notes. The seductive rustle of the bookie's wife and the fluttering, nervous thrill of backing a racehorse and listening to it actually win.

The wretched, mealy-mouthed characters who were technically in charge of my education, regarded my presence in this paradise, especially in school uniform, as some kind of moral outrage. Their pious indignation and Rotarians' wrath merely had the effect of making me decide that anything they objected to that violently had to be worth passionately embracing for the rest of my life.

Part of the joy of actually going racing is that you're surrounded by such an extraordinary mixture of people. Toffs and Spivs. Villains and Swells. Brasses and Classy Ladies. All of whom appear to have no difficulty whatsoever in being at Lingfield or York on a mid-week afternoon, knocking back the Bollinger and throwing their money away on beautiful thoroughbred racehorses.

English flat racing has managed to retain its many historic, diverse and contrasting venues, which range from the great flat heath of Newmarket to the switchback gradients of Epsom Downs. Over the last fifteen years though, the centuries-old sport has also become an industry, and for the leading protagonists the stakes today are immensely high and truly international in scale. Yet thanks to the obsession of one or two major players, like Robert Sangster and the Maktoum brothers of Dubai, the quality of racehorse competing in England each summer has probably never been higher. Most ordinary punters couldn't begin to afford even a hair in the tail of a modern Derby winner but they are still hooked on the spectacle and suspense of finding out annually which are the best and fastest horses.

American racing is often looked down upon by English conservatives. Partly for its supposed lack of tradition and partly for the controlled 'medication' programmes, i.e. drugs, that are tolerated in almost all states outside of New York. In spite of this serious controversy, turf and dirt-track racing in America is, at its best, fast, furious and terrifically exciting. What's more, many of its leading personalities are accessible and flamboyant figures far removed from some of their English counterparts, who often seem depressingly incapable of breaking out of the standard uniform of top hat for Ascot, trilby for Newbury and flat tweed cap and Husky for the Newmarket September sales.

In keeping with all the other commercial developments that have originated across the Atlantic in the last quarter of a century, flat racing's most spectacular occasion in the late 1980s is no longer the Derby at Epsom or the Prix de l'Arc de Triomphe in Paris. It's America's new 'ten-million-dollar championship', the Breeders Cup. The Cup may have been originally devised as a boost for the American racing and breeding industry but in five short years it's become a major attraction for the Europeans too and in the words of *Timeform*, the most durable and respected of formbooks, it now offers the thoroughbred 'the biggest stage of them all'.

This book is partly an attempt to account for some of the characters and events that have helped to shape the flat's new commercial order. It's also an attempt to bring to life for the non-racing outsider some of the atmosphere, humour and excitement of the turf on a handful of its most lavish and important days in Europe and America. Most of the events described took place over a twelve-month period between the fourth Breeders Cup race-meeting at Hollywood Park, Los Angeles in November 1987 and Breeders Cup Five out in Louisville, Kentucky in 1988. *Emperors of the Turf* is not intended to be a comprehensive record and no especial significance is claimed for this particular racing cycle. By the time the book is published most of the winners and losers from this period will be part of history. The races are simply a key into the obsessional worlds of the people who own, train and ride the best and most expensive horses and into the equally daft and obsessional world of those of us who follow their fortunes from track to track.

People say, 'Why romanticise a racehorse?' Why not? In many cases the thoroughbred often seems to be a far nobler creature than a human being. They carry our hopes, our dreams and our fantasies. How many times have we wished, metaphorically, that we could give the whole gang of bank managers, bailiffs, tax inspectors and prosecuting counsel a ten-length start and still cut them all down with a devastating burst of speed inside the final furlong?

We may never be as light on our feet as Nijinsky . . . but at least we can remember him winning the 1970 Derby.

I should like to thank the following for their generous support and co-operation; Breeders Cup Ltd, the Budweiser Corporation, Claiborne Farm, Coolmore Stud, Bob Egan, Marjorie L. Everett, Gainesway Farm, Jimmy Gluckson, Marten Julian, The Keeneland Association, Jim Marsh, Brian Molony, Phoenix Park Racecourse, Carl Schmidt, United Racecourses, Stanley Vereker, R. James Williams, Windfields Farm, Churchill Downs Racecourse, Louisville, Kentucky and Hollywood Park Racecourse, Los Angeles, California.

I should also particularly like to thank my editors, Kyle Cathie and Tom Weldon. Without their help this book would not have been possible.

1 : The Road to Hollywood Park

Saturday morning was hot, sunny and glaringly bright. You could feel the power of the sun as it hit the tarmac boulevards and bounced off the windows and wing mirrors of the enormous automobiles rolling up to the front entrance of Hollywood Park. Chevrolet, Buick, Cadillac, Thunderbird, Dodge. Mercedes, Porsche, Ferrari, Rolls-Royce. A steady flow of deluxe traffic waiting to be valet-parked by the red-jacketed staff. There are no grass car-parks outside an American racecourse. No strips of mud presided over by a few middle-aged men with white coats and wheezing coughs. The Hollywood car-park is constructed on an epic scale like the back of some enormous suburban shopping-centre supermart.

The suited and lipsticked smart set were out in force and all of them, it seemed, heading in under the canopied awning of the Turf Club entrance. (Which is not the kind of club in which Lieutenant-Colonel Sir Piers Bengough, the Queen's Representative at Royal Ascot, would automatically feel at home.) A group of excited young English racegoers, all clutching three-day-old copies of the *Sporting Life*, looked on in thrilled amazement as a trio of fabulously sexy, richly bejewelled and no doubt frequently married Beverly Hills ladies swept past them in a cloud of scented indifference. As enthralling and financially about as unobtainable as a potential Breeders Cup-winning racehorse.

For those without prepaid seats in the top part of the stand, the most expensive admission price on the day was the $7 entry fee to

1

the Cary Grant Pavilion or Pavilion of the Stars. This is even cheaper than the Pesage prices for the Prix de l'Arc de Triomphe at Longchamp and less than a third of what it would cost to enter the Members' Enclosure on an equivalent day's racing in England. The pavilion is a concrete and glass tower and was one of the 'innovations' built by the racecourse executive for the original Breeders Cup meeting in 1984. Inside the foyer an orchestra was playing Count Basie and Duke Ellington while up on the mezzanine floor, just in front of a huge display of Breeders Cup souvenir merchandise, a man who wasn't Frank Sinatra was tripping his way through 'Chicago', 'High Hopes' and 'Come Fly With Me, Come Fly, Come Fly Away'. At Epsom on Derby Day you have to pay a pound for a racecard. On this Breeders Cup day the racecards were free and every racegoer, be he Sheikh Mohammed or a cab driver from Oxnard, was also being presented with a complimentary Breeders Cup baseball cap as well.

Photographs of Edward G. Robinson, Ingrid Bergman, Gary Cooper and Archie Leach himself were all around the walls and stairways of the Cary Grant Pavilion. Some of the racing fans carried on up to the Sky Terrace and restaurant on the top floor. Others spread out through the bars and eating areas and down along the rails. There are an abundance of *pari mutuel* windows as well as places to eat and drink on each floor of an American racecourse grandstand. The food concessions at Hollywood Park are quick, cheap and by no means all of the junk food variety. American hamburgers and hot dogs compete with Italian pizza, Chinese pancakes and sweet and sour ribs, Mexican tacos and enchiladas and even dishes of Polynesian curry and fish stew. Giant Budweiser signs catch the eye at every turn and every racegoer seems to be clutching a *Daily Racing Form* in one hand and a huge carton of chilled beer or a little opaque tumbler of ice and club soda with Scotch or bourbon whiskey in the other.

When you arrive at some ordinary race-meetings throughout the season you feel a comfortable enough sense of anticipation but your heart is hardly in your mouth. You know that you are about to partake in an event of great enjoyment and importance to yourself but probably of little significance or interest to most people outside the frankly enclosed race-track community. When you arrive though at a few select occasions in the racing year – for the Derby at Epsom and now at this monstrously hybrid Breeders Cup – you immediately sense an entirely different level of nerve-tingling tension and apprehension. You know that momentous events are going to take place over the next four hours and that you, and thousands of others like you have gathered like members of a religious congregation to be present at one of those decisive moments in the turf calendar, when horse-racing takes its pulse in full view of the world and beneath the beady and self-interested eye of every leading player in the industry.

Standing down by the running rail at Hollywood Park an hour before the start of the fourth Breeders Cup the atmosphere felt exciting all right but it also seemed slightly intimidating and alien. Outside of the Derby you rarely see as many as 57,000 people at an English race-track. How would English and French racehorses, used to thick green grass, rain, grey skies and polite applause around the unsaddling enclosure, cope with this strange arena? With its flat, sharp track? Its heat, huge crowd and jet planes roaring by overhead?

The choice of a Californian location, with all its attendant associations of razzmatazz and real or supposed glamour, was a by no means insignificant element in the planning and marketing strategy of the men who originally dreamed up racing's $10 million 'championship'. Breeders Cup Ltd is actually comprised of some of the richest and most powerful breeders and stud farm owners in America. Emperors of the Blue Grass. Lords and rulers of the old Kentucky Home. Its first list of officers included Charles Taylor, son of E.P., the man who owned and bred the king himself, Northern Dancer; Leslie 'Big Daddy' Combs II and his son Brownell; Brereton C. Jones, a Lieutenant-Governor of the state of Kentucky. Seth Hancock, son of Bull Hancock and master of Claiborne, the most famous stud farm in the world (Seth was suspicious of the concept at first but he's in with them now); and at the centre of them all, the fifty-seven-year-old breeding aristocrat John R. Gaines, whose family's Gainesway Stud Farm, just off the Paris Pike a few miles north east of Lexington, is the home of more than thirty commercial stallions including such élite names as Blushing Groom, Riverman and Northern Dancer's son Lyphard, himself the sire of the champion European racehorse of the eighties, Dancing Brave.

Throughout the late seventies and the early to mid eighties, the American horse-breeding industry went through a boom of spectacular proportions. Such was the demand from European-based buyers in particular that the prices for yearlings and stallion shares and syndication fees soared to unprecedented levels. Yet with the exception of one-off events, like the Kentucky Derby and the other two Triple Crown prizes, race-track attendances in America were not great. TV coverage was often minimal and horse-racing's image in the eyes of the healthy, sports-loving American public was rather seedy and disreputable: a pastime for winos, gamblers and other degenerates, not a suitable activity for the true competitor. Gaines and the rest of the Good Old Boy network appreciated more keenly than most that this image had to be reversed and American racing upgraded as a TV and spectator sport. It was, after all, essential to their own commercial future. For years the mint juleps had been flowing in Lafayette and Bourbon County as freely as iced water in a Holiday Inn. The view from Lexington's airport, Blue Grass Field, was one of immaculate white- and black-rail paddock fences stretching all the way to the horizon. Yet the Emperors knew that they couldn't afford to rely on the Arabs and leading European owners coming over to the Kentucky sales circuit for ever: if their prosperity was to be preserved, if that view was to remain unblemished by other less attractive forms of real estate, then new owners and new money had to be involved. The kind of buyer they were aiming at would most typically be a new-rich American who had made his money in one of the Western or Sun Belt states. Alternatively it might be an individual or group of individuals who had formerly been active in the market but who had dropped out in the face of the soaring prices of the boom years. The question was . . . how to get at them?

There is no one body in overall charge of American racing. The states all have their own different laws and commissions. Not that this worried the Emperors. They didn't want some ossified central body deciding in advance what decisions they could make and what limits they could go to. In the true spirit of maverick, corporate free enterprise, they had already resolved to take the situation into their own hands. The scheme they had devised was as simple as it was ingenious. It revolved around the magical, irresistible allure of money. Big, megabuck, prize money.

They came up with the idea of an annual championship day's racing which would comprise seven races, each worth a minimum million dollars in prize money to the winning horses. What's more, these massive prizes would be put up by the Emperors themselves and their fellow breeders. If they wanted their horse or horses sired by their stallions to be eligible to run in the new programme, then they would have to pay a percentage of their annual stallion and foal nomination payments to a special Breeders Cup Fund. This would be self-perpetuating and used only as purse money for the big seven prizes.

The idea was to try and attract the cream of the nation's bloodstock to compete against one another in the same place and on the same day. After all, healthy Americans all loved to find a winner in any field. They liked their professional sports to be conducted as gladiatorial combat. The new Breeders Cup races would give both the railbirds and the ordinary spectators a unique opportunity to see the best racing against the best and to find out who really owned the hottest and fastest horses in the country. The seven-race programme would include a six-furlong sprint, a mile race for two-year-old fillies and another for two-year-old colts, a ten-furlong race for fillies and mares and the lavishly endowed $3 million Breeders Cup Classic, the richest race in the world, also over ten furlongs, for fillies and colts of three years and up. All five of these races would take place on the dirt. The other two contests, also for three-year-olds and upwards, would be a million-dollar event over a mile and the two-million-dollar Breeders Cup Turf over a mile and a half. As the name implies, both of these races were to take place on grass, which is the traditional surface for all major horse-racing in Europe but which is only used for a minority of the big events in America. With the benefit of an all-important four-hour live telecast, coast to coast, negotiated in advance with NBC Television, it seemed as if racing would indeed be presented to the American public in the most attractive and favourable light possible.

The two turf races were an important part of the programme. The Cup was primarily intended to give a major boost to American racing but the Emperors were also keen to try and attract some of the top European horses across the Atlantic to take on their home-based runners. This was not entirely connected with any concept of sportsmanship. They knew that their own domestic audience was not necessarily the most sophisticated, the most historically aware or the most globally conscious in the racing world. Yet they also well understood that it was good commercial sense for the new racing to partly reflect the international flavour of the breeding industry that depended on it. In 1989 the most powerful European owners, especially the Arabs, have the money, the brood mares and the stud bases to keep their best stallion prospects in England, Ireland and France. In 1982 most of the really successful stallions standing in the world were all still based at stud farms in Kentucky. Many of them had been campaigned in Europe as racehorses and then sold back to the Emperors at the end of their racing career. Each year since about 1975 many of the pick of these stallions' annual crop of yearlings had in turn been bought by European-based interests to take back again and aim at the English, French and Irish classic races. This exodus of the choicest and highest-priced lots had not always delighted some of the rougher and redder-necked of the Good Old Boys. At the same time the smarter men amongst them, the Gaineses and Hancocks, the outrageously hustling Tom Gentry and the socially impeccable Will S. Farish jun., understood precisely that it was because of this burgeoning European market that they had been making such galloping megabuck fortunes. Success for the offspring of American-based stallions in top European Group One races was of enormous significance in determining the continued upward revaluation of those stallions' position in the American and international marketplace. If the best European horses could now be persuaded to compete in the Breeders Cup races, then the series would become one of those few select racing events worldwide, like the Kentucky Derby and the Epsom Derby, in which victory for a horse would automatically have a dramatic effect on the price of a share in that horse's sire and on the average price per head of his next crop of yearlings to appear in the commercial sales ring.

To sweeten the Europeans, a European Breeders Fund was set up to enable cross-registration of English, French and Irish stallions in the Breeders Cup scheme. It was estimated that in the first year this would raise about £450,000 in England alone with France and Ireland doubling that total. This would go to additional prize money in European racing, albeit to horses sired by stallion participants, and to new Breeders' prizes.

These were the ideas, the bold, exciting, money-spinning ideas, that Gaines and the other Emperors first unveiled to the rest of the commercial racing and breeding industry in the spring of 1982. This, they said, was the face of the future. The dynamic and competitive future of international horse-racing. Their American audience seemed both excited and impressed. Some of the Europeans were markedly less so and very soon the foreign-based objections started flooding in.

First there was a dispute over the proposed date and setting for the first Breeders Cup series which had already been scheduled for California in early November 1984. As far as the big-money boys like D. Wayne Lukas, the most successful trainer in the world, were concerned, November was no problem. November was beautiful. November was AOK. Most, though not all, American trainers agreed with him. That it was right at the very end of the European flat-racing season was not their business. The top American horses tend to run far more often than is usually the case in Europe anyway. A high-class three-year-old trained by Lukas or Woody Stephens could be competing in a classic prep race in Florida as early as January, in the American Triple Crown in May and June and then running maybe ten or twelve times up to the end of the fall campaign on the East Coast. It is very rare for English classic horses to race so often.

There are just five classic races in England each season: the 1,000 and 2,000 Guineas, which are for three-year-old fillies and three-year-old colts respectively and which are run over a mile at Newmarket in the spring; the Derby, which is for three-year-olds, over a mile and a half, and which takes place at Epsom on the first Wednesday in June; the Oaks, which is for three-year-old fillies only and which also takes place at Epsom on the Saturday after the Derby; and the St Leger, which is for three-year-old colts and fillies, over a mile and three-quarters at Doncaster in September.

All five of the classics automatically enjoy what is called Group One status (Grade One in America) in the racing calendar. Then there are a number of other famous and prestigious contests which, although not literally classics, also merit Group One rank. These are special championship events that have been designed over the years to pit the best horses of one generation against the best of the older horses that have remained in training. It's a tough and congested schedule. Trainers who have to work hard to get a three-year-old ready in a wet spring for a tilt at the 2,000 Guineas in April, then have the Derby to aim for in June followed by the big midsummer races like the King George VI and Queen Elizabeth Diamond Stakes at Ascot in July. Their natural end-of-season target would be the Prix de l'Arc de Triomphe, or the Champion Stakes at Newmarket in October. The instant objection of many of these top-drawer English trainers was that it would be impossible for them to keep their best horses at peak condition until November.

It was also claimed that the new races couldn't possibly be a fair test of international merit as the Americans wouldn't have to leave their native climate and training areas. The Europeans would be expected to fly ten thousand miles and then acclimatise quickly to a level of heat and humidity virtually unknown to them during the damp North European summers. On top of that they would have to adapt to being stabled in the American-style barns adjacent to the courses and to being exercised on the track itself in conditions far removed from the lavish off-the-farm facilities available in most European training centres.

These were the immediate reservations of some serious and even seriously ambitious European horsemen. Then there were the objections of the turf traditionalists of whom none were more glacially sceptical than the Jockey Club of Great Britain, for more than two centuries the self-perpetuating, ruling oligarchy of British racing. You could literally feel the might of the English establishment closing ranks and rising up in indignation against this upstart new concept. As far as most Jockey Club members were concerned, the Derby, steeped in years of history and prestige, was *the* horse race of the year and Royal Ascot the Number One race-meeting and that was an end to it. Where was the history to be made on a flat dirt-track in brash California in November? Money, they claimed, should not be allowed to distort the pattern and these new races would simply be putting even more money into the hands of very rich men – exactly the kind of men who had already commercialised racing to an unacceptable degree by making the protection of a horse's stud value more important than fully and fairly testing it on the track.

Listening to some of the arguments emanating from Portman Square, the London head offices of the Jockey Club, was like listening to a re-run of the great debate over Kerry Packer's cricketing revolution in 1977. To many people at Lords, the Packer phenomenon was, and still is, anathema: a commercial wide-boy and blackmailer placing money before tradition and picking on the worst and most abrasive aspects of the Australian style of cricket and adding to them gimmicks such as floodlights, white balls and coloured clothing. For their part the mainly much younger band of international cricketers who accepted Packer's money believed that they were not just insuring their own financial future but also in some measure contributing to an exciting and innovative new phase in the development of cricket as a spectator sport.

Just like Packer, the Emperors of the Blue Grass made no attempt to disguise their commercial motives when revealing their plans to the American public. They wanted to be taken seriously after all. At the same time the Emperors and the glittering team of PR and marketing people that they had hired to sell Breeders Cup Ltd were loud in their remonstrations to the European powers that they too were establishing a hallmark for the future in their efforts to attract a whole new audience of racetrack devotees.

As the arguments over money, dates and locations raged backwards and forwards there was one other, as yet only half-stated, European suspicion that began to gain steadily in volume and intensity until it gradually became the focus of all non-American distrust of this new Breeders Cup idea. Shared by owners, trainers and administrators it was even felt by some of those European horse-dealers whose own commercial futures were already heavily interlinked with American stallions and stud farms. It concerned the contentious use of 'medication', i.e. drugs, in American racing.

California, where the first Breeders Cup series was due to take place, was one of many states outside New York, which permitted trainers to use 'enabling' drugs such as Lasix and Bute. Lasix, or furosemide, is used primarily to treat horses who are 'bleeders' or who suffer from some kind of circulatory problem. The drug is thought to reduce the blood pressure in the lungs, which may accordingly reduce the risk of a horse who suffers from breathing problems under stress having a lung haemorrhage during a race. It is administered by intravenous injection at least four hours before a race takes place and works like a powerful diuretic so that any unwanted fluids are washed out of the body with the horse's urine. Bute, or phenylbutazone, is used as a painkilling anti-inflammatory drug to treat bruises, sprains and muscle injuries. Usually administered by injection for three days up to a race with the last dosage being given twenty-four hours before competition, its effects can last for up to forty-eight hours after the treatment has ended. It works therapeutically by taking the heat out of an inflammation and lessening the swelling and therefore the discomfort.

In Europe, racehorses are not allowed to run in a race with these substances in their bloodstream. The English racing authorities have been going to great lengths for generations to stamp out all forms of 'dope', not just the use of doping by criminal gangs as a means of stopping horses for betting purposes but any attempt by an over-ambitious stable to improve their runners' chances by giving them Lasix, Bute, anabolic steroids, blood transfusions or any other illicit veterinary assistance in the run-up to a big race. Keeping racing drug-free has been projected as of paramount importance to both the image of the sport and the well-being of the breed. Running a horse on Bute, it is claimed, might actually aggravate its injuries rather than help them to heal, while diuretic drugs like Lasix could, it is suspected, be used to disguise other more sinister substances in a horse's bloodstream.

Some English breeding experts and establishment figures have even gone so far as to assert that allowing horses to 'race on drugs' is not only cheating on the racecourse but possibly permitting congenital weaknesses to be passed on to those horses' offspring via the breeding shed, with severely deleterious long-term effects for the future of the thoroughbred. The idea has been seriously postulated that some supposed champions, highly favoured by the hype of the not always scrupulous commercial breeding industry, might be both defective and unsound.

Needless to say, the Emperors of the Blue Grass, not to mention the ordinary Joes of the American racing press and railbird community didn't quite see it this way. It was quickly pointed out that there was no racing organisation in America that could have resolved the situation even if it had wanted to. In the land of democracy, states rights and litigious free enterprise, an autocratic body like the Jockey Club would have been quite unable to hand down a centralised ruling on what owners and trainers could and could not give their horses. It would be challenged in all the courts in every state in the union. The special demands of the American racing programme, with racing taking place all year round on hard dirt surfaces, would be bound to place a greater strain on a horse's constitution. The American owner believes that as long as he's paying the bills he's damned well entitled to value for money and that means seeing his horses out there on the track as often as possible. Without frequent racing, it was maintained, the cost of ownership would be totally prohibitive and the states who ran the courses would go without valuable betting revenue. So of course, the corollary implied, without the use of Bute and Lasix frequent racing would be impossible.

As far as some of the Emperors were concerned, if it was okay for a tennis player, a golfer or a pro-footballer to be treated with a pain-killing spray during a competition, then why not afford the same facility to a racehorse? American vets were wheeled out to testify that perhaps up to 60 per cent of all racehorses bled during a race anyway and that if Lasix, a generally safe drug sometimes used to treat human heart disease, could overcome the problem it should be welcomed not rejected. They also claimed that the advantage that Lasix was supposed to give was not so marked as to enable an inferior horse to suddenly beat a superior one who was running without the benefit of medication.

There were also plenty of arguments to counter the breeding issue. For more than twenty-five years, it was said, enabling drugs had been permitted in US racing. Yet there was no conclusive evidence during that period that stallions who had been medicated on the racecourse were as a matter of course passing on infirmities to their progeny. Was not St Simon, one of the greatest English racehorses of the nineteenth century and one of the most influential sires of all time, a notorious bleeder? Had not the outstanding classic sire Blandford, himself unsound as a racehorse, become the father of four different Derby winners, including Blenheim, who was to prove equally successful as a stallion, and Bahram, the 1935 Triple Crown winner who retired to stud both sound and unbeaten? Were not the paddocks of famous owner-breeders throughout history filled with fillies who were unable to fulfil their potential on the racecourse due to physical limitations but who became first-rate brood mares without giving birth to a whole series of defective animals?

The problem for the English was that they were beginning to sound as if they were not so much anti-medication as just plain anti-American. Quoting to a Brooklyn sports journalist the remarks of a long-term Jockey Club member, Sir John Astor, about some aspects of American racing being 'ridiculous' and about Ascot having to stage a festival of its own 'to stop horses having to go to the USA' was rather like confronting an audience of colonists in 1776 with a letter to *The Times* by General Sir Johnny Burgoyne to the effect that this Washington chappie would never make a soldier or a leader of men. The English were told that they did not have a monopoly of high moral principles. Were they not simply piqued that a new idea was taking place outside their country and outside their control? Some Americans had forceful views about English racing and didn't all share the conviction of the stewards of the Jockey Club that life on the turf in Britain had reached such a stage of blissful perfection that further improvement was neither possible nor desirable. The English could stay at home if they wanted ... and pass on the big bucks. Nobody was going to force them to participate. On the other hand if they did decide to come over then they couldn't expect the Americans to make concessions for them that would never be extended if the situation were to be reversed.

And so it was that the first Breeders Cup race-meeting did take place on schedule at Hollywood Park in November 1984. More than sixty thousand spectators turned up to watch and they wagered a Californian record eleven and a half million dollars on track. There were numerous American equine stars on display and, in spite of the doubts and suspicions, quite a few European challengers too. The Aga Khan's three-year-old colt, Lashkari, trained at Chantilly by Alan de Royer Dupré, won the inaugural running of the Breeders Cup Turf. And when Robert Sangster's exceptionally game mare Royal Heroine, who had been second in the 1983 1,000 Guineas but was now trained out in California by John Gosden, won the first Breeders Cup Mile, her owner collected more prize money in one go than he had ever received for a single horse-race in Europe. And here was a man who had won two Derbys and three Prix de l'Arc de Triomphes.

The 1985 Breeders Cup was staged not on the West Coast but at Aqueduct racetrack which is in the Ozone Park district of the borough of Queens in New York City – about as far removed from the sunlit glamour and pzazz of LA as it's possible to get. The outstanding European feature of the 1985 series was the brilliant performance by the four-year-old filly Pebbles, owned by Sheikh Mohammed, trained at Newmarket by Clive Brittain and ridden by Pat Eddery. Her thrilling and dramatic victory in the second Breeders Cup Turf resulted in her being voted older filly of the year at the subsequent American Eclipse Awards. These are a kind of racing Oscar ceremony that has far more status in America than any equivalent racing award ceremony in Europe.

For 1986 the Cup was back in sunny LA, not at Hollywood this time but at beautiful Santa Anita which is in the Arcadia district at the foot of the San Gabriel Mountains. The biggest draw of the 1986 Breeders Cup meeting was considered to be the presence of Europe's undisputed racehorse of the year and one of the true champions of the decade, Dancing Brave. Winner of the 2,000 Guineas and the Prix de l'Arc de Triomphe, his American target was the one-and-a-half mile Breeders Cup Turf. Like Pebbles, 'the Brave' was Arab-owned. Not by the Maktoums this time but by Crown Prince Khalid Abdulla of Saudi Arabia. He was trained down at Pulborough in West Sussex by the forty-seven-year-old public-school educated garage proprietor's son, Guy Harwood, and he would be ridden by Pat Eddery.

To have an Arc winner of this calibre competing in only the third running of the Breeders Cup was a spectacular coup for the Emperors of the Blue Grass. On the other hand there were many traditionalists who feared that this was exactly the kind of horse who would not be able to show his true form so far away from home so late in the season. The fact that he had already been syndicated to stand at the Maktoums' Dalham Hall Stud near Newmarket for no less than £14 million yet was now travelling on to California five weeks after his Longchamp showdown was surely taking 'Bravery' to the point of folly. The great weight of expectation riding on the horse's shoulders seemed too much for anyone to bear.

Sadly, inevitably perhaps, Dancing Brave did not show his true form at Santa Anita. While another French-trained colt, Last Tycoon, won the third running of the Breeders Cup Mile, Dancing Brave, whether dehydrated, jet-lagged or just worn out after all his earlier races, could finish only fourth to America's two top turf-horses, Manila and Theatrical. At the post-race press conference Manila's owner, Bradley Shannon, came out with some decidedly abrasive comments. Dancing Brave, he said, was no big noise. The Europeans had taken a beating. Next time they ought not to talk so big and so on. One or two English journalists responded by going to the opposite extreme. Dancing Brave's defeat, they said, proved incontrovertibly that the Breeders Cup was simply a commercial gimmick, that European horses didn't need it and that they would never be able to flourish in it anyway, thanks to the brinkmanship of the American hosts. Especially if they had to race against drugged horses etc. etc.

The Emperors diplomatically declined to get involved in the argument except to say that nobody had ever expected that any great racing power would make it easy for foreign-trained horses to come over and win their big races. As if to underline their point they had already announced that the 1987 Breeders Cup series would take place once again in the Golden West at Hollywood Park. What is more, the date for the 1987 running had also been moved back three weeks to 21 November. This was at the behest of the all-important TV companies who didn't want it to clash with a series of big college football games. After the Dancing Brave humiliation of 1986 most European trainers might have been expected to complain furiously at such a late running date and blame it on the disproportionate influence of television in the new American racing set-up. But not in the least. When November came round again there were no fewer than fourteen European-trained horses, nine from England and five from France, back on that plane to California.

The truth was that the Breeders Cup was now simply too big to resist. Stallion syndication fees, like yearling prices, had dipped since the boom years of the early eighties. Once again racehorses were being compelled to fully prove themselves on the track before the market-place would tolerate their claims to exalted status. In almost every sphere American racing trends had been setting the pace commercially for more than twenty years: in the progressive devaluation of English distance races like the St Leger and the Ascot Gold Cup; in the emphasis on ten furlongs as the optimum winning distance for the classic racehorse. In the requirement that a prospective stallion should have shown speed and winning form as a two-year-old at around six or seven furlongs. Now, too, the Breeders Cup was an idea whose time had arrived. All the leading international racehorse players wanted a piece of that action. And the show business element inherent in the whole concept was going to affect the marketing of the sport in every premier racing country in the world.

2 : D. Wayne and Mr Klein

Hollywood Park racecourse isn't actually in Hollywood at all. It's in an area of Los Angeles known as Inglewood which is chiefly distinctive for being underneath the flight path of the incoming 747s about to make a landing at LAX. Approaching the track from the direction of the San Diego Freeway at La Brea Avenue you feel as if you're driving up to a large modern greyhound stadium with palm trees. The flat, counter-clockwise circuit with its sharp turns is only about nine furlongs round and the turf course is on the inside of the wider and somehow more noticeable dirt surface which is closest to the stands.

Out in the centre of the course are the *pari mutuel* totalisator boards which on racedays flash up the betting pool and the odds for each race. Beyond the back stretch, a row of strikingly tall movieland palm trees partially obscure a complex of grey, concrete training barns from the spectator's eye.

In America, almost all racehorses are stabled in barns adjacent to a major track. Tracks like Hollywood Park stage meets of more than forty days at a time and trainers from outside California may bring . in a whole string of horses and rent space for them in the training barns for the duration. This is where the Europeans and most of the non-Californian-trained American Breeders Cup challengers were housed for the week leading up to 21 November.

The practice of taking racehorses out of their stables for early morning exercise is pretty much the same in every country, and each morning, between the hours of six and nine, some of the world's most valuable bloodstock was out 'breezing' along the back stretch. US racing is obsessed with speed. The sectional times for each quarter are often called by the course commentator during a race and the horses are all trained literally on the clock. Owners, work-watchers, touts and trainers alike are always hanging around the training barns with a stop-watch in their hands, timing their charges through a series of short, sharp, three-, four- and five-furlong workouts.

Inglewood may not be the most glamorous location in California but it's still Los Angeles after all, 'Capital of the fabled Southland' as the Emperors' promotional trailers kept describing it. There was certainly no lack of atmosphere down by those training barns on those late fall November mornings. Each day seemed to begin with a clear blue translucent sky, with the sun pushing up over the distant white Hollywood sign by 7 a.m. and a marvellously fresh and dewy smell in the air winning out over the aeroplane fumes and the sound of the automobiles on nearby Century Boulevard. From some of the stable barns and grooms' quarters came the crackle of Spanish language radio stations and cassettes mixing in with the sound of snorting horses, of muttered exclamations, and of early morning fumbles and swearing. The smell of horse shit doesn't change much from Europe to America but some things definitely improve. From across the other side of the track came the delectable aroma of grilling bacon, pancakes and hot coffee from where a part of the racecourse catering facility had been opened up to provide breakfast for the large gallery of attendant work watchers. Many of the American sports journalists present were doing their best to live up to their celluloid image as a cross between Walter Matthau and Frank Sinatra in his *Pal Joey* era. One sharp little George Burns lookalike with a cigar and a pork-pie hat took a long, hard look at one of the English outsiders for the Breeders Cup Sprint and then rasped at his sidekick: 'Don't they know it's a long way to come for a day out?'

Not all the Americans though were behaving like characters out of *Guys and Dolls*. This was California after all and some of them looked and sounded more like Werner Erhard than Damon Runyon. 'Have you ever asked yourself what it is about you that enables you to excel in this sphere?' was the question one *Revenge of the Nerds*-type, with pony-tail, goatee beard and open-toed sandals, put to Michael Stoute. Fortunately Stoute seemed to be the English trainer least bothered by either the questioners or the surroundings. In fact no one was more intent on serious business than the forty-four-year-old policeman's son from Barbados. Was he not after all one of the top two trainers in Newmarket, his lustre only slightly diminished by comparison with his sallow-faced neighbour, Henry Cecil? Was he not the man who had trained Shergar to win the 1981 Derby? The man who had amassed a record European prize-money total in 1986 only to see that record shattered the following season by his chain-smoking Newmarket rival? With Cecil almost ostentatiously ignoring the Breeders Cup for the fourth year running, this was the perfect moment for Stoute to step back into the limelight and prove that his was the more adventurous and internationalist approach to modern racing.

With his large busy face and his incisive manner of speaking, Stoute may appear to be cast more in the mould of an impatient Thatcherite entrepreneur than an old-fashioned English racehorse trainer. In fact his approach to competition is at least partly based on a more traditional model than simply the fashionable virtues of self-help and robust individualism. Almost from the moment he could walk Michael Ronald Stoute has been a passionate lover of cricket. Especially the way the West Indians play it. And Stoute found the cricketing metaphor a particularly attractive one as he considered the forthcoming Breeders Cup challenge. He wasn't thinking of losing gracefully though. He was thinking of attacking the enemy with aggression and flair.

Stoute reasoned that if the MCC had refused to play in Australia more than a century before on the grounds that for the English cricketers it would've been at the end of a long domestic season and that the heat would've been too much for them, then the great England versus Australia cricketing rivalry would've been stillborn. Of course it wasn't the same playing the Sydney Cricket Ground under lights as it was playing at Lords in June but the kudos of winning there was just as great. So why not the same with horse racing? And the Breeders Cup races were not the first example of English, French and Irish horses travelling out to North America at the turn of the year. Laurel Park racecourse in Maryland had been staging their Washington, DC, International since the early fifties and that had been won by many illustrious European names. The 1968 winner Sir Ivor was appearing for his ninth race of the season when he contested Laurel Park; a season that had already included the 2,000 Guineas, Derby, Irish Derby, Eclipse Stakes, Prix de l'Arc de Triomphe and Champion Stakes. Hadn't English horses been running in Chicago's Arlington Million since 1981 and hadn't two of them won it? Well, now the Breeders Cup programme existed too and considering that the prize money, right down to sixth place, was out of all proportion to most European Group One races, Stoute reckoned that the English racing fraternity ought to be taking this new concept extremely seriously indeed.

That meant identifying the kind of horses who might adapt best to American tracks and conditions and training them specifically for those races instead of sending them across the Atlantic as an afterthought at the end of a long European campaign. With that end in view Stoute had been training Sheikh Mohammed's four-year-old filly Sonic Lady for the 1987 Breeders Cup Mile all year long. Twelve months earlier he had sent her out to Santa Anita at the end of an exhausting English season and she'd flopped badly. This time he'd given her just three races in England and, along with Milligram, his other Group One-winning filly, the daughter of Nureyev had been sent out to California several weeks early in order to give the two horses every chance to acclimatise. To the horror of some English commentators the uncompromising trainer had even indicated his willingness to play it by American rules and permit his two horses to be treated with Bute and Lasix if he thought it would significantly improve their chances.

There seemed to be every possibility of exactly that happening when a chance mishap befell Milligram, only three days before the race. On the Wednesday morning, she pinched a foot while being shod and although Stoute was insisting that it wasn't of 'major concern' his outwardly sanguine view of things was not shared by the representatives of the big London bookmaking firms. As far as they were concerned, Milligram's chance had already gone and they were beginning to push her odds out accordingly.

Elsewhere, Stoute was leaving nothing to chance. Sonic Lady was to be ridden by the Panamanian-born but Californian-based senior rider, Laffit Pincay jun. The stable-jockey Walter Swinburn, who had been on the filly the previous year at Santa Anita, had recently been involved in an unfortunate incident at Silks restaurant in London in which the twenty-six-year-old 'choirboy' had fallen foul of a wine waiter and then been ambushed by a predatory photographer from a popular newspaper. This was not the sort of coverage to endear itself to teetotal Arab owners and in spite of official statements about Pincay being the local boy and logical choice there was no lack of speculation amongst outside observers that the angelic-looking Swinburn was being punished for his misdemeanours.

Not all Europeans had followed Stoute's example and travelled their horses early. The English and French 1,000 Guineas winner Miesque, like Sonic Lady engaged in the Mile, had left Chantilly just a week in advance while the Arc winner Trempolino, whose target was the Breeders Cup Turf, wasn't even clearing quarantine until the day before the race. The majority of the other English runners had arrived together on the Monday morning after the kind of horror-stricken plane journey more usually associated with stories of plucky Brit holidaymakers battling their way through a maze of striking air-traffic controllers to get to their place in the sun. After all these delays and quarantine problems the prospects for most of these horses didn't look bright. One or two of their trainers too looked pink-faced and out of place in the bright Californian sunshine, especially without their usual uniform of flat tweed cap and Husky. 'No one, but no one, wears a Barbour in Los Angeles at seven o'clock in the morning,' affirmed the Crawley-born bloodstock agent David Williams, now a naturalised citizen of San Diego.

Sheikh Mohammed's racing manager, Anthony Stroud, was on hand to watch Sonic Lady at work. Stroud has a very white, rather pasty-faced complexion and to see him on a racecourse in England in his grey suits and blue and white striped shirts you'd think he was a caricature merchant banker or young City whiz-kid. Out in LA in his short-sleeved casual clothes he looked more like a public-school prefect on his way to a cricket match in mufti.

The Newmarket trainer Clive Brittain, a one-time head lad to the celebrated English trainer of the post-war years, Noel Murless, rarely if ever wears a flat tweed cap, or a brown trilby hat for that matter. The irrepressible Brittain, never afraid to run his horses in Group One races no matter how chary the press may be of their chances, had come over with three prospective runners including the four-year-old colt Bold Arrangement, who had achieved the remarkable distinction for an English racehorse of finishing third in the 1986 Kentucky Derby. Unfortunately he'd shown little worthwhile form since the start of the 1987 season and the Americans were merciless about his chances. 'Why he has been shipped over for this, is something only God and his owners know. Perhaps they're into humiliation,' cracked Jack Hingle of *Daily Racing Form*. 'Bold Arrangement has proved he can lose races in England. Why cross the Atlantic to prove the same thing here?' quipped Bob Mieszerski of the *Los Angeles Times*.

It was noticeable that nobody was making too many jokes about Miesque or her trainer, François Boutin. Like Sonic Lady, a bay filly by Nureyev, Miesque was owned by the Greek shipping tycoon

Stavros Niarchos. She had only ever been beaten twice in a ten-race career and in 1987 alone she had already won four Group One races including the two classics. On each occasion she had blinded her rivals for speed.

The English press were quick to point out that the French filly had grown a thick winter coat since her last run in Europe but Boutin countered that the strength and power were still there and that, having had a seven-week rest since her surprise defeat by Milligram at Ascot, she was now showing him the same kind of form that she'd displayed before she'd won the Prix Jacques Le Marois at Deauville in August. The silver-haired Boutin, a tall, broad-shouldered and commanding man, always smartly but relaxedly dressed, looked totally at ease in these supposedly unfamiliar surroundings. With his elegant, dark-haired daughter Patricia accompanying him everywhere, he had a winner's look about him which wasn't lost on the Americans and which was hardly surprising considering his career record in France. He'd only recently added to that tally as a result of a profitable stop-over at the Festival of Turf Racing at Laurel Park in Maryland in which his two-year-old filly Minstrel's Lassie, just below the top class in France, had picked up $150,000 for winning the Selima Stakes. 'Why wasn't Cecil there?' asked one disgruntled English correspondent, referring to the English champion trainer Henry 'Gucci Shoes' Cecil. 'Why isn't he here now?'

The fifty-one-year-old Boutin began life with few of Cecil's natural aristocratic advantages. His father was an ordinary farmer in the small Norman village of Beaunay and Boutin had to rely on talent rather than patronage to develop his career. As a young man he became an accomplished showjumper, trotting race driver and amateur rider. Like Cecil he served a short spell on Elizabeth de Couturié's Haras de Mesnil stud farm in the Sarthe district near Le Mans. His first serious racing job came in 1961 as assistant trainer to the great Etienne Pollet. Amongst other champions Pollet saddled the 1965 Derby and Arc winner, Sea Bird, who, like Ribot and Nijinsky, was one of the really great racehorses of the twentieth century. At the end of that year Boutin went into business on his own and his first classic winner came three seasons later.

Boutin, a widower, devotes his spare time to his three children. The daughters, Patricia and Nathalie, and his son, Eric. At Hollywood Park M. Boutin claimed to speak no English whatsoever and rather craftily left all translating matters in the hands of the glamorous Patricia. Yet there was sometimes a wily look in his eye, especially when the conversation turned to one of his best horses and its career earnings or future stud plans, which suggested that he actually understood a great deal more than he was letting on. He did occasionally break out with a line of disparaging English but that seemed to be done more for theatrical effect than as a serious indication of his command of the local patois!

The ritual down by the training barns would be the same each morning. Every half an hour or so another smooth, power-steered limo would glide up to the barn area and out would get another party of what Raymond Chandler would've described as 'the Big Rich'. American owners and their friends come to watch their horses at work. Some of them would be in tennis shorts and sneakers, some in expensive short-sleeved golfing shirts and smoothly pressed check trousers. Almost everyone it seemed had a baseball cap and a pair of shades. From time to time a silver or gold Cartier watch-chain would flash through the air as another Cool or Winston Lite was tipped out of its pack and the well-coiffeured heads nodded in agreement or stared uncomprehendingly at the latest reports of trainers' assistants and racing managers.

The doyen of all Californian racehorse trainers is the seventy-six-year-old Hall of Famer, Charlie Whittingham. Charlie, spry, sharp and shiningly bald, is known throughout the sport as the Bald Eagle. His record of achievement in American racing, especially on the West Coast, has earned him the kind of status and universal respect enjoyed by the seventy-two-year-old Vincent O'Brien in Europe. Whittingham, yet to train a Breeders Cup winner, was looking after the 1986 Kentucky Derby winner, Ferdinand, who was the hottest favourite of all for the 1987 series. Ferdinand, a handsome chestnut son of Nijinsky, had gone with only one victory in nine starts after his Churchill Downs triumph but in a six-week period, starting in the late summer of the 1987 season, Whittingham had succeeded in bringing the horse right back to his very best form. He was coming to Hollywood Park off a winning streak in three Grade One races in which he'd never been seriously extended. 'Who is going to beat him?' Charlie asked the press on the Wednesday morning. 'All I have to do is keep him breathing for three more days.'

For many years one of Charlie's principal rivals in the US training tables has been another supremely tough and astute septuagenarian, the New York-based Woodford C. Stephens, known to one and all as 'Woody'. The son of a family of poor Kentucky tobacco farm workers – 'we worked from when you couldn't see to when you couldn't see' – Woody Stephens has won every big race prize in America . . . other than a Breeders Cup. The trainer of five consecutive Belmont Stakes winners – and like Whittingham a member of US racing's Hall of Fame – Woody would most controversially not be represented in the 1987 Breeders Cup. The races, he said, came too late in the year. There was no way he was going to ship his star two-year-old, Forty Niner, all the way from New York to California in the third week in November. He was saving it, along with his other best horses, for a nice warm winter in Florida where they would be gradually trained up for the 1988 Triple Crown races. Not everyone agreed with Woody's argument.

'There are lots of reasons why one might not want to race. But this business about 21 November being too late is the weakest excuse of all.' The man who so crisply delivered himself of that opinion was undoubtedly the man who most visitors to Hollywood Park, be they Americans or Europeans, wanted to look at, listen to and write about. He is currently the most successful, the most compulsive and just about the most fascinating racehorse trainer in the world. His name is D. Wayne Lukas.

As he came into the 1987 Breeders Cup series, D. Wayne had already won 315 races that year for total prize money of more than $58 million. Even in a land of year-round racing and, by European standards, lavishly endowed purses, that's still a staggering record. By comparison England's 1987 champion trainer, Henry Cecil, had sent out 180 winners of £1,882,314 worth of prize money. If you were to caricature Cecil as a typical example of the European racehorse trainer as an upper-class English fop, then you'd have to describe Lukas as a typical example of the American sportsman as self-made Hollywood star.

Now fifty-four years of age (Cecil is forty-six), Lukas looks strong, tanned and awesomely healthy. With his silver-grey hair, his tinted glasses, his thirty-two-carat smile and his near perfect row of glittering white teeth he would have been an ideal role for, say, James Coburn at his peak. Like Cecil, his English counterpart, D. Wayne is always nattily dressed but sharply so – usually in what Americans would describe as a tailored sports coat and tight-fitting pants. If you didn't think he was a movie star or a well-shaven TV detective you might as easily mistake him for a major league basketball or pro-football coach of the kind we see stalking the NFL touchlines during the winter.

Lukas grew up on a farm in Gritigo, Wisconsin and began buying and selling farm horses while he was still a teenager. The experience, he says, taught him as much about hustling as it did about horseflesh. Encouraged by his parents 'to make a contribution to society and not just loaf around racetracks' Lukas became a high school and college basketball coach in his early twenties. He was immediately successful at it and his players not only had to work harder on the court than anybody else they also had to sit through plenty of positive thinking and motivational sessions from the coach. Lukas has made that kind of psychological self-awareness approach an integral part of his game plan as a racehorse trainer too.

D. Wayne was and still is an avid follower of all mainstream American sports but it was always horses that were his passion. While he was on the coaching staff at the University of Wisconsin he started racing quarter-horses in his spare time. Travelling all over the Midwest to the little country meets and state fairs where the cowboys and their sprinters were in opposition. In 1967 he decided to make quarter-horse training his full-time occupation – to dazzling effect: in ten years he broke every single record that existed in the quarter-horse business. By the late seventies there were eighteen quarter-horse races a year in California worth more than $100,000 to the winner. For three years running, Lukas won every single one of them. His phenomenal success was only partly due to his high motivation and his almost religious drive. He was also beginning to display to the world his remarkable gift for assessing the physical conformation and potential of a racehorse and his talent for getting inside the horse's mind and thinking out the way to develop its potential to the maximum effect.

In 1978 Lukas began to turn his attention to thoroughbreds, taking with him the same team, the same methods and many of the same owners. That season he won $942,786 worth of prize money. By 1983, the first year that Lukas led the country in purses won, that figure had jumped to $4.2 million. In 1986 it escalated again to a remarkable $12.3 million dollars. Throughout his spectacular rise D. Wayne has continued to behave like Dale Carnegie with a deadline. He frequently pushes himself through a twenty-hour day beginning at 4 a.m. each morning. His stable has divisions in all the major racing centres around the country. Each division is in the charge of an assistant who consults with the trainer by phone at least once every twenty-four hours. Lukas's chief assistant and most trusted aide-de-camp is his son, Jeff. Juggling with the health and training programmes of all these fabulously expensive horses in four different time-zones leaves little time for sleep (or for partying). Lukas doesn't drink and he doesn't smoke and, in a sport not renowned for the abstemiousness of its leading participants either here or in America, that doesn't make him universally popular. Especially with some of his less successful colleagues.

Lukas's main training barn is not at Hollywood Park but at nearby Santa Anita. By comparison with many other of these rather grey and anonymous buildings D. Wayne's set-up is spotlessly clean, neat and tidy. The dirt in front of the creamy green lawns is regularly raked in a precise herring-bone pattern while the smartly painted green and white panels on the barn walls all bear the same proud, but by Californian standards not ostentatious, monogram: D.W.L.

On the wall by D. Wayne's office there is a rather touching and neatly typed list of what are described as the trainer's 'Daily Dozen'. They are a list of maxims, encouragements to self-improvement, rather like Jay Gatsby's list of General Resolves written in the back of the old copy of *Hopalong Cassidy* that Mr Gatz shows Nick Carraway at the end of Fitzgerald's novel. 'The value of time' the list begins. 'The success of perseverance. The pleasure of working. The dignity of simplicity. The worth of character. The power of kindness. The influence of example. The obligation of duty. The wisdom of economy. The virtue of patience. The improvement of talent. The joy of originating.' You almost fear for Lukas at times. There's something about his intense need to succeed, to be recognised, to be acknowledged, that makes you feel that one day the strain he's putting himself under could lead to a major breakdown, or worse, to the kind of archetypal American Dream turned American Tragedy scenario, much like the fate of Gatsby himself.

Somehow you don't have the same type of nervous apprehension about Eugene V. Klein, the former owner of the San Diego Chargers football team and the man who has been Lukas's principal owner and partner in his assault on the thoroughbred industry. Klein's conquest of the commanding heights of American capitalism has been almost as impressive an example of self-motivation and drive as the career of his trainer.

Gene Klein was born in New York City in 1921, the youngest child in a family of six. He grew up in a background of what he describes as very, very average means. Smart enough to enrol in the engineering school at NYU he supported himself as a door-to-door encyclopaedia salesman before walking out of college the day after Pearl Harbor to enlist in the US Air Force.

At the end of the war the newly married Klein followed the example of thousands of other Americans before and since and moved out to California where he set up in business as – what else – a used car salesman. By 1951 he'd got so smart at it too that he'd begun importing the first Volvos from Sweden to Western America. From automobiles he moved on rapidly to banking and real estate and then became President and Chief Executive of the National General Corporation, a nationwide chain of movie theatres. Within a few years he'd turned it around from being a major loss-maker into a highly profitable concern with assets of over a billion dollars.

Up until this point in his life Gene Klein had shown little interest in horse-racing. His passion was football. In the mid sixties he purchased a major interest in one of his local pro-outfits, the San Diego Chargers. A decade later he sold National and General to devote his full attention to the fortunes of the team. To nobody's great surprise he came out smiling from that deal too. In 1983 a couple of heart attacks compelled him to shave a few rough edges off his high-intensity approach to life. So he sold the Chargers – for thirty million dollars more than he'd paid for them a decade earlier.

Supposedly under orders to relax, Klein had no plans to put his feet up in what he calls a polyester retirement home. In 1982 his second wife Joyce had purchased a half-share in three brood-mares and one morning that summer she took her husband down to the beautiful Del Mar race-track just north of San Diego, to watch some of her friends' horses working out. Big Gene met D. Wayne and a famous partnership was born.

In 1983 Lukas gave Klein eleven winners for prize money of $500,000. The next year Klein's blue and gold silks – emblazoned with a thunderbolt like the strip of his former ball team – were carried to victory in thirty-five races for winnings of more than $2,400,000. Amongst the 1984 crop was the brilliant filly, Life's Magic, who won the following season's Breeders Cup Distaff, a race in which Lukas and Klein were successful again in 1986 with another great racemare, Lady's Secret. (When Klein decided to disperse some of his breeding stock at Keeneland a week before the 1987 Breeders Cup, the two mares were sold for a combined total of nearly ten million dollars.)

The history of flat racing is filled with celebrated owner-trainer relationships from the 14th Earl of Derby and George Lambton to Sir Victor Sassoon and Noel Murless to Robert Sangster and Vincent O'Brien. Gene Klein's teaming up with Wayne Lukas, though as yet of shorter duration, involves many of the same ingredients that made the Sangster-O'Brien syndicate so successful and, just like O'Brien, Lukas is a major shareholder in most of the horses he trains. Klein's first partner was the solid waste disposal tycoon, Mel Hatley, who had been associated with Lukas since his quarter-horse days. Nowadays most of the Klein horses are owned by himself, Barry Beal and L. R. French jun., who, as befits a citizen of Midland, Texas, is a big man in cattle and oil wells. These three supply the finance, the commercial backing and the trust. Every single aspect of the training and care of the horses is left to Lukas's judgement. Although the whole team revel in the atmosphere of the big yearling sales in Kentucky and Saratoga, they have rarely spent as lavishly as Sangster or the Arabs. They may have been underbidders in one or two epic bidding duels but on average a Lukas-selected and Gene Klein-purchased yearly is just as likely to cost $300,000 as $3 million. There are sometimes exceptions.

In 1984 they had an Alydar colt called Saratoga Six who'd been purchased as a yearling for $2,200,000. He was undefeated in four straight races including a Grade One before he fractured a sesamoid bone in his right ankle while at exercise one morning and had to be immediately retired. As yet he could hardly be said to have vanquished the best in the land but such was already the vaunting power of Lukas's reputation that he was successfully syndicated as a stallion by North Ridge Farm, a new and rapidly thriving Blue Grass empire, for no less than $14 million – the same price as the 1988 valuation of Risen Star, a proven top-class three-year-old colt, who had won two legs of the American Triple Crown.

Robert Sangster and his partner John Magnier had already pulled off the same kind of syndication coups on several occasions, most notably in 1981 with Storm Bird, an outstanding two-year-old who failed to train in the following year, but who was syndicated for an enormous sum of money. This was partly due to his breeding and two-year-old form and partly due to the awesome reputation of his trainer, Vincent O'Brien. Any trainer who can regularly demonstrate to an owner that he can turn his speculative purchase into a lucrative stallion commodity, will continue to get more and more owners and more and more money to spend each year. Some aggrieved and less wealthy members of the training profession would claim that it's not difficult to top the statistics tables when you can automatically buy the best-bred and the best-looking horses on the market. Confidants of Lukas and O'Brien as well as of Cecil, Stoute, Boutin and Woody Stephens would quickly retort that only the best in the business can continually succeed in winning big races with highly strung thorough-bred horses. And Gene Klein has certainly never had any doubts whatsoever that D. Wayne Lukas is the best.

Unlike some other American owners, now and throughout the century, Klein has no current plans to race a stable in Europe. Although he says that if he ever had a turf horse good enough he'd love to bring it over for the Arc. With the kind of disarming grin that you don't often see in Sangster or the Aga Khan, the sixty-seven-year-old Klein insists that he's in racing for fun. He's been up and down the sidewalk of life a few times now, he says. He knows it isn't all pretty but at his age if it doesn't look inviting he's no longer interested. And buying, owning and racing horses is just about the most fun thing he can think of.

With his grizzled face, his shock of white hair and his white moustache, Klein may look like a Macy's Father Christmas but for all his affability he hasn't lost one ounce of the fierce competitive energy that originally made him a fat-cat tycoon inside five years. As Lukas himself says of the combination, 'Mr Klein and I are in business to win million-dollar races.' To win all three legs of the American Triple Crown; to win all seven Breeders Cup races on the same day; to break every track record in the country. Having survived well enough to nearly seventy, you feel that Klein is both emotionally and financially entrenched enough to weather any possible downside or reverse in his grand designs. By comparison some people have claimed to see an indication of Lukas's potential vulnerability in his up-and-down relationships with the American press.

When D. Wayne first began training thoroughbreds back in 1978, he quickly became a media darling. They loved everything about him. His look, his smile, the cut of his clothes and not least the way that he communicated with them about racing events by using analogies with other sports. Many American sports reporters may have heard of the Kentucky Derby but they know surprisingly little about horse-racing for the other fifty-one weeks of the year. Lukas made their life much easier by comparing the Breeders Cup to the Superbowl and the Keeneland July Sales to the National Football League's annual college draft. American sports-writing thrives on the crisp one-liner. Whole articles depend upon them. It's part of a tradition that infuses some of the best novel- and screenplay-writing of the twentieth century. Lukas began by giving the press juicy one-liners every week. Then all of a sudden, things started to go sour. The resentment that some older members of the American training profession already felt about this prodigy in their midst started to filter through to the journalists. How could anyone be so successful so quickly? There had to be something wrong somewhere. There just had to be a flaw. In the classic manner of so many contemporary overreachers, brilliant or otherwise, Lukas had been built up in the media as a genius. Now he had to be knocked down too.

Writers started opining that he was overtraining his horses. A high number did seem to be breaking down only a short way into their racing careers and, although a racehorse is every bit as vulnerable to injury at any time as a human athlete, Lukas was virtually accused of causing the injuries by his training methods. Saratoga Six broke down at the end of his two-year-old career in 1984. Lukas's 1980 Preakness Stakes winner, Codex, ran disappointingly in the Belmont Stakes next time out and never raced again, while his 1985 Preakness winner, Tanks Prospect, was also retired after breaking down in the Belmont.

To put this into perspective it's important to remember that injured or prematurely retired horses aren't confined to American racing or the Wayne Lukas stable. Storm Bird wasn't the only one of Vincent O'Brien's top two-year-olds of the seventies and eighties who failed to train on at three. Try My Best, Danzatore, Gold Crest and Tate Gallery all failed to live up to the high expectations held for them over the winter while Sangster and O'Brien's 1982 Derby winner, Golden Fleece, never raced again after his Epsom victory. Cynics would say that this was because it was more convenient for the owners to keep the horse off the track as an undefeated stallion prospect than to risk it again on the racecourse but O'Brien's staff are always at pains to document the numerous genuine problems that prevented them from training Golden Fleece for further races. Lukas and O'Brien may have the whiff of commercialism and controversy about them but Henry Cecil is a wholly acceptable establishment figure. At the end of the 1987 season in England he had no fewer than four two-year-old colts in the top seven horses quoted in William Hills ante-post list for the 1988 2,000 Guineas. For various reasons, all connected with injury, slow development or loss of form, none of them even made it to the start the next spring. Neither would Cecil have a runner in the 1988 Derby.

Lukas's reaction to the charge of overtraining was that his methods got more races out of good horses than the policies adopted by more defensive trainers. Life's Secret ran a staggering fifty-four times in a three-year racing career which would be unthinkable for a classic filly in England. Yet in doing so she recorded five Grade One victories and amassed more than $2,250,000 for her owners.

To the end of the 1987 racing year Lukas's jinx race had been the most traditional and distinguished blue riband classic in America. The 112-year-old Kentucky Derby. Lukas had run twelve losers in the Derby in a seven-year period and how the old-timers loved to taunt him about it. His 1986 champion two-year-old colt, Capote, was the warm ante-post favourite for the 1987 Derby but he became ill during the winter and, unusually for American racing, Lukas was only able to get two small prep races into him in the run-up to the classic.

When Lukas and Capote arrived back east at Churchill Downs a week before the Derby, it seemed as if everyone, including some of his fellow trainers, was out to get him. 'He'll run last and we'll never hear of him again' was what Woody Stephens had to say about Capote. Lukas insisted that Capote was well, that his legs were sound and that he had every chance after two dazzling work-outs in California before leaving for Kentucky. The critics refused to be convinced. 'Lukas's horses may break down or disappear from view before they reach a ripe age,' wrote Phil Norman of the *San Diego Tribune*, 'but the man is the epitome of glitter and always has enough money to buy a new pair of pants. Still the SPCA (Society for the Prevention of Cruelty to Animals) has a right to frown on the system.' Lukas was furious. He started turning up at his training barn in the company of his good friend Bob Knight, a basketball coach from the nearby state of Indiana. Knight's almost fanatical competitiveness has made him a notorious figure even in the take-no-prisoners world of American sport where winning is usually the only thing. He was once thrown out of a basketball arena for hurling a chair on to the court in the middle of a college game against a team from the Soviet Union.

Lukas and Knight made an imposing double act. 'Over here, Bob, are the horses,' said D. Wayne as he pointed out his string coming back in from work. 'And over there . . .' he switched on his best orthodontist's grin and waved in the direction of the press '. . . are the horses' asses.'

Sadly for Lukas, Capote finished second to last in the 1987 Kentucky Derby and was eventually retired without having won another race all year.

Six months later in the run-up to Breeders Cup Four, Lukas, who is always patient and courteous in response to what he considers an intelligent question, was still hurt as much as angered by what he regarded as the malign untruths and just plain inaccurate reporting that he'd been subjected to. He smiled momentarily at the cameras and threw out the occasional sharp crack but for most of each morning he cut out the press and remained in close consultation with his son Jeff, with Gene Klein and with his work riders and other owners.

As Lukas moved around briskly from Santa Anita down to Hollywood Park, out on to the track and back again, the confidence in his walk, his manner and his bearing was quite extraordinary to witness.

He almost seemed to glow around the edges. Lukas had already trained four Breeders Cup winners in five runnings of the series, along with five seconds and a third, and all worth some $3,243,000 in prize money. The imminence of further competition seemed to have buoyed up his determination still further. This coming Saturday D. Wayne would start a further fourteen horses. This was racing's Superbowl after all. And this time around the winning trainers and jockeys would even be presented by the Emperors with a fourteen-carat gold Breeders Cup ring, just like the football players each January. Others might sneer at the concept but on 21 November and then through the coming twelve months at least, D. Wayne was determined to have the last word.

Lukas wasn't the only man with pressure on his shoulders. For their part the English contingent, still prickly about the Dancing Brave episode, were keen to post at least one more winner if only to demonstrate to the Americans that their horses really were as good as they claimed and that, after all the comments about the 'Bleeders Cup', they weren't just racing's equivalent of whingeing Poms. For Gaines and the Emperors of the Blue Grass the pressures were the greatest of them all. To further establish the Cup in the media and entertainment spotlight they needed a big crowd, record betting and a good day out for the TV executives and their guests. Of course they wanted results from the leading representatives of their own stallion stations but they were also looking for a prominent display from at least one European horse and the right balance of close and competitive finishes and clear-cut winners to further vindicate their concept's claim to championship status.

On the night of Friday 20 November there was a special Breeders Cup Gala Ball at the Beverly Hilton Hotel. A superbly kitsch and glitzy Hollywood occasion it was too. The co-chairmen of the ball were 'Dynasty' star and lifelong racing enthusiast John Forsyth, and Barbara Grant, wife of the late Cary Grant, himself a former director of Hollywood Park racecourse. The 'event committee' also included Forsyth's 'Dynasty' co-star 'Crystal' (Linda Evans), Walter Matthau, Robert Wagner and soap opera production king Aaron Spelling. While the guests chomped their way through Crab Louis, Catalina Lobster and Santa Barbara fried chicken 'Spanish Style', one of those ludicrous feuds that ensure that lawyers are the best-paid citizens in America was eating up the legal fees in a suite on the top floor. Two owners, supposedly involved in a partnership deal, couldn't decide whose colours their horse should run in.

Theatrical, ante-post favourite for the Breeders Cup Turf, was originally owned exclusively by real-estate developer Bert Firestone, whose racing interests are split between Ireland and America. Firestone bred Theatrical himself at his Gilltown Stud in County Kildare and raced him in Europe as a two- and three-year-old. He always looked a good horse and was Lester Piggott's final Derby ride when unplaced at Epsom in 1985. The following year Firestone shipped him out to the States and he'd finished second to Manila in the 1986 Breeders Cup Turf at Santa Anita. In the run-up to the 1987 series the son of Nureyev had established his own claim to be regarded as the best turf horse in America with impressive victories in the Man O'War Stakes and the Turf Classic in New York.

Half-way through the 1986 season Firestone had sold 50 per cent of Theatrical to Allen Paulson, another self-made millionaire and would-be Blue Grass Emperor whose career and racing ambitions have much in common with those of Gene Klein. Paulson, the son of a struggling Iowa farmworker, had to start supporting himself at the age of thirteen and worked his way through the standard litany of jobs of the American poor boy who is bound to make good. Newspaper salesman, men's-room cleaner, cowhand. Paulson did them all. In 1938 he came by one-third of a $100 raffle ticket and used his share to buy a one-way train ticket to California. Fifty years later Paulson is the president, chairman and chief executive of his own corporation, Gulfstream Aerospace, which is America's largest manufacturer of business aircraft.

Like Gene Klein, his principal American rival in the racing sphere, Paulson only became seriously involved in the business of ownership in the early 1980s. He's been a leading buyer at Keeneland now for five or six years but although his total purchases reach well over the fifty-million-dollar mark he's been as reluctant as Klein to get regularly involved in the really high-priced action with Sangster and the Arabs. Paulson's associates have frequently assured the world that their man is totally hooked on the beauty and excitement of thoroughbred racing. Not that his outward manner exactly exudes fun-loving enthusiasm. As befits a regular member of Forbes 500, supposedly the annual list of the richest men in America, Paulson welcomes being described as hard-boiled. Thickset and partially balding he even looks like a hard-boiled egg. Unlike Klein he's yet to be anywhere near as successful on the racetrack as he has been in his commercial life. Up to November 1987 his biggest success had been with the former French-trained filly Estrapade, purchased for $4.5 million and winner of the Arlington Million, one of America's richest turf races, in Chicago. Paulson's favourite ploy is to buy a share in a good horse with a leading chance in an upcoming race and then to buy out the other owner in due course. That was the plan with Theatrical.

According to the rules of the New York State Racing Commission, ownership of a horse must be limited to one person and one stable name. When Theatrical had run there at Aqueduct and Belmont Park he'd been registered in Firestone's name so he'd raced on the track wearing Firestone's colours. Now that they were out in California it was Paulson, the majority shareholder, who wanted Theatrical to run in his colours. Firestone, although reputedly retaining just a 12½ per cent stake in his horse, insisted that he and his wife had also retained managerial rights in Theatrical's training career and that if they so wished it the horse should continue to run in their green and white check silks. On the Thursday before the Cup the Hollywood Park stewards came down in favour of Firestone. Paulson, his supposed partner, promptly took his case to the California Horse Racing Board who overturned the stewards' decision and ruled that Theatrical must run after all in the red, white and blue colours of Paulson. For a while it was beginning to look as if Theatrical's chances would never even get beyond the jockeys' changing room.

As the eve-of-race banquet moved on towards the dessert course, two tuxedoed teams of lawyers for the Paulson and Firestone camps were 'still trying to work this thing out' upstairs. Using the kind of newspeak language that only seems to exist in the world of American litigation, Paulson's racing manager, George Scott, explained the situation to a breathlessly waiting world: 'Our people had a meeting with their people to see if we could have a meeting with the people from Hollywood Park. Now we have a proposal to put to the Breeders Cup committee which we hope will be amenable to the legal people from both sides . . .' etc., etc. In the end it was Paulson's people who won. Whether worn down by brilliant legal argument or just so distressed at missing all their dinner that they couldn't bear the thought of passing on the cabaret too, the Firestone people eventually threw in the towel or the black tie or whatever. This little ego war was over. Theatrical would run in the colours of his new exclusive owner, Allen E. Paulson.

'Welcome to California,' croaked Neil Diamond to his audience of celebs back in the Hilton ballroom down below.

The real entertainment was about to begin.

3 : 'Who is this Super-filly?'

At the top of the grandstand the Hollywood Park stewards were all in place, seated in their especially designed observation booth complete with phones and TV monitors. In California and most other American racing states the stewards are all under sixty and are all paid professionals. In the event of an objection or enquiry the jockeys talk to them by phone, in full view of the TV cameras, by picking up the receivers down by the unsaddling area.

In England, Ireland and France, going to the paddock and watching the ritual of walking the horses around before the jockeys arrive to mount up is one of the most cherishable moments of the afternoon. The paddock at Ascot, shaded by elegant horse chestnut trees with the old red-brick nineteenth-century stabling boxes in the background, is one of the most beautiful racecourse settings in the world. The paddock at Hollywood Park is simply a small, sunken oval in front of the clubhouse. A crescent of green turf in the centre surrounded by a smooth dirt horse-walk. The saddling-up boxes are around the outside and there's one exit on to the track and another into the Wembley tunnel-like entrance to the jockeys' weighing room. The horses are brought down from the training barns adjacent to the track before each race and then saddled up and walked briefly around in the paddock area itself which rapidly fills up with the rich, the powerful, the nervous, the astute, the egomaniacs and all those other *aficionados* and freeloaders who pass for racing 'connections' the world over.

The horses are led out on to the track to parade like greyhounds three or four times in front of the stands. The runners are accompanied on to the course by a posse of mounted grooms in dark glasses. At the head of this procession is the bugler. At Hollywood Park this gentleman is a Bob Hope type character complete with shades, top hat and hunting pink. It is his job to sound those few immortal chords that even the most casual turf enthusiast or 'Top Cat' and 'Sergeant Bilko' fan will always associate with American racing.

The 11 a.m. post time isn't normal in California. It had been forced on the Emperors of the Blue Grass by the all-important TV producers to put the races out at an acceptable transmission time back east. With some very big college football games like the Cornhuskers and Sooners clash (Nebraska and Oklahoma State) competing for attention, the NBC executives weren't being particularly optimistic about likely viewing figures but they all seemed determined to enjoy themselves none the less.

For the first race, the six-furlong Breeders Cup Sprint, America's undisputed champion speed-horse, Groovy, was the Las Vegas oddsmakers' red-hot 5-4 on favourite. The four-year-old Texan-bred had been an even hotter 5-2 on favourite for the previous year's Sprint at Santa Anita in which he'd been an expensive disaster. Since then Groovy had spent five months off the track with a knee injury but after returning to the course in June he'd run up a sequence of six straight victories and to most local judges his triumph in 1987 was merely a formality. Groovy's owners were after an Eclipse award as Horse of the Year and they were going at it like movie producers hyping up a film to the media. 'Groovy is the fastest thing I ever put my ass on,' said jockey Angel Cordero helpfully. The owners had even hired a PR company called 'Feeling Groovy' to promote their horse's chances and those who took up the invitations were treated to a cocktail party in his honour on the eve of the race.

Like many grandly conceived commercial scenarios the end-product didn't quite work out to plan. Groovy, drawn on the inside, was struggling all the way up the back stretch and at the far turn it was the three-year-old filly Very Subtle, a 16-1 shot ridden by Pat Venezuela, who had forced her way to the front. That's where she stayed too. Flashing past the wire no less than four lengths in front of her thirteen rivals of whom Groovy at least managed to finish second. Very Subtle's owner, Ben Rochelle, and her trainer, Mel Stute, who themselves looked as much like a pair of movie big shots as their evocative names suggest, were jubilant in the winners circle.

Very Subtle had just taken her career record to ten wins from sixteen starts with purse money of more than $1,250,000. Groovy's trainer, José Martin, looked devastated. Two of the three English entries, Governor General and Sharp Romance, couldn't adapt to the dirt surface at all and finished last and second to last but the Epsom-trained Sylvan Express put up a much more creditable performance to be eighth, some nine lengths behind the winner.

The race was all over in little more than a minute. About one minute eight and four-fifths seconds of fourteen thoroughbreds covering three-quarters of a mile at upwards of forty-one miles per hour. Americans start cheering their horses from the moment the stalls open and the noise of the cheering, of the horses' hoofs and of the heavily amplified commentary mixing in with the flashing silks and the flying dirt and whips, makes each race a truly exhilarating assault on the eyes and ears.

Events moved on briskly. No sooner had Ben Rochelle collected his prize than the twelve all-American-trained runners were moving out to parade for the second million-dollar race on the card. The Fillies Juvenile. This was to be D. Wayne Lukas's first big challenge of the day. Lukas had run Pine Tree Lane unplaced in the Sprint but no fewer than five of the twelve two-year-old fillies were entries from his stable including three daughters of leading American sire Mr Prospector and four runners wearing the colours of Eugene V. Klein. The Klein entry had the call in the morning line at 8-5 favourite with Classic Crown the 'outsider' of the party on offer at 4-1. The only filly being seriously backed to upset Lukas's plans was Jeanne Jones, a most attractive bay daughter of Nijinsky, trained by Charlie Whittingham for Golden Eagle Farms who'd named their horse after the author of a series of American cookery books. An easy winner of her maiden and then a game second to colts in her only other outing, Jeanne Jones was being supported by more than just Lukas-haters. In the saddle was the fifty-six-year-old Bill Shoemaker, as enduring, as gifted and as legendary a rider in the history of North American racing as Lester Piggott has been in Europe. Astonishingly short even by the standards of the flat race weighing room and as leathery now as any Marlboro cowboy, Willie the Shoe, the son of a Texas sharecropper, had, up to November, 1987, ridden more than 8,600 winners in an extraordinary thirty-eight-year career. He had yet to win a race in the Breeders Cup.

For seven of the eight furlongs of the Fillies Juvenile that duck looked sure to be broken. With Jeanne Jones no fewer than six lengths clear at the distance the outcome seemed likely to be every bit as decisive as Very Subtle's victory half an hour beforehand. Then suddenly, pulling away from the rest of the pursuers on the outside of the field . . . there was a challenger. A 33-1 outsider called Epitome ridden by the youthful Pat Day, a top Midwestern-based jockey no more than thirty-four years Shoemaker's junior. With half a furlong to run Jeanne Jones seemed to jink away from the photographers lining the rail. That and tiredness probably caused her to wander slightly off a straight course. To tumultuous cheering from the crowd the two fillies went past the wire together neck and neck. The subsequent photo-finish print recorded that in the very last stride of the race Epitome had got up by a nose which is a winning distance that doesn't exist in England where the closest verdict – apart from a dead-heat – is a short head. Epitome's owner-breeder John A. Bell III was as ecstatic as Ben Rochelle had been before him. Owner of Jonabell Farm, one of Kentucky's oldest commercial stud farms located within shouting distance of Keeneland and Blue Grass airport, Epitome's victory put the sixty-eight-year-old Bell back in the racing limelight and he was manifestly grateful for it too. Off a record of three wins in eight starts, Epitome's career earnings had now jumped to $553,991 thanks to the $450,000 she'd just won. Her victory was the narrowest yet in the short history of the Fillies event.

D. Wayne Lukas may have been twice out of luck already but his moment was rapidly approaching. With only six runners, the ten-furlong Breeders Cup Distaff, for fillies and mares of three years old and up, looked on paper to be the easiest race of the day. The favourite was another Charlie Whittingham-trained prospect. A five-year-old Chilean-bred mare called Infinidad owned by Seth Hancock's older brother Arthur Boyd Hancock III and ridden by the eighteen-year-old Corey Black. Yet many serious railbirds reckoned that odds of 2-1 about one of Lukas's runners, the three-year-old Raja Baba filly, Sacahuista, were an invitation to buy money.

Lukas had farmed the last two runnings of the Distaff and once again he was reckoned to have assessed it perfectly as the weak link in the series and a golden opportunity to collect a million. Sacahuista, a losing favourite in the 1986 Fillies Juvenile, had been running well without winning much all season. Game and consistent, she had every chance of success against possibly inferior opposition. And so it proved. Jockey Randy Romero broke from the gate in first place and dictated the entire race from the front. The novelty of a smaller field and further to travel meant that the connoisseurs in the stand had plenty of time to observe his masterful control and judgement of pace. It was a perfect demonstration of the style of race-riding that has won Steven Cauthen so many admirers and so many big prizes since he first came over to England in 1977. Just like the 'Kentucky Kid' it seemed as if Romero had a clock in his head. Never easing up his grip on the race for a second even though he was going progressively slower through each quarter of a mile he had a comfortable two and a quarter lengths to spare at the wire. Infinidad never showed.

In two minutes and two seconds Sacahuista had boosted her career winnings to over $1,300,000. Lukas greeted his winner not with emotion but with the cool confidence of the ex-basketball coach who has just watched his preordained game plan executed to perfection. As he strode around, purposeful but relaxed, between the saddling-up area and the track, it was quite impossible to take your eyes off him: the check jacket and black trousers, immaculate; the not too short hair, immaculate; and those extraordinary tinted glasses bouncing back every glare of the sun and every resentful stare from the public or the press. Like Vincent O'Brien and Lester Piggott in the era of Sir Ivor and Nijinsky. Like the fictitious cool players on whom he seems to have modelled himself – Steve McQueen playing poker in *The Cincinnati Kid* or Paul Newman shooting pool in *The Hustler* – Lukas's genius lies in making extremely difficult things, like successfully training highly strung thoroughbred racehorses, seem deceptively easy.

If D. Wayne was celebrating Sacahuista's victory, then Randy Romero was certainly in on the party. He was probably toasting the fact that he'd been able to ride in the race at all. In 1983 he suffered second and third degree burns over 65 per cent of his body after a freak accident in the slimmer's hotbox at Oaklawn Park racetrack in Arkansas. Unconscious for three weeks he was given only a 20 per cent chance of survival and told that even if he lived it would be at least a year before he could ride again. Yet just fourteen weeks later he was back on the course and he won with his first ride back too.

The Louisiana-based Romero's best-ever season was in 1986 when his 223 winners netted him $8,075,672 in the national money-earnings table. The money table is *the* crucial factor that determines a jockey's position in the American industry. Racing takes place all year round right across the nation, though the top jockeys tend to base themselves mainly in one particular region of which California and New York are the toughest and the most lucrative. With so much racing – there were more than 69,000 contests in 1987, of which 80 had a value to the winner of over $100,000 – it's not difficult to win a large number of races numerically but you have to be right up there with the best to win five or six million dollars at Belmont or Hollywood Park.

Even the best riders have no stable contracts or permanent retainers with specific trainers. It's a totally free market in which the jockeys' agents, who take 25 per cent of their clients' earnings, play a much more active role than they do in Britain. The top names in California are Shoemaker, Chris McCarron, Gary Stevens and Laffit Pincay. The top man in New York, the most powerful, competitive and intimidating jockey in the nation, is Angel Cordero jun. The big joke about the flamboyant Angel, who was born in Santurce, Puerto Rico in 1942, is that he doesn't just ride his own horse, he rides *all* the horses in the race. His combination of strength, aggression and enormous natural skill has made him one of the most successful riders in racing history. Aside from Shoemaker and Pincay he's the only other jockey with lifetime earnings of over $100 million. He's won the Kentucky Derby three times and the coveted Saratoga jockeys' title twelve. Over the weekend of 28 February–1 March 1987, he flew coast to coast for D. Wayne Lukas to win the $450,000 Flamingo Stakes at Hialeah in Florida and then the $300,000 Santa Margarita Handicap at Santa Anita, California.

He's also been known to give a less than cordial welcome to aspiring new boys on the New York circuit, and journalists too have learnt to approach him with caution. A couple of English writers, accompanied by a Breeders Cup publicity aide, were introduced to Angel down by the training barns at Hollywood Park. They stood there rooted to the spot and mouthed a few platitudes about his fearsome international reputation. The Puerto Rican fighting cock stared at them for a moment or two and then suddenly showered them with a stream of Spanish expletives. The Englishmen smiled limply. Angel smiled back and then strutted away, tapping his boot with his riding whip. 'That's great,' says the grinning aide. 'No really. That means he likes you!'

Lester could handle Angel. Pat Eddery can handle him. How would the Frenchman, Freddie Head, cope when he rode Miesque against Angel on Le Belvedere in the Breeders Cup Mile?

With three races down and the clock past midday it was extremely hot now out on the track. The NBC TV crew, looking cool and laid-back in their matching blazers, were sailing through it all with unruffled calm. They even had Channel 4 racing's English anchorman, Brough Scott, with them as token Limey for the day.

The Channel 4 team have had their critics but they have also made enormous strides in recent years in their efforts to make horse-racing accessible and entertaining to a much wider audience than just the trilby hat brigade. Scott, a former professional jump-jockey, seemed much shorter than his American co-hosts. But neither lack of inches nor the heat nor the unlikely setting could deflate his terrier-like energy and enthusiasm. He kept marching up and down past the winning-post in full view of the sun with a clipboard in one hand, a microphone in the other and what looked like a giant television aerial attached to his back. The whole effect made him seem rather like an extra at the climactic scene of *Close Encounters of the Third Kind*. Not that the Americans could've been anything but impressed by his professionalism. 'OK, Mel . . .' one of them would drawl, 'nothing much happening up here by the clubhouse, so . . . (a three-second pause) . . . let's hear from Bruffscot.' And there on cue would be an inset of the splendid Bruffscot. Bubbling with enthusiasm like Basil Brush and giving his glazed Californian colleagues the low-down on why Clive Brittain's Cruise Ship was an unlikely candidate for the Colts Juvenile.

One crucial piece of news that Bruffscot was able to relay was that in spite of her injury Milligram would definitely take her chance in the Breeders Cup Mile. Take her chance maybe but, according to both the London offices and the Las Vegas bookies, with little or no chance of winning. Her trainer still had Sonic Lady though. Michael Stoute arrived in the paddock looking almost as crisp and business-like as D. Wayne Lukas. Wearing his Goodwood cream suit and bareheaded as he almost always is in England, no American was lightly underestimating this competitor. A mile on turf is a rare experience for American racing fans and it may need to be said that, of the fourteen runners for the 1987 Breeders Cup Mile, the nine American-trained horses were mostly, though not all, some way below the class of the best nine-furlong dirt horses in their own country, let alone the best turf milers from Europe. The three European fillies dominated the PMU market with Sonic Lady, whose single-minded training campaign had impressed the locals, best at around 11-4 favourite. Charlie Whittingham's pair, Le Belvedere, owned by Paulson and Temperate Sil, who was to be ridden by Shoemaker, were both 5-1 shots. Yet to some big-time European gamblers (of whom there were more than a few present, especially from Ireland) odds of more than 7-2 about Miesque, a six times Group One winner, were one of the stand-out bets of the year.

Miesque's sire Nureyev, also owned by Stavros Niarchos, won the

1980 2,000 Guineas at Newmarket in brilliant style only to lose the
race in the stewards' room as the result of an instant's reckless riding
by his jockey. Nureyev himself is a son of the 1964 Kentucky Derby
and Preakness Stakes winner, Northern Dancer, who is not only the
most successful and prepotent sire of the post-war period but quite
possibly the most influential stallion of the century. Like her grandfather, Miesque is not over-large but she's neat and strong and full of
quality. Ideally suited you might think to the sharp turns and fast
pace of American racing. And who could forget the devastating
speed that she'd shown at Newmarket, Longchamp and Deauville?
In the paddock the winter coat observed by the training barns was
certainly noticeable but then so was her strong, muscular physique,
her relaxed temperament and the equally relaxed and outwardly
confident manner of her elegant trainer, François Boutin. Miesque's
jockey, Freddie Head, came out of the weighing room tunnel with
the thirteen other riders and very quickly they all got the leg-up from
their trainers and followed the bugler out on to the track.

Freddie Head is one of the most gifted and experienced riders in
the world yet in the past he has frequently been cruelly and unfairly
roasted by the English racing press. Son of the great French trainer
and breeder, Alec Head, and brother of the equally talented trainer
Criquette, the smooth-faced Freddie first burst on to the international
racing scene in 1966 when he won the first of four Prix de l'Arc de
Triomphe, on Bot Mot trained by his grandfather, William. Two of
his other famous Arc victories on Ivanjica for his father in 1976 and
on Three Troikas for his sister in 1979 confirmed that he had joined
Yves St Martin at the very top of his profession in France and that,
along with St Martin and Lester Piggott, he was now among the élite
of the world's big-race jockeys. Yet at least to begin with, his efforts
in England and especially at Epsom rarely seemed to meet with the
same success as at Longchamp.

Riding with an almost exaggeratedly short style, his bottom even
higher in the air than Piggott's, and frequently dropping his horses
right out and coming from way off the pace, Freddie looked an artist
when he won but was labelled an artist of a very different kind by
the English punters when his tactics backfired, his mounts got boxed
in and he couldn't get a run. Then there was the problem of steering.
Epsom is one of the most difficult racecourses to navigate in the
world, made all the harder because of the fact that there are so few
race-meetings there each year. Riding Lyphard for his father in the
1971 Derby, it appeared that Freddie lost control coming down the
hill to Tattenham Corner. Lyphard veered away to the right and

ended up on the stands-side rail, any chance of victory gone. English jockey Geoff Lewis joked afterwards that 'if Freddie Head comes to Epsom again the gypsies'll be demanding danger money'.

Yet there have also been memorable days when Freddie has made fools of the English. When he rode Ma Biche for his sister in the 1983 1,000 Guineas at Newmarket, many of the local racing correspondents insisted that as he was bound to hold the filly up he'd never get a run and that he must be opposed. Ma Biche won brilliantly by one and a half lengths. Discussing Miesque's chances in 1987, the same journalists were still claiming that Freddie's riding tactics were bound to cost him the race and that the English jockeys would gang up on him and bully him. Miesque came with an electrifying late run ... and won by one and a half lengths. 'You cannot come wizout zee horse,' said Freddie afterwards. 'Today I have zee horse ... so I come.'

With his light-brown hair, his suave, slightly arrogant good looks and his faintly supercilious manner, Freddie makes the perfect fat frog Frenchman that every upright English racegoer loves to hate. No European or big international race-meeting where English and French horses are in competition would really be complete without him. Whenever there's an English-trained favourite for a race like the Prix de l'Arc de Triomphe, some sections of the domestic racing press always insist on describing it in excessively patriotic terms as honest, brave, courageous, etc. The leading French fancy is by comparison sneaky, arrogant, low-down and ridden, of course, by Freddie.

The sensible jockeys in the stand were full of pre-race advice and doubts about how Freddie could possibly be trusted to win round Hollywood Park. You couldn't ride a horse off the pace in America, they said. He'd never get a run, never get through. The race would be over before he was even in top gear. What about that first bend? Fourteen horses swinging sharp left-handed after barely a furlong would be like negotiating the first turn in a greyhound race. Miss the break or the inside rail and you could be knocked as wide as the five-dog at Harringay. And Freddie was never one of the first out of the stalls, now was he? Laffit Pincay, Angel Cordero and our own – well Ireland's actually – Pat Eddery would make Freddie look like an amateur, like an apprentice. Hah! Just see how they would. Only then they didn't ... naturally.

As the runners paraded in front of the crowd for the last time, Freddie looked around him in what seemed to his admirers and detractors alike to be his most overweeningly self-confident manner.

When the stalls opened, he and Miesque came out like finalists in the Olympic 100 metres (no ambiguity intended). They took that all-important first turn in about fifth place just one horse off the rail. As the leaders sped away down the back stretch, Miesque was right on their heels. Coming up to the turn on the far side there was no more than a three-and-a-half length gap between Shoemaker on Temperate Sil and Freddie Head with Pincay and Sonic Lady frantically trying to get on terms. You could practically feel the hearts beating in the European contingent – even the English were Europeans now – and you could hear the muttered, believing but disbelieving prayers of the gamblers and lovers of the track. 'Go on Freddie. Go on my beauty. She can do it. She can. She can win it from here. I really think she's going to do it.' As they came into the straight with just a quarter of a mile left to run, Marcos Castaneda on Show Dancer moved off the inside rail. It was the decisive moment of the race. Miesque, suddenly asked for that blinding burst of acceleration that she'd displayed so many times before, went through the gap in a second. And that was it. With Head crouched low over his filly's neck but riding only hands and heels and never once touching her with his whip, the dual Guineas winner shot clear of the field, putting instant daylight between herself, the valiant but tiring Show Dancer and the desperate finishing run of Sonic Lady. As she stormed towards the wire more than three lengths clear of her pursuers the reaction of the crowd was ecstatic. Hardened French, English and Irish racing-lovers shouted themselves hoarse with jubilation. At last all the jibes and sneers of the Americans could be flung off like the cramping harassment of a playground bully. The supreme moment of vindication had arrived and to a racing-lover the sight of that beautiful filly going so explosively through the gap on the inside straight would always be as emotional and unforgettable a memory as the moment when Eric Liddell slams the Americans in his 400-metre final in *Chariots of Fire*. A European classic winner had come to LA in November, seven months after her opening run at Maisons Laffitte in the suburbs of Paris, and had upheld the status of European racing in a quite glorious and spectacular way.

Patricia Boutin flung her arms round her father as, along with Niarchos' racing manager, Alan Cooper, they vaulted over the rail and raced towards the returning heroine. Anthony Stroud insisted that the Maktoums were in no way disappointed with Sonic Lady's performance; Michael Stoute, who looked desperately disappointed, was assured by everyone that his filly was really the second-best horse in the race. Looking unimpressed, Stoute confirmed that Sonic

Lady would now be retired and go to Kentucky to be covered by one of the élite stallions. Milligram finished second to last. As Cooper accepted Niarchos' trophy from Linda Evans (who may not have enjoyed being described by the announcer as the second most beautiful filly on the track), there were suggestions that Miesque, who in spite of having won two classics in Europe had just increased her lifetime prize money by one third again to $1,308,740, might stay in training as a four-year-old.

The Americans were impressed too. Oh, they were impressed all right. 'Who is this super-filly?' shrieked a chubby, therapy-group leader from Malibu. 'Are there many more like her back home?' asked a tanned Don Johnson clone who'd even taken off his shades and broken his pose by the running rail to leap on to a chair and cheer Miesque home. Other local spectators leafed frantically through their racecards as if clues to this horse they'd never heard of before might suddenly come to light. You could feel the crowd still buzzing as the jockeys arrived in the paddock to mount up for the next race. The French – or as the English insisted 'European' – victory had brought new respect from the bleachers, and the fans were a little closer together now in spirit. As far as John Gaines and the Emperors of the Blue Grass were concerned, the day was already a hit whatever else happened. In fact for everyone, not least the two brothers from Cork who'd backed Miesque to win more than a quarter of a million dollars, the excitement had embarked on an exhilarating upward curve and it would get still higher before the business was done.

Half an hour after Miesque's victory Wayne Lukas and Gene Klein were back in the winners circle when Success Express, one of their three-strong entry in the Colts Juvenile, scored by one and three-quarter lengths from the Canadian-bred Regal Classic with another Lukas-trained runner Tejano back in third. Incredibly this was Lukas's sixth Breeders Cup triumph which, when you consider there had been just twenty-eight races in the series to date, gives further confirmation of D. Wayne's extraordinary ratio of winners to runners when the big money's down.

'Ladies and gentlemen,' called the racetrack announcer. 'Please welcome Mr Merv Griffin.' Lukas and Klein stepped up to collect their trophies from the durable Merv and, as the runners for the Breeders Cup Turf began to make their way into the saddling-up area below, the NBC cameras roamed back over the balcony seats by the Directors' Lounge intercutting celebrity-spotting with a spot of station identification.

For the Europeans another moment of truth was approaching.

There seemed to be a bigger contingent of owners and connections assembling now on the small grass oval than for any of the afternoon's previous races. Dancing Brave's owner Prince Khalid Abdulla was there but merely as an onlooker. Accompanying him was one of his two principal English trainers, the rotund, sixty-two-year-old, Jeremy Tree. The impeccably mannered Old Etonian, with his large jowls and bloodshot eyes, would actually pass muster with many Americans as a Sydney Greenstreet or even Orson Welles figure. Not a Southern police chief maybe but certainly a powerful industrial magnate or head of some 'old money' investment bank. Tree could afford to look relaxed as he had no runners at the meeting and was only there for the sunshine and the Californian wine. Some of the more involved English trainers hovered uncertainly on the edges of the action looking like new arrivals at a party who don't really know any of the other guests. Paul Cole and Barry Hills were there to saddle Bint Pasha and Sir Harry Lewis. Accepting that dress codes are rather different in Los Angeles than they may be at Newbury they had each of them laid aside their customary brown trilby hats and they almost seemed normal people without them. Bareheaded, the greying Hills looked remarkably like the wily-faced Ladbrokes boss, Cyril Stein, while Cole in a plain, dark suit had the stiffer, more upright manner of a prep school headmaster from the Home Counties. Perhaps they'd read the comments about them in *Daily Racing Form*. Cole barely got a mention but, whereas Michael Stoute had been described as a 'world-class conditioner', the entry on Hills was more oblique. 'Barry Hills is an Englishman who lives in Wiltshire,' said the paper.

In truth the eyes of most ordinary spectators and racing professionals alike were not on either the Irish Derby winner or the heroine of the Prix Vermeille but on the two horses that had dominated all the pre-race speculation. America's Theatrical and Europe's Trempolino. To call Theatrical American at all was stretching it considerably in view of his Irish breeding and the fact that he'd actually finished second to Law Society in the 1985 Irish Derby. None the less, his seven graded-race victories since coming to America were a perfect advert to other European-based owners of the rewards that could be gleaned from shipping a horse out to a different environment to compete against supposedly weaker opposition. Having been completely bought out by his former partner, there was no Bert Firestone down there in the paddock watching Theatrical saddle up. Only Paulson and his 'people'.

The local handicappers may have been making Theatrical favourite but after Miesque none of them was underestimating Trempolino.

Unlike Guy Harwood's two-week acclimatisation programme with Dancing Brave, the 1987 Arc winner had only arrived in LA the day before the race. It had been seven weeks since the Arc but, so far from looking tired or over the top, Trempolino seemed fresh and well and to have improved in strength and condition since Longchamp. His dashing owner, or co-owner as he now was, the grey-haired senior Société d'Encouragement member, Paul de Moussac, was clearly revelling in the big-race American atmosphere. Having already won the Arc and then struck a more than satisfactory deal with Bruce McNall you could say he was entitled to. De Moussac, tall, slim and slightly foppish and McNall, short and smooth with dark glasses and what looked like his own set of designer bodyguards, made an interesting combination, if outwardly a more equitable one than Paulson and Firestone had been.

The Americans revere the Arc almost as much as the Derby at Epsom and as an Arc winner it was assumed that Trempolino was automatically a champion. In fact his European form, though good, hardly placed him in the Miesque class. Prior to the Arc his best performance had been his narrow defeat by Natroun in the French Derby but at Longchamp he looked to be no better than a genuine outsider. The hot favourite for the 1987 Arc was the English Derby and St Leger winner Reference Point, who as usual went off at a furious gallop. Whether due to an injury possibly sustained during the race or to the effects of too many hard battles earlier in the season, Reference Point was done for when they turned into the straight but, thanks to the pace he'd set, so were many of his rivals. Trempolino, who had been dropped out at the rear early on by Pat Eddery, closed on the tiring leader about three furlongs out and then burst into the lead showing an acceleration that had not been apparent in his earlier races. The Italian horse Tony Bin was second. An alternative view of the 1987 Arc was that, of twelve tiring horses, Trempolino was simply tiring less quickly than the others. Yet whatever his detractors believed, he did seem to have improved through the autumn and the fact that his trainer, André Fabre, thought that in European conditions he only just stayed a mile and a half seemed to make him a natural for the same distance round the easier, sharper Hollywood circuit. Certainly Pat Eddery, whose previous Breeders Cup Turf experiences on Pebbles and Dancing Brave had been decidedly mixed, was as determined as ever he is to prove to the pampered Americans that the English jockeys' championship is the best and toughest riding school in the world.

Pat Day, the Christian Fundamentalist jockey who was riding

Theatrical, was considered to be in fair need of divine assistance to overcome the natural disadvantage of his number twelve outside draw, which in local parlance is reckoned to be about as helpful as being somewhere out on Century Boulevard. Clearly mindful of the problem Day came out of the stalls almost as forcefully as Freddie Head had done on Miesque earlier on. He took the first turn in fourth place and held that position through the first six furlongs where Day moved him up and then over on to the inside rail giving him the lead for the first time at the all-important far turn. Pat Eddery, showing no panic at all in the face of the fierce early pace, was playing it almost by European standards for the first half-mile and riding Trempolino from well off the pace as he had done at Longchamp. With the horse relaxed and running well for him Eddery started making up ground down the back stretch. For a while the course commentator lost sight of him but there were thrilled gasps of excitement from the Europeans in the crowd as they saw McNall's blue and silver colours appearing out of the pack on the outside. Theatrical tried to kick on but he couldn't lose Eddery as the Arc winner first loomed up to join him and then swept into the straight full of running and apparently with the race in his sights. A furlong and a half from home it seemed as if Trempolino was going to go past, that he was going to do it, that a French-trained horse was going to pull off the unprecedented Arc de Triomphe/Breeders Cup Turf double in the same season. Only, Theatrical wasn't done for. Two years older than Trempolino, tough, fit and every inch a stayer, he put down his head, stretched out his neck and battled for dear life up that inside rail. André Fabre's fears that his horse wouldn't quite get home in a true-run mile and a half race suddenly seemed to be fulfilling themselves in front of his eyes and try though the English and French might to roar and roar and lift Eddery up past the leader they saw Day pull away again inside the final one hundred yards and flash past the wire still a precious half a length to the good. Theatrical's 1987 earnings had just rocketed to an incredible $2,250,000, a record for any racehorse in one year running solely on the turf.

Once again the sixty thousand spectators were swaying dizzily with the excitement of it all. Pat Day insisted that with racing luck and the good Lord prevailing he always knew that he'd do it. Paulson got his moment in the winner's circle. 'He looks like a fat old alligator, don't he?' said Florida's Van Grayson. John Gaines and his Imperial committee got more of the confirmation that they'd so desperately wanted. Theatrical had won first prize but Trempolino had performed heroically and demonstrated beyond doubt that his Arc victory was anything but a fluke. Who could possibly say now that the top European-trained horses couldn't show their best form in unfamiliar surroundings and couldn't retain their ability so late in the year? And André Fabre had thrown all conventional ideas about acclimatisation right out of the window. The chubby therapy-group leader was ready to salute the French effusively. 'They only stepped off the plane yesterday, for Christ's sake. They fly in. They do the job. And then they're out. Fantastic. It's a fucking dream!'

Six races down and only one race left of the original magnificent seven. The Breeders Cup Classic. Ten furlongs on dirt. For a total purse of three million big ones and first prize winnings of $1,350,000 making this by far the richest horse-race in the world. With that kind of money at stake, even some of the wealthiest American owners were looking a little nervous. Down in the paddock the Las Vegas comedian Tim Conway was trying to loosen them up. Conway joked that his two horses had reached the point now of walking around their stable box. 'Which has to be an improvement,' he added. 'They are also undergoing swimming therapy. If the track ever has a three-furlong backstroke event I'll be rich.' So why had he got involved with thoroughbreds in the first place? 'Horse-racing gives celebrities the opportunity to spend the inheritance before the kids grow up.' Conway's colours have the words 'No Passing' emblazoned on the back. 'It doesn't do any good,' he said. 'All the other horses ignore it.' The visiting press loved it but the connections of the leading participants were all too edgy to laugh.

Surprisingly – or inevitably, according to the critics of his training methods – there was no D. Wayne Lukas runner. In the days before the race one other trainer, Jack Van Berg, handler of the Kentucky Derby winner Alysheba, had been taking almost as many digs and wisecracks down at his training barn as Lukas had been getting himself. Alysheba, a bay son of Alydar, the luckless and narrow runner-up to Affirmed in each leg of the historic 1978 Triple Crown series, had given Van Berg and his jockey, Chris McCarron, their first-ever Derby victory in Louisville's 'Run for the Roses' earlier in the year. Alysheba had gone on to take the Preakness Stakes at Pimlico racecourse in Maryland but in the third leg of the Triple Crown, the Belmont Stakes at Belmont Park in New York, he was completely overrun by a horse called Bet Twice who had himself been well beaten by Alysheba in the previous two races. The significant and possibly disturbing fact about this was that, before the Derby and the Preakness, Alysheba had been treated with Lasix.

In the Belmont Stakes he had had to run without it since the use of such drugs is restricted by the New York State racing authorities. Van Berg gave his colt a long rest after the Preakness fiasco, bringing him back for a winning return in a Grade One race in Louisiana, another state permitting Lasix, in September. Grilled by the press boys as to whether Alysheba was really a deserving winner of the Derby and whether he could win big races without medication, Van Berg insisted that his colt had gained his victories entirely on merit, and that the Belmont had simply been too far for him especially after his earlier tough schedule. Then he added that he would be treating Alysheba with Lasix before the Breeders Cup Classic.

There was no doubt that most non-partisan onlookers were rooting not for Alysheba but for the previous year's Kentucky Derby winner, Ferdinand. As well as being Whittingham's first-ever Derby victor, the Nijinsky colt had also been Bill Shoemaker's first triumph in the race since 1965. A whole flood of popular support forced Ferdinand down to even-money favourite before the off, with Alysheba next best at around 7-2, the 1986 Classic winner Skywalker at 8-1 and Clive Brittain's Bold Arrangement out with the rags at 200-1.

The first six furlongs of the race were almost a carbon copy of the Breeders Cup Turf half an hour before. Candi's Gold with Corey Black and Judge Angelucci ridden by Eddie Delahoussaye broke very fast from the gate and led the field through the first turn. Shoemaker, coming out of the number six draw expertly, took Ferdinand up quickly into fourth place just a length or two off the leaders. As they raced away down the back stretch, McCarron seemed to be riding like a European and he and Alysheba, who had been drawn nine, were just to the rear of the main chasing group in about seventh position. At the far turn Shoemaker moved Ferdinand to the outside with just Judge Angelucci and Candi's Gold in front of him now, and seemingly both horses covered. Except that Alysheba was coming too. Making up ground rapidly like a potential Champion Hurdle winner coming down the hill at Cheltenham, McCarron appeared on Shoemaker's outside as the four horses swept round together into the straight. For a moment it seemed as if 'The Shoe' only had to press a button for Ferdinand to accelerate into a decisive lead but all of a sudden Judge Angelucci wasn't giving way and Alysheba still appeared to be going as well as any of them. The crowd weren't just on their feet. They were standing on their chairs. They were jumping and straining for a view and roaring and punching the skyline and yelling their hearts out. The final moves of the race and the rising crescendo of noise had everyone in a state of almost indescribable excitement. At the furlong pole Shoemaker had it. Judge Angelucci seemed beaten and with 'The Shoe' perfectly balanced and never once picking up his whip, the Ferdinand entourage must have believed that the wire, posterity and $1,300,000 were only seconds away. If they did they were reckoning without Alysheba. Chris McCarron, riding for all he was worth, simply wouldn't give in. Rousting his mount closer with every stride, he kept coming and coming and inching his way up until the two horses and their riders, a tumultuous gash of colour and noise and straining muscle, galloped past the winning post together, virtually inseparable.

The crowd were beside themselves. To have seen two successive Kentucky Derby winners locked in battle and giving everything in the dying strides of the richest race in the world was a script that not even the corniest film-writer would've dared to come up with. After a minute's deliberation and examination of the photo-finish print the judge called the names of Ferdinand, Charles Whittingham and William Shoemaker the winners. By a nose. The fans erupted once again. The baseball caps and stetsons flew high into the air, and celebration wasn't confined to the bleachers either. Some of the big shots were trembling and weeping and hugging each other in scenes reminiscent, to European eyes, of the Irish mare Dawn Run's historic Cheltenham Gold Cup victory in 1986. Even the most cynical and conservative observers freely admitted that they'd just witnessed the most exciting single day's racing of their lives culminating in possibly the most dramatic and emotional climactic race imaginable. In those final two breathtaking minutes the dream of John R. Gaines and the Emperors of the Blue Grass had surely been vindicated for all the world to see.

The Breeders Cup was over but there were actually still two races left on the nine-race programme. Not million-dollar races but $100,000 handicaps none the less. A stark contrast to, say, Derby Day at Epsom where the three contests following the big one are a string of mediocre second-eleven races worth less than £50,000 between them. Of course the really beautiful people from both the racing and the movie world were already beginning to leave. It's always a mark of attaining celebrity status on the racecourse when you're seen heading for your helicopter just after the big race. At Hollywood Park that meant sweeping out of the Turf Club entrance towards the line of valet-parked limos that were gliding back up to the front steps. The Beverly Hills wives and mistresses marched back past the same groups of gawping onlookers that had greeted their arrival earlier. For them the horse-racing had been just a momentary interruption in their normal flow of conversation about agents, florists and the catering arrangements for a charity breakfast party the following day. One older and more anarchic-looking lady, no doubt contemplating the first highball of the evening, paused momentarily on the top step. Oozing that air of sexual ruthlessness immortalised by Anne Bancroft in *The Graduate* she suddenly took a large wad of dollar bills out of her handbag, flicked through them briskly and then slipped the entire amount down the front of her dress.

As the several thousand British and Irish racing-lovers who'd made the trip to California also began to file out into the shadowy blue light of the Los Angeles afternoon they had plenty to think about as well as Hollywood fantasies. How would England and Ireland's centuries-old racing programme compare in the year ahead with the thrilling events that they'd just witnessed here? So Hollywood Park was ugly and featureless compared with Epsom or The Curragh. So American racing had a contentious drug policy too but how could you discount the excitement, the noise, the showmanship and the sheer effortless professionalism and razzmatazz? Why should tradition, the existing pattern of racing and other apparently inviolable concepts be allowed to prevent a similar single-day epic in Europe? Why did it have to be so expensive to go racing in England and why did some racing occasions still feel as if they were being staged for a private coterie of the right people with the general public tolerated at best? If the prize money was on American lines would the racing be any better? And why were English racecourses still divided up on such an outdated and snobbish basis with their Members' Enclosures, Tattersalls Enclosures and Silver Rings?

For the professionals too there were many important matters to ponder over. Just how good were the horses who'd been competing in Southern California that late fall day? Would any of the two-year-olds, especially the Lukas horses, train on the following year? Would Ferdinand, Alysheba and Miesque, all of whom were to stay in training, in spite of the enormous costs and insurance premiums, be able to hold their form through another season? Why had the French done so well and the English, for all their excuses, performed so poorly? And was there really any difference, as the Americans claimed, between these enabling race-track medications and the real, enhancing drugs that would come to cast such a shadow over the world of athletics nine months later?

The Emperors of the Blue Grass were more than satisfied with the

actual racing. The crowd had been enormous. Thirteen million
dollars had been wagered on the track and a further twenty-three
million at off-track locations around the country. The live telecast
had been taken by thirty-eight countries around the world and the
US TV audience alone was estimated at twenty million people.
Several of the big Kentucky stallion farms like Walmac, who stood
Nureyev, and Claiborne, the home of Nijinsky, had particular cause
for satisfaction while any Blue Grass Empire with a major concentration of Northern Dancer blood, be it Claiborne again or Robert
Sangster's Coolmore Stud in Ireland, could relax in the knowledge
that their money was still safely invested in the right place. For the
Emperors though, the crucial question was whether the success of
the racing would genuinely boost the bloodstock market and lead to
new owners getting involved in the industry. With Wall Street's
Black Monday still only a very recent memory they were bound to be
worried but to find out the answer to their question they would have
to wait until at least the big yearling sales the following summer.

And what of the fat cats who actually owned the top horses? How
would they fare in 1988 in both Europe and America? Would the
Arabs draw further away? Could Sangster's apparently depleted
empire fight back or might they even go under altogether? Could
Wayne Lukas and Gene Klein win a Kentucky Derby at last? For
the bloodstock gambler and the ante-post punter alike it was all the
same obsessive speculation. Which of them and their trainers, jockeys
. . . and horses, would be able to call themselves a winner when it
counted the most: at Newmarket, Epsom and The Curragh; at
Pimlico and Belmont Park; and at Churchill Downs, Kentucky? The
following May and then again at the season's end on 5 November
1988? For Breeders Cup Five.

4 : A Small Businessman with an Overdraft

It began really, this astonishing transformation of a traditional sport into a big-time international industry, back in 1975. And the prime mover, the player whose actions would have a far-reaching effect on events on both sides of the Atlantic, was the then thirty-eight-year-old, Repton-educated, Robert Edmund Sangster, son of Vernon Sangster, founder of the nationwide pools company. This Robert Sangster was a lucky man. He was passionately interested in horse-racing and he was already involved in owning and breeding horses from his base up at Swettenham Hall near Congleton in Cheshire. But now he wanted to go in on a much bigger scale. Only unlike most people who have ever entertained dreams of empire-building on the turf he had a large wad of inherited money with which to try and make those dreams become reality. He also just happened to know a dynamic young Irish stud-farm manager, called John Magnier, who just happened to be about to get married to one Susan O'Brien, whose father, Vincent O'Brien, was at the time the most famous and successful racehorse trainer in the world.

Sangster and Magnier had collaborated over a few horses with O'Brien before. They had won the Wokingham Stakes together at Royal Ascot with Boone's Cabin. Now Sangster proposed to O'Brien that along with Magnier and one or two other selected partners they should form a new kind of racing syndicate. A syndicate that with the help of Sangster's capital, O'Brien's judgement and expertise and Magnier's energy and commercial flair, would go out to Kentucky that summer and attempt to buy the best-bred and best-looking yearlings they could find. In particular they'd be looking out for colts from the bloodline of Northern Dancer, sire of O'Brien's brilliantly fast 1970 Derby winner, Nijinsky. These horses would be brought back to O'Brien's stable at Ballydoyle in County Tipperary, and raced in Europe with the specific intention of 'making them' as attractive stallion prospects rather than simply trying to win prizes with them on the track. The aim was to buy a sufficient number of quality yearlings each year to ensure that if just one of them made the grade and developed into another O'Brien-trained European classic winner, like Nijinsky himself, then the chances were that they could sell that horse back to the Americans for more than the whole yearling batch had cost them altogether. And if the operation really became a success, then the possibility existed that instead of always selling on they could begin to keep some of the better horses at their own stud base at Coolmore, less than ten miles from Ballydoyle, so that when Northern Dancer and his older American-based sons were played out they could start to operate as rivals to the Americans in their own right.

Sangster's reasoning was that the traditional concept of racehorse ownership as a luxury sport for men born to privilege was an idea whose time had passed. He wanted to exploit the commercial and economic possibilities of the newly expanding international bloodstock market. Of course there were high-class stallions standing at stud in Europe too. You could purchase their yearlings at Tattersalls Sales at Newmarket and at Goffs in Ireland each autumn. The real financial muscle though, the ability to syndicate a stallion for serious money, only existed in the States. And if you wanted to get a piece of that action you had to be buying and running horses in the first place that had built-in breeding potential for the American market. The infinite power of the dollar had been enough to purchase numerous European racehorses for a track and stud career in America throughout the twentieth century and the Blue Grass was now home to the largest collection of blue-blooded stallions anywhere in the world. Then there was the fact that the best of the progeny of these Kentucky-based sires seemed to possess both the speed and the fluency congenital to American dirt-track racing. Qualities which might well give them an invaluable edge in future competition against the more stoutly bred and stamina-influenced European thoroughbreds.

It would be quite wrong to imply that when he set up his operation, Sangster in any sense 'bought' Vincent O'Brien. None the less when the pools heir succeeded in getting in with the fifty-nine-year-old Irish trainer he was attaching his money to a genius and to a racing record beyond compare. In a career that had begun in the early 1940s O'Brien had already scaled just about every single height that a trainer could aspire to. Three successive Grand National winners. Three successive winners of the Cheltenham Gold Cup and victory in almost every major flat race in the calendar including no fewer than four triumphs in the Derby at Epsom. And two of those horses, Sir Ivor in 1968 and Nijinsky in 1970, were considered to be amongst the greatest Derby winners of the twentieth century.

Nijinsky's Derby was a decisive turning-point for O'Brien personally and for European racing in general. Nijinsky's most striking characteristic was his dazzling speed which he seemed to have inherited from his father, the Canadian-bred Northern Dancer, who won the 1964 Kentucky Derby and Preakness Stakes. Northern Dancer was himself a grandson of Nearco who had been owned and bred by the celebrated Italian, Tesio. Nearco was one of the best European racehorses of the pre-war years. Unbeaten in fourteen races, his most famous victory was in the 1938 Grand Prix de Paris. At stud he became one of the most influential stallions that racing has ever known. Vincent O'Brien believed that Northern Dancer himself was also a sire of such quality that it was entirely possible that he would continue to transmit the same speed that he'd imparted to Nijinsky to others of his sons and that they in turn might continue to pass it on to their own progeny. Robert Sangster realised that if the American-breds did indeed do well in European racing a new commercial fashion could be initiated. Other big owners would also want to buy them as yearlings. The yearling prices would rise and so would the prices the Americans would be prepared to pay to buy back the most successful of them as stallions for their own stud farms in the States. The crucial element in Sangster's plan, the factor upon which everything else would depend, was the unrivalled skill of Vincent O'Brien.

The hallmark of the trainer's success had always been his quiet, painstaking professionalism and his astonishing eye for a horse. To a degree unequalled by any other agent or trainer he could look at an unraced yearling and assess and imagine its likely development over the next two years. Then, when the horses were actually in training at Ballydoyle, O'Brien would often demonstrate an almost magical, intuitive understanding of a horse's mind and mental landscape. This ability, shared by Wayne Lukas and understood if not possessed by many other Irishmen, was what marked O'Brien out from some of those unimaginative English trainers who could only stick to the simplest rules. What's more, Sangster was offering O'Brien a kind of trainer's paradise. A relatively small number of superbly bred horses to which the Master could devote infinite time and patience, unlike some of the big English stables where with nearly 200 horses in the yard the trainers may personally encounter some of their charges about once a week if they're lucky. O'Brien would have a personal financial shareholding in every horse he trained and all of those horses would be jointly owned by just a small group of people, limiting arguments over priorities and cutting out different owners insisting on different things. Sangster's commercial aspirations were likely to make one or two Jockey Club members choke on their port but that didn't bother O'Brien who, while an outwardly shy and thoroughly respectable man, had never been an establishment figure anyway.

Vincent O'Brien was born and brought up in County Cork and has lived all his life down in Cork and Tipperary, part of the province of Munster, which has always been a staunchly Catholic and conservative but Republican region of Ireland. In the 1920s it suffered horribly at the hands of the Black and Tans and O'Brien can remember as a small boy dodging and hiding along the wooded banks and hedgerows on his way home from school in order to avoid the Tans in their big Crossley tenders who used to swagger around this beautiful landscape like Sherman's Yankees on their march through Georgia.

Later on in O'Brien's life the idea of a Catholic trainer from Tipperary doing so well in the big Irish flat races and steeplechases seemed to threaten the traditional superiority complex of what Brendan Behan described as the 'horse-arse Anglo-Irish' from Kildare and Meath. O'Brien has always displayed considerable acumen and shrewdness in all matters relating to money. Starting out as a trainer with little capital behind him, he decided that the only way forward in life was to bet on his horses and this he did over a great many years with astonishing success. The care, guile even, with which he laid out his runners and planned his coups would be the envy of many a lesser gambling trainer today. But it often brought O'Brien within the disapproving gaze of the Irish and English racing authorities. At the same time you can see in those gambles, in the cool way that he chose his targets, trained his horses to his satisfaction and then put his money down, exactly the kind of judgement and nerve to back up that judgement, be it in the sales ring or on the race-track, that would be the instrument of Robert Sangster's success.

Some of that latent resentment aroused by O'Brien in the forties and fifties lasts even to the present day. Especially in England where some conservative racing writers have been very hard on the Ballydoyle stable over the years. In 1972 when O'Brien trained Roberto to win the Derby at Epsom he was almost mobbed afterwards by angry top-drawer types who gathered around the unsaddling enclosure to accuse him of unsportsmanlike behaviour. Roberto was the property of an American, John D. Galbreath, who had bred him himself at his Darby Dan stud farm in Kentucky. The horse was named after Roberto Clemente of the Pittsburgh Pirates baseball team. Galbreath owned them too. He was to have been ridden in the Derby by the Australian jockey Bill Williamson, who had recently recovered from a broken arm. On the eve of the race Williamson was jocked off in favour of Lester Piggott. Piggott and Roberto won. By the shortest of short heads. And that's when the trouble started. O'Brien was actually thwacked and walloped with handbag and umbrella by one or two fat old female upper-class dragons who considered that decency and the right sort had themselves just taken a thumping blow to the solar plexus. The trainer could reflect that his decision had been vindicated where it mattered most. Roberto had won and the prize money and the stallion career had been secured for the horse's owner. It was exactly that unflappable ability to get it right in the tightest and most crucial of tight corners that made O'Brien's involvement so essential to Sangster if he was to justify to himself the enormous financial investment that he was about to make. Yet there was more to it than just money.

As well as the all-important commercial and pragmatic advantages, what Robert Sangster got for himself by his connection with Vincent O'Brien was access to a whole world of Irish, and specifically Tipperary- or Munster-based, racing men and women. Down in the Golden Vale, around Slievenamon and the Knockmealdown Mountains and as far away as Limerick, Waterford and Cork, Vincent O'Brien is racing's accredited patron saint. Every publican, bookie, stable lad, jockey and priest has his story of where Vincent used to drink in the old days on his way back from Punchestown or Naas. They'll all tell you which bar it was or which hotel in Clonmel where Vincent and his brother Phonsie hatched the Good Days/Dry Bob gamble over the Irish Autumn Double at The Curragh in 1944. And they'll show you the spot where Father Francis Hourigan blessed the horsebox carrying Alleged on its way to Shannon Airport for the 1978 Prix de l'Arc de Triomphe. Nuns like Sister Martha Hannafin of the order of St Brides in Cahir still giggle like schoolgirls at the thought of the convent rebuilding fund going on Sir Ivor in the 1968

Derby. There are the racing pubs like McCarthys in Fethard and the Horse and Jockey in Thurles. There are the celebrated vets like Demmi O'Byrne and the celebrated bookmakers like Limerick's J. P. McManus and Tipp's own Eamon O'Brien. There's the former champion point-to-point rider turned bloodstock agent, P. P. Hogan, and there's the former champion steeplechase jockey turned stud farm owner and flat-race trainer, Tommy Stack. And there are the cattle dealers and gambling brothers like Seamus and Michael Purcell and Jim and John Horgan, who was a major player in the Gay Future coup. The fathers of some of these men can be picked out wearing flat caps and funny old coats in the black and white photographs of O'Brien's first great steeplechasing heroes being led in at Cheltenham in the early fifties. Nowadays their sons are as familiar with such venues as Hialeah and Hollywood Park as they are with the traditional action at Thurles and the Junction. But what unites them all across the generations is their massive degree of affection and respect for Vincent O'Brien. It was this wealth of humour, understanding and gambling-mad passion for horses and racing that passed in to Robert Sangster's rather shy and tight-lipped orbit as a result of the formation of that syndicate in early 1975.

It was in the July of that year that the partners first descended on the Keeneland Select Sales in Lexington, Kentucky. Keeneland was already well established as the premier yearling sale in North America but there were some European owners and trainers who had never even heard of it at the time. Over the next five or six years the activities of the Sangster/O'Brien syndicate and then of their Arab rivals would change all that forever. Back in 1975 many top European racehorses were still privately bred by long established gentlemen owner-breeders. At Keeneland the opportunity existed to buy on the open market into some of the very best bloodlines in America.

At the 1975 'vendue' as the locals call it, the syndicate bought twelve yearlings including a little chestnut son of Northern Dancer whose dam, Fleur, was a daughter of Nijinsky's dam, Flaming Page. The chestnut had a prominent white blaze and four white socks or white markings on his legs. In the view of some breeding purists he was 'flashy' and therefore unacceptable. O'Brien, who was more worried by his size or the lack of it, paid $200,000 to take the horse back to Ballydoyle. They called him The Minstrel.

The Minstrel won his first two races in Ireland in 1976 and by October was considered good enough to come across to England to contest the Dewhurst Stakes at Newmarket which Nijinsky had won in 1970. The Dewhurst had emerged as the leading English two-year-old race of the season not least due to O'Brien often running his best juvenile in it. The Minstrel won the 1976 Dewhurst comfortably enough and was duly installed as ante-post favourite for the following year's 2,000 Guineas. His first race of the 1977 season was the Guineas trial run at Ascot on appallingly heavy going on 2 April. The Minstrel slogged his way through the mud to record a thoroughly genuine if unspectacular victory. In the paddock before the Guineas at Newmarket there were still many people who questioned his lack of scope, and the memory of O'Brien's expensive disappointments in the race with Apalachee in 1974 and Roberto in 1972 were as much in their minds as the prospect of witnessing another Nijinsky. The Minstrel didn't win the 2,000. He finished an honourable third to another Irish-trained runner, the 20-1 outsider Nebbiolo, with the Middle Park Stakes winner, Tachypous, in second. A few weeks later he tried again in the Irish 2,000 at The Curragh. This time he came off second-best to a horse called Pampapaul but he did manage to reverse Newmarket form with Nebbiolo who finished third.

None of these three races seemed to indicate that The Minstrel was in quite the top class and he was surely no Sir Ivor or Nijinsky. His next three runs which were to be the climax of his career forced people to regard him in a very different light. Up until the Irish Guineas, O'Brien had never seriously contemplated running The Minstrel in the Derby. Then in one of those mumbled and economical moments that were the clearest encouragement any trainer could get, Lester Piggott suggested that the chestnut was not really a top mile-horse but more a potential middle-distance type who needed to go further out. If that were true, then the Derby had to be his target. Once the news was confirmed that the Derby would indeed be The Minstrel's next race and that Piggott would ride him, the ordinary punters started to pile on the money.

The professional's choice for the 1977 Derby was the Aga Khan's French-trained colt, Blushing Groom, who had been a brilliant winner of the French 2,000 Guineas. Yet Blushing Groom was even less certain to stay a mile and a half than The Minstrel. What's more he was going to be ridden by a French jockey, an insuperable disadvantage in the eyes of the great British racing public. Piggott had already won the Derby seven times and five of the last nine Derby winners had won or been placed in the English 2,000 Guineas. At around 3.38 on the afternoon of Wednesday 1 June 1977, The Minstrel made it six out of ten. And where Piggott and O'Brien had been booed after winning on Roberto in 1972 this time they were the toast of Epsom Downs. The winning margin was only a head and it

was one of the most powerful and inspired finishes in Piggott's long
career. The Minstrel's guts as much as his class carried him through.
Within seconds of passing the winning-post the son of Northern
Dancer was valued at a conservative $4,500,000. Sangster had broken
the bank at his first attempt.

Three and a half weeks later The Minstrel completed the classic
double in the Irish Derby at The Curragh. A month after that came
perhaps his finest moment when he took on and beat the best of the
older horses, including five classic winners, in the King George VI
and Queen Elizabeth Stakes at Ascot. Once again the winning
margin was minute. The shortest of short heads with Piggott again at
his powerful and invincible best and both horse and jockey simply
refusing to give in. Eddie Taylor, the Canadian industrialist who had
bred both The Minstrel and his sire, was already on the lookout for
new young stallions to follow in the older horse's footsteps. He made
Magnier an offer and the syndicate didn't refuse. Shortly after the
deal had been struck O'Brien discovered that due to an outbreak of
equine metritis in the USA the American ties were on the point of
banning all imported horses from Europe. The Minstrel's racing
career was over and he was flown out of Ballydoyle and back to
Windfields Farm, Maryland within hours of the ban coming into
effect. His new purchase price was nine million dollars.

In spite of the evidence of the metritis problem in America and
even though the horse had already demonstrated abundant courage
in his final three races, there were still some racing journalists and
English establishment figures who cavilled at the new valuation and
especially at the way in which the horse had, as they saw it, been
whisked away from under their very noses. Why wasn't he staying in
training as a four-year-old? they demanded. Economically impossible,
mumbled the poker-faced Sangster. Why wasn't he at least waiting
for the Arc then? they asked. O'Brien had a good answer to that.

Alleged was the son of another American stallion, Hoist The Flag,
himself a grandson of another great European racehorse, Ribot, who,
like Nearco, was bred by Federico Tesio. Alleged wasn't purchased
at Keeneland. He was bought out of a two-year-olds-in-training sale
in California by Sangster's American-based talent-spotter, the Irishman Billy Macdonald, and he was intended as a partnership horse
between Sangster himself and the Californian chemicals magnate Bob
Fluor. He was originally going to be trained in the States until
Sangster decided to send him over to Ballydoyle where he came
quietly through his two-year-old year just running and winning once
in a small back-end race at The Curragh in November.

It wasn't until his second race as a three-year-old when, starting as a 33-1 outsider in the Royal Whip at The Curragh, he easily defeated two better-fancied stable companions, that the yard started to appreciate his potential. For his next race, the Gallinule Stakes also at The Curragh, he was made an 11-10 favourite and Piggott rode him for the first time. Once again he won easily. After the Gallinule, Fluor wanted Alleged to be aimed at the Irish Derby but O'Brien had other ideas. He already had The Minstrel primed for that race. The trainer kept Alleged, who was said, unusually for an American-bred, to dislike very firm going, off the track for nearly three months while The Minstrel established his claim to be considered the champion middle-distance horse of the season. Then at York's Ebor meeting in August he brought Alleged back to score a stunningly facile victory in the Great Voltigeur Stakes. The racing public gasped with incredulous admiration. Could O'Brien conceivably have an even better three-year-old than the dual Derby winner?

Alleged was automatically promoted as the short-priced favourite for the final classic of the season, the one-and-three-quarter-mile St Leger at Doncaster in September. O'Brien wasn't really that keen to run Alleged in the St Leger. It was only three and a half weeks before the Arc and sometimes running at Doncaster first over the extra distance could wear a good horse down and blunt its speed. Nijinsky had run in and won the 1970 Leger at his owner Charlie Engelhard's behest. O'Brien always maintained that the effect of that race, coming after an attack of ringworm, played some part in Nijinsky's narrow and heartbreaking defeat in Paris. In the event Alleged was beaten at Doncaster, and for the only time in his ten-race career. And it was one of the few occasions in their long partnership when the Ballydoyle staff felt moved to criticise Piggott's judgement. In the Leger they believed that he took the running up too early in the long straight and then let himself be outstayed by the Queen's dour Oaks-winning filly Dunfermline. If Alleged had been held up longer and ridden for speed the implication was that he'd never have lost.

1977 was the year of the Queen's Silver Jubilee and the more royalist members of the racing press were beside themselves with frantic expectation of a Royal victory in the Arc which it had been decided would be Dunfermline's next race. But Alleged was going there too. And the big Irish gamblers and racing professionals who were close to the Ballydoyle stable and who knew about Alleged's real ability were confident of a very different outcome.

Lester Piggott had suffered mightily after the Longchamp disaster on Nijinsky in 1970. He'd gained some revenge when he'd won the 1973 Arc on Rheingold but there were still plenty of critics of his riding out in France. In 1977 Piggott taught them all a lesson that they'd never forget. He didn't make all the running as is sometimes stated but he did ride the horse very close to the pace. As they turned down the hill out of the far side, he was already in second place. When the field swept into the straight he was suddenly in the lead, the horse starting to stretch out elegantly and magnificently and Piggott superbly balanced as always and totally in control. He just kept galloping faster and faster. Nothing could come abreast of him. Piggott even seemed to ease him down again inside the final furlong and the final winning margin was just a length and a half. It didn't begin to reflect his superiority.

The Arc was the climax of an unbelievable season for Sangster. He had won the two biggest races in Europe with two different horses. And the O'Brien stable had also won the Waterford Crystal Mile with another Northern Dancer colt, Be My Guest, the Eclipse and Sussex Stakes with Artaius and then in October the 1977 Dewhurst Stakes with yet another son of Northern Dancer called Try My Best. This colt had shown such promise as a two-year-old that he had been instantly installed as ante-post favourite for the 1978 Guineas and Derby. On top of all this the syndicate decided to keep Alleged in training as a four-year-old – a strange decision seemingly, in view of the unsentimental and purely economic lines on which the business was supposedly being run. The Minstrel had been sold as a stallion for nine million bucks. What price his brilliant stable-companion? O'Brien argued, not at all sentimentally, that Alleged had not yet reached his full potential whereas The Minstrel had fulfilled his in July. Alleged had not been hard-raced as a three-year-old and if he could win a second Arc, not to mention other valuable races along the way, think what he might be worth then. It was the first and just about the only time in the history of the syndicate that a champion Group One-winning three-year-old was not retired to stud at the end of his three-year-old career.

So the opening of the 1978 season seemed to herald great things for the team. Within six weeks they had taken a disastrous plunge. If the 1977 2,000 Guineas had been a disappointment for O'Brien, then the 1978 race was a fiasco. Try My Best, who made an encouraging reappearance in Ireland, was still the red-hot favourite. His form, his breeding and the aura surrounding his trainer were enough to guarantee that. A few days before the Guineas it was said that a quarter-share in the colt had changed hands for something in the region of £750,000. Then the rumours started. The horse had a respiratory problem. He'd been held up in his training due to other mysterious and unspecified ailments. The syndicate had already negotiated a deal with a stud farm in America and the Americans' own vets were flying in to decide whether or not the colt should even be allowed to run at Newmarket. Racing thrives on this kind of gossip but whatever the truth of it Try My Best did run and still went off a warm 15-8 favourite in a field of nineteen. And the result? First: a 28-1 outsider named Roland Gardens ridden by that ageing dwarf, Frankie Durr. Last: the 15-8 favourite Try My Best ridden by Lester Piggott. The stunned crowd could hardly believe their eyes when Try My Best first seemed to be struggling as soon as Piggott began to try and put him in the race after four furlongs. With a quarter of a mile still to go the favourite was going backwards fast. He crossed the line, more than twenty lengths behind the winner. It was Apalachee all over again. Yet at least Apalachee had been placed. This performance was surely too bad to be true. The horse had to have been sickening for something. But what price that quarter-share in him now?

Many people had backed Try My Best ante-post. Not just for the Guineas but for the Derby too which was now only five weeks away. No serious professional believed that Try My Best would even run at Epsom let alone win. Yet one or two announcements in the racing press supposedly indicated that the Derby was still his target. Unscrupulous bookmakers continued to quote the horse as low as 5-1 for Epsom and some mug punters continued to back it. Of course Try My Best didn't run in the Derby. In fact he never ran again and towards the end of 1978 it was quietly announced that he had been retired to stud.

The Try My Best affair gave O'Brien's critics a field day. Some people seemed to derive immense satisfaction from seeing that 'money doesn't always win'. And when the horse departed to stud, there were fresh allegations that he'd failed to train on and that therefore his progeny might fail to train on too. He was not proven sound as a racehorse and it was claimed that any attempt to exploit him at a high fee as a stallion prospect would be damaging the breed. O'Brien was certainly stung by the criticism and prefers not to discuss the matter to this day. Try My Best was certainly afflicted by quite normal setbacks of the kind that can occur to any horse at any moment at any time of the year. Nijinsky had gone down with an attack of colic on the eve of the 1970 Derby but the public were not informed. The problem cleared up and Nijinsky won brilliantly. And it could at least be argued that even though Try My Best had failed to win a classic his breeding was still impeccable and that there was every chance that he would pass on the qualities in his pedigree to his own offspring. If anyone deserved censure it was surely the bookmakers who had continued to cynically lay the horse even when they knew that all was not well. But if anyone thought that this episode would wipe out the syndicate they were quickly proved wrong.

Vincent O'Brien won three Group One mile-events for Sangster in 1978 with an ex-French purchase called Jaazeiro while another syndicate member, the LA based attorney Danny Schwartz, saw his red and black colours carried to victory in three Group One sprints by Solinus, champion speed horse of the year. Not to be outdone Sangster's English trainer, Barry Hills, saddled Hawaiian Sound to be second in the Derby and then to go on and win the Benson and Hedges Gold Cup at York. And then there was Alleged.

The Arc winner reappeared on schedule at The Curragh in May to win the Royal Whip for the second time. Then the problems set in. The Curragh race had been run on fast ground and as a result it seemed that Alleged had jarred himself up. On top of that he was knocked out by a virus which beset many of the stable's horses that summer and which was probably responsible for finishing off Try My Best. As King George day came and went, the decision to keep the horse in training began to look more and more questionable. The veterinary and insurance bills were mounting and the Americans were possibly wavering over the amount that they were prepared to pay for him. It seemed that only another Arc victory could salvage his four-year-old career. The pressure on O'Brien was enormous.

It wasn't until mid-September that Alleged was considered ready to return to the racecourse. There were no suitable races for him in England or Ireland so he was flown across to France to contest the Prix du Prince d'Orange over ten furlongs of the Arc course at Longchamp. After such a long lay-off everyone imagined that he would be badly in need of the run. No one expected him to win. He not only won, he broke the Longchamp course record. It was one of the most extraordinary triumphs in O'Brien's long career and the crowning moment was still to come. All the big players and gamblers came charging in now with a roar. They sensed that the horse would be unbeatable in the Arc in fourteen days' time. There was still to be one more drama. For two solid days and nights before Sunday 1 October 1978 it rained in Paris. Alleged may have been unsuited by really firm ground but the possibility of the other extreme, of the Arc being run on heavy going, worried some of the syndicate just as much. At the age of four Alleged seemed faster than ever. How could he produce that speed in a quagmire?

Longchamp is one of the great racing amphitheatres of the world. By the first weekend in October the leaves on the horse chestnut trees in the surrounding Bois de Boulogne are just beginning to turn. When the Arc field parades before the race in front of the packed stands with a whole season on the line it's a moment of tension, beauty and emotion every bit as intense as the prelude to any Derby or Breeders Cup. On that Sunday in 1978 Alleged matched up in every way to the majesty of the occasion. He had always been renowned as a tough, even aggressive, animal by the stable. On the track he looked fit, sharp and trained to the minute, his big, intelligent head surveying the crowd and the photographers with unperturbed calm. Piggott of course was totally cool, impassive, ready. In the race itself the syndicate and their supporters never had an anxious moment. Piggott was never very far away from the leaders in the first half-mile, and as they began the right hand downhill swing towards the home turn he was going easily in about fifth place with no worries about getting blocked in or impeded by tiring horses, which is often a problem for English jockeys at Longchamp. About two furlongs out Alleged hit the front and the Irish cheers began. As the whole racecourse began to realise that O'Brien's champion was about to make history by becoming only the sixth horse ever to win the Arc for a second time so even the normally partisan French joined in the roars of approbation. Alleged went past the winning-post by almost exactly the same victory margin that he'd enjoyed in 1977.

It was an emotional moment all right. As horse and jockey returned beneath the trees into the paddock unsaddling enclosure, even Piggott was smiling. O'Brien walked in behind the horse smiling sheepishly and acknowledging the tributes of the crowd by continually and almost deferentially touching the brim of his hat. 'Bravo, bravo, bravissimo,' cried some of the French, saluting him as if he were a great opera conductor appearing on stage for the final curtain. The cheering was hardly a display of warmth for Sangster personally but the reticent owner had plenty to cheer about none the less. A few weeks after the Arc it was announced that Alleged was to be syndicated by Walmac International Stud Farm of Lexington, Kentucky for $13 million. Admittedly it takes up to four years for the vendors to receive the balance of that fee but technically at least the money was in the bank. Now the men from Ballydoyle could go to war on an even bigger scale.

The age of the million-dollar yearling had arrived.

5 : Winning Big

The first horse to be sold for the magical seven-figure sum was a colt by the phenomenal 1973 American Triple Crown winner, Secretariat, who won that year's Belmont Stakes by no less a margin than thirty-one lengths. His yearling son, bred by Nelson Bunker Hunt out of the mare Charming Alibi, went for $1.5 million at Keeneland in 1976 and was purchased by a group of Canadians who named him, appropriately enough, Canadian Bound. His racecourse achievements were modest.

In the summer of 1978 a Northern Dancer colt out of the mare Special was sold for $1.3 million at the same sale. Interestingly though, the buyer was not Sangster or O'Brien who were the underbidders but the Greek shipping tycoon Stavros Niarchos. With his silver-grey hair, his elegant suits and his enormous wallet, Niarchos was like a caricature figure from a Sidney Sheldon novel. The one with a yacht and a bank account in every port. He'd been involved in racehorse ownership before but not in a serious way since the mid 1950s. Now he was returning to the big time. He owned Marcel Boussac's old stud farm, Fresnay le Buffard, in Normandy and he'd got François Boutin to train for him. Yet his racing ambitions were never really to be quite on the same level as Sangster's. Niarchos was the classic example of the rich man who can buy anything he wants and decides that he's bored with houses, islands and oil tankers so he'll buy beautiful and expensive thoroughbred racehorses instead. Partly because their very unpredictability intrigues him. Not that he liked to lose.

The Special colt was to be none other than Miesque's sire, Nureyev, and in 1980 he put up a top-class performance to win the 2,000 Guineas at Newmarket in which he demonstrated all the characteristic speed of his family. Unfortunately his jockey, Philippe Pacquet, was deemed to have impeded some of the other horses when making his run. Nureyev was disqualified by the Newmarket stewards and Niarchos angrily asserted that he would never run a horse on an English racetrack again. He soon got over that and by the early eighties he had horses in training with Jeremy Tree, Henry Cecil and Guy Harwood. But to the disappointment of the racing public Nureyev really was making his farewell appearance. Due to an injury his racecourse career was already over and after just three races in his entire life he was whisked off to Walmac International who had syndicated Alleged two years before.

At the end of the 1979 sales-round Sangster and Magnier persuaded Niarchos to come in with them and become a full partner in the Ballydoyle syndicate. To outside observers the purchasing power of the richest men in racing now seemed disturbingly invincible. The syndicate could surely corner the market in Northern Dancer year-lings if they wished. In fact the Ballydoyle stable had a relatively quiet 1979 at least until the autumn when O'Brien produced another champion two-year-old. This one was called Monteverdi and he was a son of Lyphard and therefore a grandson of Northern Dancer. At Newmarket in October he became O'Brien's fifth winner of the Dewhurst Stakes. Now it was his turn to be ante-post favourite for the following year's classics. But once again the punters' money had gone astray.

Without equalling the embarrassment of Try My Best two years earlier, Monteverdi at least bettered – or worsted – The Minstrel's record in 1977. Beaten in his reappearance race at The Curragh he was then brought over for the Greenham Stakes at Newbury in April in which he finished second to a horse called Final Straw. The form was actually not at all bad as Final Straw ended up as one of the season's top milers but it was felt that if Monteverdi couldn't beat him at Newbury with the benefit of a previous outing then there was no point in taking him to Newmarket. The Lyphard colt was rerouted to the Irish 2,000 Guineas at The Curragh but he failed to get into the first three. You might've thought that the wretched horse would now be quietly retired to stud but some members of the syndicate, with no obvious alternative in sight, were keen that he should try and emulate The Minstrel and take his chance at Epsom.

Piggott was the syndicate's jockey and so it was Piggott who was pressed to ride. But Lester wasn't happy. He was famous for sniffing around before big races in an effort to find out whose horse might give him the best chance of victory. His decision was often the most important signal that a punter looked for but in May 1978 L. Piggott was convinced that Monteverdi was no Derby winner. He did ride the horse at Epsom . . . and they finished down the field. As Lester dismounted he supposedly remarked to a fortunate journalist, who just happened to be within earshot, that Monteverdi was 'useless'. A genuine comment or not it was widely quoted in the racing press and hardly made sweet reading for the syndicate. Whatever Monteverdi's failings as a racehorse his breeding alone still made him a salvageable stud prospect. Indeed the economics of the operation demanded that he be sold on at the best rate possible. In that context Piggott's off-the-cuff remark was hardly a helpful prelude to any syndication arrangements. Monteverdi did make the trip to Kentucky in the end though hardly with the same aura about him as The Minstrel and Alleged. But in spite of the syndicate's success in eventually getting their money back, 1980 was to be Piggott's last as the Ballydoyle stable jockey. The Monteverdi incident wasn't the official reason for the rift but it was symptomatic of how mutually unsatisfying the most famous partnership in racing had suddenly become.

When the news became public in the autumn that Piggott and the syndicate were dispensing with each other's services, some members of the racing community professed their astonishment. If any of them thought that Lester had been in some way hard done by they soon had to reappraise that view once he formed a new and equally invincible jockey and trainer alliance with his ambitious Newmarket neighbour, Henry Cecil. Piggott's new retainer was only one side of the major transformation that took place in racing's top riding arrangements at the end of the 1980 season. Millions of pounds were now tied up in the Ballydoyle operation. The considered judgement of the trainer and his staff of vets and bloodstock advisers was sought and pored over at every stage of that operation but in the end the fate of all the money came down to the ability and the temperament of the horse on the one hand and the skill of the jockey on the other. And if Ballydoyle couldn't have Lester Piggott, there was clearly only one alternative in Europe in 1980. Pat Eddery.

The phrase 'dead behind the eyes' could've been invented to describe the then twenty-eight-year-old Irish champion jockey's son, Patrick James Eddery. He'd already won the English jockeys championship four times between 1974 and 1977 as well as the Derby on

Grundy in 1975. He was considered to be almost as strong and gifted in the saddle as Piggott and to share the older man's unswerving dedication to riding horses and winning races. He was also known to give nothing away in interviews and to actively dislike talking to journalists. There seemed little chance of any of the syndicate's secrets escaping in a rash or unguarded moment from Pat's mouth.

At the start of the 1980 season Eddery was still officially contracted to ride for the Lambourn stable of Peter Walwyn, the man with whom he'd shared his championship years in the mid seventies. Walwyn was and is a highly distinctive personality, whose eccentric, not to say apoplectic, mannerisms had earned him the nickname of 'Basil Fawlty'. He'd enjoyed few big-race successes in the three-year period leading up to 1980 and to predatory outside observers it appeared that his fortunes were irretrievably on the wane. Several prominent members of his staff had left to set up on their own and Pat was said to be restless. Sangster knew that Walwyn's owners couldn't possibly match his kind of money but 'Basil' wasn't happy. Jockey hiring and firing by the big owners has never been quite as smooth or agreeable a process as it's sometimes portrayed and this was no exception. Walwyn's new rider was to be the immensely experienced but no longer youthful Joe Mercer, who had been Piggott's predecessor at Warren Place. The official line was that all three trainers were getting an equally good deal but the market thought otherwise. Walwyn was perceived to be on the way down and 'Uncle Joe' Mercer was just looking for a few final quiet years before his retirement. Cecil was the coming man and Piggott was anticipating what he thought would be the last great lucrative phase of his riding career at Newmarket. But it was Vincent O'Brien who was still at the top and not surprisingly Pat Eddery felt that for him the best was yet to come. In the new world of million-dollar yearlings and stud syndications it was an open secret that jockeys could expect to get ever more lavish 'presents', percentages and perhaps a share of a horse's stallion earnings if they helped to make it on the track. Once again some members of the establishment were affronted. Once again Ballydoyle was setting the pace.

One of the factors that had swayed Sangster in opting for Eddery was that there was ample evidence from his Grundy period that he was an outstanding rider on the big occasions who always put a horse in a race with a chance. Less than a month after signing his new six-figure deal Eddery was required to put that reputation on the line and he came through the test magnificently. At Longchamp at the beginning of October he gave Sangster his third Arc victory in four years when he brought the French-trained filly Detroit with a devastating trouble-free run on the outside of a strong field. Two weeks later he was riding for Sangster in a Group One race for the second time. Once again, Vincent O'Brien had brought his top two-year-old over for the Dewhurst Stakes. The colt was yet another son of Northern Dancer and he'd been bought at Keeneland for a million dollars the previous summer. His name was Storm Bird.

Storm Bird's Dewhurst was one of the most exciting races, two-year-old or otherwise, of the whole 1980 season. In a field of five his main opponent was another unbeaten colt called To Agori Mou who was owned by Mrs Audrey Muinos and trained by Guy Harwood. In contrast to Storm Bird's glamorous father, To Agori Mou was by the somewhat less glittering English sire Tudor Music and had cost a 'mere' 20,000 guineas as a yearling. Harwood, though, had already proved that in partnership with the bloodstock agent James Delahooke he was a shrewd man at picking out likely prospects at an attractive price with good conformation if less fashionable breeding. This facet of his character along with his bluff straightforward manner and his upright stance, not to mention his remarkably sheer and upright hairstyle, made him very much the right, indeed the preferable, type in the eyes of some racing correspondents: he was modern and businesslike; he was open and honest about his horses and it was felt that he made the whole thing less mystifying than some of his more secretive colleagues. Cynics might say that he didn't have enough imagination to be mystified about anything in the first place but the contrast with 'Sangster's Gangsters' was heavily inferred if not stated.

In the event it was the equine millionaire and not his much cheaper rival who came out on top in the Dewhurst although Storm Bird had to work hard to get there. To Agori Mou, ridden by the grizzled forty-one-year-old Greville Starkey, known to one and all as the 'Dog Barker' for, naturally enough, his dog impersonations, got first run and didn't seem to be stopping when the race began in earnest. Eddery though, riding with great patience at first and then with considerable determination, unloosed Storm Bird's speed as they raced down into the dip and the American-bred got on top in the final furlong. There was half a length in it at the line. It was Storm Bird's fifth successive victory and the *Timeform* men were to write in their 'Racehorses of 1980' that he had impressed them as much as any of O'Brien's previous Dewhurst winners since Nijinsky. Storm Bird now had the fateful honour of being the latest Sangster-owned horse to be winter favourite for the Guineas and the Derby.

Only this time it really did seem as if the hype was justified and that a new king was about to be crowned.

The events that followed and that overtook not only Storm Bird himself but also O'Brien, Sangster and Harwood over the next twelve months were to be amongst the most controversial in even O'Brien's sometimes contentious career. More than anything else they were to demonstrate once again both the glorious unpredictability of thoroughbred horse-racing and the astonishing levels of commercial gamesmanship that it had now been raised to.

Even before the 1981 season had begun, a disaffected stable lad, who had been dismissed from O'Brien's employ some time before, broke into Storm Bird's box and hacked his mane and tail with a pair of shears. The incident received considerable unwelcome publicity but the horse seemed to recover from his trauma remarkably well. Unfortunately the stable lad incident was only the prelude to a whole catalogue of disasters. O'Brien wanted to run Storm Bird in his favourite classic prep race, the Gladness Stakes at The Curragh. At the beginning of April the colt appeared to be slightly lame in a hind leg and on the advice of the vets he was withdrawn from his intended engagement. No sooner was he sound again than he started to cough in mid-April. The English and Irish Guineas went by but Storm Bird remained at Ballydoyle. He also remained at the forefront of the betting on the Derby which, it was said, was still his big target. Then the Derby came and went too. So did the Irish Derby and the Eclipse Stakes. Sangster mumbled his way through a series of laughable encounters with Bruffscot and company and continued to insist that his colt was progressing well. Everybody else began to snigger and describe Storm Bird as 'the Invisible Horse'.

1981 was the summer of Shergar who followed up his two Derby victories with a four-length success against the older horses in the King George VI at Ascot. Shergar was patently a champion and before his Ascot win his owner, the Aga Khan, had announced the details of his syndication at his own stud farm, Ballymany, in Ireland, for a valuation of about £10 million. This was considered to be less than half of what he could have got for the horse if he'd been willing to sell it to, say, Claiborne or Gainesway in Kentucky.

Within days of Shergar's Ascot triumph the racing community gasped and choked with astonishment – and in one or two cases anger and indignation – when it was revealed at the big Goodwood meeting that the Storm Bird syndicate had sold a majority of the shares in their horse to a group of Americans for upwards of $30 million. At the then rates of exchange that made him worth about

£16 million. In other words a horse who had not yet run as a three-year-old, who had never won a classic race and who might not have trained on at all, was being valued at a higher rate than an outstanding dual Derby winner. Some people practically implied that it was immoral of Sangster, Magnier and O'Brien to have taken the money. Sangster's attitude was that a thoroughbred, like any other commodity, was worth what you could get for it and that if the market was prepared to pay thirty million then thirty million was a fair price. The horse was by a provenly great sire of two Derby winners. He'd beaten the 1981 2,000 Guineas winner as a two-year-old and there was every chance that whatever else he did on the racecourse he would impart his inherited speed to some of his own offspring.

Whatever the validity of the various arguments, the pubs of Cashel, Clonmel and Tipp' were alive with colourful stories about the negotiations. It was said that John Magnier had decided that $12 million was what they should try and get for the horse. When they walked in to face the opposition the Americans' opening gambit was supposed to have been that they wouldn't go a cent above $15 million. At this point, according to these entertaining if undoubtedly embellished scenarios, Magnier sat there with a perfectly straight face and responded nonchalantly that anything below $45 million was wasting his time. And that's how they came to split the difference. True or not it's become a part of the Coolmore myth that people still believe in, not only in Ireland but in parts of America too. From such stories was the legend of the apparent invincibility of the Ballydoyle syndicate being created.

The saga wasn't over yet either. The new American owners enthusiastically announced that Storm Bird was fine and coming along well, that he was staying in training and that his new target was the Arc in which they eagerly anticipated him taking on Shergar. The bookmakers eagerly anticipated taking lots of money on this improbable event and put up Storm Bird as a 16-1 shot for Longchamp. He never got there. At least not to the Arc. York's Benson and Hedges Gold Cup came and went. No Storm Bird. The St Leger was out of the question but then at long last a Ballydoyle stable spokesman revealed that the son of Northern Dancer would run in the Prix du Prince d'Orange in Paris, the same race that Alleged had gone for in the build up to his second Arc in 1978. On the strength of some rumours that Storm Bird had worked brilliantly at home with Kings Lake, the O'Brien horse was cut from 16-1 to 6-1 for the Arc in a matter of days. Not for the first time the ante-post gamblers lost the lot. Storm Bird finished seventh of nine at

Longchamp and was promptly retired. O'Brien, who had been understandably tense beforehand, looked relieved that it was all over.

Storm Bird's 1982 covering fee was set at $175,000 live foal which was only $50,000 less than that of his sire. Vincent O'Brien had always been the first to emphasise that while Northern Dancer was still the blood to buy into, not all million-dollar yearlings could be guaranteed to recoup their cost on the track. Sangster's view was that in gambling at this level you were backing a genius like O'Brien to come up every year with one horse that would be good enough to pay for the flops and put them all into profit. In 1981 Storm Bird achieved just that even though he only appeared once on the racecourse. What's more he subsequently went a long way to justifying his stallion valuation by siring the brilliant classic-winning filly Indian Skimmer in only his second crop of foals. And by the time the 1988 Keeneland Select July Sales catalogue was printed, Storm Bird had become the sire of no fewer than five Grade One winners. To Agori Mou's record as a stallion by the same date was negligible.

The syndicate's most successful representative on the racetrack in 1981 was not a son of Northern Dancer but a grandson of the astonishing stallion by his 1970 Derby winner, Nijinsky. This horse was called Kings Lake. A neat, bay colt, Kings Lake won two small races as a two-year-old. Nothing spectacular maybe but he looked like the type to improve the following season. He was third over ten furlongs on his first run at three and that was enough to persuade O'Brien that his immediate future should be over a mile. To Agori Mou had already showed that he'd trained on, scoring a convincing win in the English 2,000 Guineas at Newmarket. He was odds on to do the double in the Irish Guineas at The Curragh with Kings Lake a 5-1 shot in a field of thirteen. With two furlongs to run Kings Lake took up the running near the inside rail, with To Agori Mou, who'd been held up in the early stages, starting a run on the outside. As they approached the furlong marker both horses were reaching the climax of their effort, each jockey uncompromisingly intent on victory. It was at this point that Pat Eddery changed his whip from his left to his right hand and as he did so Kings Lake appeared to veer momentarily towards To Agori Mou, although in the opinion of *Timeform*, who had two race-readers at the scene, the horses didn't collide. Throughout the last furlong the duelling pair seemed to bump several times with Starkey, no innocent lamb in the hard business of big-race jockeyship, giving as good as he got. A few yards from the line Starkey actually stood up in his irons as if to theatrically telegraph a point to the stewards that his mount had been interfered with. The photo finish showed Kings Lake the winner by a neck. There was an immediate announcement of a stewards' enquiry. As the Curragh stewards examined the camera patrol film and interviewed the jockeys concerned, the bookmakers down on the rails were betting even money on the two. When the result came it was announced that, in the opinion of the stewards, Kings Lake had interfered with To Agori Mou. There was to be no action taken against Eddery so presumably whatever interference did take place was regarded as accidental. None the less the placings were reversed and To Agori Mou was awarded the 1981 Irish 2,000 Guineas. And that was only the beginning.

A few days after the Curragh race the Kings Lake syndicate decided to take up their right to appeal against the verdict of the Curragh stewards, directly to the stewards of the Irish Turf Club. This was certainly an unusual if not an unprecedented move. In Ireland as in England the authorities liked to convey the impression that the stewards' word, no matter the doubts that professionals might have about their competence, was always final. To ask the Jockey Club or the Turf Club to overturn a local stewards' decision was usually doomed to emphatic rejection.

After a six-hour enquiry at the Turf Club's Curragh headquarters it was announced that the original stewards' decision had been overturned. Kings Lake was after all the official winner of the 1981 Irish Two Thousand. The English racing press erupted almost to a man in a throbbing mass of righteous indignation. The decision, they shrieked, was scandalous. Kings Lake had interfered with To Agori Mou. The rules stipulated that interference must be punished by disqualification. How could O'Brien's horse have possibly got the race? The whole furore seemed to be in no small part affected by the steadily deteriorating relationship between the press and the Ballydoyle stable in general, especially over the well-being of Storm Bird who at this point was still technically an intended Derby runner. The way some correspondents were writing about it, made O'Brien quietly furious. It was as if they expected that his first priority each morning was to get on to the *Mail* or the *Sun* and inform them of the latest intimate details of his horses' well-being and likely running plans. For a while he reacted by imposing a black-out on all statements relating to his stable. Of course that simply made the hacks more indignant than ever.

There was the fact that the syndicate had been represented at the enquiry by an experienced QC, who, so the stories went, really put the Curragh stewards through the wringer. What had they observed at the time of the race? Had they written it down? And where were they when it happened anyway? The camera patrol film was inconclusive. Greville Starkey was bound to say that he'd been interfered with. So the stewards must have remarkable eyesight to have been able to spot so much from so far away. This cross-examination, or 'inquisition' as the rags depicted it, was, so the racing public were told, completely unsporting. A silken-voiced smoothie-chops assassinating the integrity of honourable and independent men. One steward was supposed to have been virtually reduced to tears. And Major Victor McCalmont, the archetypal Anglo-Irish hunting and racing man and the Senior Steward on duty on the day of the race, went so far as to resign from the Turf Club in protest although he did subsequently change his mind.

Over the next few weeks the issue was stoked up still further in the letter columns of the racing papers and on television. The almost unanimous view was that it was the Harwood stable who were the injured party. Then on the first day of Royal Ascot – the absolutely perfect setting in every way – the moral majority got their revenge. To Agori Mou and Kings Lake met again in the St James' Palace Stakes over Ascot's old mile. Before the off Sangster was interviewed by the BBC racing correspondent, Julian Wilson. Wilson seemed to be heatedly suggesting that Sangster wasn't playing by the rules. The owner retorted that the BBC's paddock commentator, Jimmy Lindley, was very 'in' with Guy Harwood so how could his opinion be fair or impartial either? The race itself was run on fast ground and, given an inspired ride by Starkey, the English Guineas winner put up an outstanding performance. Kicking on at the turn into the home straight, 'The Dog Barker' poached an invaluable advantage and, try as they might, Eddery and Kings Lake could never quite close the gap. The winning distance was a neck. A majority of the Royal Enclosure crowd were beside themselves with delight. Harwood the decent, upright chap with the inexpensive horse had deservedly triumphed. The smart money had at last got its comeuppance.

As he went past the winning-post Starkey turned round briefly in the saddle and gave Eddery a full Harvey Smith salute. He later claimed that he'd just been making a victory sign. The Ascot stewards called him in and gave him a week's holiday for ungentlemanly behaviour in full view of the Royal Box. Whatever they said in public, in private a lot of people believed that they were secretly rather delighted. A sort of justice had been enacted.

All the talk of bounders and cheats obscured the fact that To

Agori Mou and Kings Lake were both very good horses. In their next meeting at Goodwood it was Kings Lake who got home by a short head after Last Fandango, also owned by Sangster but trained by Barry Hills, had obligingly moved off the rail to let him through. Their final encounter was at Deauville in August when To Agori Mou won their personal battle by a nose but where both horses were beaten five lengths by the crack French miler Northjet. And Northjet's grandsire? Northern Dancer. Kings Lake won one more Group One race in Ireland in September and then ran unplaced in the Arc. He was retired to Coolmore Stud. To Agori Mou, who was kept at full stretch almost throughout the season, won twice more after Deauville and then failed to stay in his final outing, the Champion Stakes at Newmarket. In spite of his racing record it wasn't possible to syndicate him at an attractive rate before the end of the year because his breeding simply didn't match his achievements. Once again the commercial logic of Vincent O'Brien had been fully vindicated when it counted. Yet if To Agori Mou has not yet been a success as a stallion it's also only fair to say that, so far at least, Kings Lake has himself failed to match up to the accomplishments of his contemporary Storm Bird or indeed to those of some of the other young Northern Dancer sires who have subsequently been added to the Coolmore empire.

If 1981 had been a year of drama and controversy for the Ballydoyle syndicate, then 1982 was to be one of spectacular and almost unclouded triumph. In the space of three and a half weeks two horses carried Sangster's now famous, even infamous, blue and green silks with the white cap with the green spots, to victory in the English, French and Irish Derbys. It was to seem like the zenith of Robert Sangster's racing fortunes. The two horses, both grandsons of Northern Dancer, were called Golden Fleece and Assert. Only one of them was trained by Vincent O'Brien.

The partners had made three million-dollar-plus purchases at the 1980 Keeneland Sales. One of them, who cost a million fifty and would race in Danny Schwartz's black and red colours, was a son of Alleged's sire, Hoist The Flag, and was called Lords. Just outstripping him in price was a full brother to The Minstrel who they called Pilgrim. Lords and Pilgrim both ran once and won once in their two-year-old season auguring, it seemed, great things for the future. Yet it was another of the syndicate's Keeneland acquisitions, a great bay colt by Nijinsky who came in under seven figures at $775,000, who was to upstage them both.

Golden Fleece also raced just once as a two-year-old, easily winning a seventeen-runner maiden race at Leopardstown in September. One of the most thrilling and aesthetically beautiful sights in racing is to see a top-class jockey sitting on a horse with real box-office sex appeal or star potential and to see them both poised on the heels of the leaders, the horse still on the bridle and seemingly only needing to be given an inch of rein to accelerate away past his rivals as if they're moving up and down on the spot. It was an area in which Lester Piggott used to be in a class of his own but, since he'd begun riding for O'Brien, Pat Eddery had never once been embarrassed by the comparison. And this was exactly the kind of display that Eddery and Golden Fleece put on for the spectators and race-readers who happened to be at the Dublin track that autumn afternoon. Once allowed to hit the front the big horse, who in the opinion of some observers looked as if he might be equally at home in the Cheltenham Gold Cup field as in the Derby, immediately quickened four or five lengths clear of the opposition and was easing down again at the finish.

Many horses can win a maiden race easily. You need to see them compete in better company to have a surer idea of their potential. Golden Fleece didn't race again in 1981 but three of the horses he beat at Leopardstown went on to win other races later in the season. The most significant of these was Assert, the runner-up at Leopardstown, who was also a grandson of Northern Dancer by the Coolmore stallion Be My Guest. Unlike Golden Fleece who was the property of a syndicate, Assert was wholly owned by Robert Sangster and he was trained by Vincent O'Brien's eldest son, David, only twenty-five years old at the time, whose own stable began just beyond the hedge at Ballydoyle where his father's land ended.

Assert had been picked out as a yearling by Sangster's inimitable talent-spotter, P. P. Hogan, who had snapped him up for 160,000 francs at the Agence Française sale in Deauville. At first Sangster was apparently disinclined to believe that a horse costing so little could really be much use to him. The Leopardstown maiden was Assert's first race too and three weeks later he won a two-year-old Group race in Ireland but then failed to show his best form when sent over to have a crack at the English juveniles in the Futurity at Doncaster. Only David O'Brien knew how good Assert really was. His father might have a yard full of blue-chip bloodstock, automatically expected to win classic races, but David, a quiet and reclusive figure completely devoted to his horses, had great expectations too.

At the beginning of 1982 and for the first time in many seasons there was no obvious Ballydoyle 2,000 Guineas horse for the bookmakers to hoist to the top of their ante-post lists. That didn't mean that the bookies and the serious gamblers alike didn't expect O'Brien senior to have a pretty good idea by the first few months of the New Year of just what his principal Derby hope might be in June. It was after all essential to the whole existence of the syndicate that they aim towards a Derby horse each year but this time, during the freeze-up weeks of early 1982, the bookies' representatives and the leading rails faces couldn't quite work out which that particular horse might be. Usually the big firms' intelligence services never missed a clue in the lead-up to the major races, and Ladbrokes in particular had always been remarkably prescient about the state of play at Ballydoyle. But in the second week of March 1982 a diligent English professional searching around for tips for the Cheltenham Festival, happened to be sitting in a pub in Cahir and discussing the triple Gold Cup winner Cottage Rake with one of O'Brien's former assistant trainers, who casually remarked that 'The Rake' had always possessed so much more speed than the average chaser. 'Speed is always what you're looking for in a potentially top-class racehorse. Like the big Nijinsky they've got up at Ballydoyle this spring. They think that he could be as quick as his sire, so I'm told. In fact, if he gets the trip, I suspect they believe that he could win the Derby. But I shouldn't be telling you about that!'

When the punter got home he leafed through *Timeform*'s 'Race-horses of 1981' and concluded that 'the big Nijinsky' could only possibly be Golden Fleece. The following afternoon he got on the phone to the offices of the big four bookmaking firms in London and, by asking for very small money each time, managed to get £500 each way on Golden Fleece at 50-1 for the Derby. It was the first serious money for the horse and for once, an exceptionally rare occurrence, the big layers had missed the connection.

When the four-day declarations were published for the Ballymoss Stakes at The Curragh in mid-April, everybody else still searching for the hidden link in the classic jigsaw puzzle was intrigued to see Golden Fleece declared as the Ballydoyle representative with Pat Eddery down to ride. The Ballymoss was over a mile and a quarter and Golden Fleece won it easily without coming off the bridle. Quoted at 25-1 for Epsom in the days leading up to the Curragh race he was promptly cut to 12-1 immediately afterwards. O'Brien hid his delight behind his usual reticent façade. If he were to have a Derby horse, he reflected pessimistically, he supposed that this could be the one.

The following month Golden Fleece ran again in the Nijinsky

Stakes, another ten-furlong classic trial at Leopardstown. Once again he won easily, demonstrating for the few brief strides that he was required to seriously exert himself the same powers of instant acceleration that he'd displayed over the same course as a two-year-old. O'Brien confirmed that Golden Fleece would now definitely be aimed at the Derby and the bookies slashed his odds again to 5-1. Yet O'Brien himself was not without reservations about the horse's chances. To begin with he was relatively short of racecourse experience having run just three times in his life. Then how could they be sure that a horse with that kind of speed would really stay the Derby distance of one and a half miles? Not all the American-breds stayed. His sire, Nijinsky, had stayed but Sir Ivor for all his brilliance had been partly guided to his Derby victory by the artistry and finesse of Lester Piggott.

There were other problems too that the outside world were only barely aware of at the time. Like his sire, Golden Fleece was a rather nervous and highly strung racehorse. Not surprisingly for a horse of his size he appeared to suffer from claustrophobia. It had taken weeks of coaxing and training by the Ballydoyle staff to get him over his aversion first to the starting stalls and then to being boxed up and taken away from home. Then there was the question of the flight to England. How would he react to being cooped up in an aeroplane for an hour? To overcome this problem the O'Brien team regularly practised taking him down to their private airstrip adjacent to the Ballydoyle gallops so that he could be loaded up on to the transporter and given a foretaste of what was in store for him. There was a potentially priceless stud career at stake now and O'Brien, forever the perfectionist, was determined to leave nothing to chance.

Golden Fleece made it safely to Epsom all right but some people took one look at him and immediately objected that such a big horse would never act on the track. Epsom is after all one of the most extraordinary racecourses in the world. If the Derby were being designed from scratch tomorrow any racecourse executive who came up with Epsom Downs as the ideal setting would probably be laughed at hysterically and then sacked. The steep uphill climb through the first half-mile, the bends and turns, the dramatic downhill descent to Tattenham Corner and then the way in which the camber of the course slopes away from the stands in the final two furlongs makes Epsom one of the hardest tracks to ride and race over in the business. Throughout the history of the Derby the course has often seemed to favour neat, compact animals with big and possibly unbalanced horses at a decided disadvantage. Some old pros and quite a few well-lubricated old bores took one look at Golden Fleece and announced that he'd never come down the hill.

As if all this wasn't enough, there were also people who questioned the value of his form. After all, they said, who had been second to him in the Nijinsky Stakes? None other than Assert. The same horse who had chased him home on his début the previous September. Since Leopardstown in May, Assert had comfortably won the Gallinule Stakes at The Curragh and was now earmarked for the French Derby at Chantilly four days after Epsom. The sceptics implied that Assert had not only needed the run in the Nijinsky but that David O'Brien had clearly been under instructions to make sure that his horse, well, took things fairly easily so as to avoid any embarrassment to the owner's number-one choice. To believe that, you had to conceive of a relationship between the older O'Brien and his son which most confidants of the family would have found impossible to credit. The truth was that the bitter and recriminatory atmosphere engendered by the Storm Bird and Kings Lake affairs the previous year had still not been entirely dispelled and there was scarcely an overflow of popular goodwill towards the syndicate.

The chief rivals to Golden Fleece in the 1982 Derby appeared to be Jalmood, who'd won the Lingfield Derby Trial, Peacetime, who'd won the Guardian Trial at Sandown and the French challenger, Persepolis. The race was run in humid, overcast conditions after a spectacular thunderstorm the night before. O'Brien's staff sat up all through the night periodically bathing their horse with ice packs to keep him cool and undisturbed. Should there ever be a film made about the rise of the Ballydoyle syndicate then Vincent O'Brien's quiet words of instruction to Pat Eddery just before the 1982 Derby should be played as a voice-over as the horse and jockey are waiting to go into the stalls. 'The longer you wait . . .' he said, '. . . the further you'll win by.' Pat Eddery executed those instructions to perfection. Golden Fleece settled for him well early on and as the eighteen runners raced down the hill to Tattenham Corner the pair had only three other horses behind them. Then Eddery switched Golden Fleece to the outside of the field and asked him to go. The response was immediate. Showing once again quite astonishing powers of acceleration, especially for such a big and heavy-topped horse, the favourite picked up the opposition in an instant and went from fourth-last to challenging for the lead in about seven seconds. Eddery simply had to keep him going as, still on the outside, he powered past Touching Wood and Silver Hawk and reached the winning-post in the fastest electronically recorded Derby time since

records began and one almost as fast as the hand-timed victory of
Mahmoud in 1932. Three days later Assert won the Prix du Jockey
Club by two and a half lengths.

The aftermath of the English Derby was, perhaps inevitably now
whenever Ballydoyle were involved, not without its share of controversy. It was at first stated that Golden Fleece would run next if not
in the Irish Derby then in the two-furlong shorter Eclipse Stakes at
Sandown which it was believed might suit him better. Both races
came and went without the Derby winner. Assert went to The
Curragh instead and beat Silver Hawk and five other largely substandard opponents with ease. After that, David O'Brien let him take his
chance in the King George at Ascot where he ran right up to his best
form but was beaten half a length by a four-year-old colt called
Kalaglow who had run in the Eclipse and won it and who, appropriately enough, was trained by Guy Harwood and ridden by the
infamous 'Dog Barker'.

In the meantime Golden Fleece had been plagued with problems.
First he'd gone down with a cough and then he'd suffered swelling
and lameness in his hind legs. The question that everybody in the
industry was asking was would he carry on racing or would the
syndicate cash in on his current valuation as a Derby winner and
artfully retire him to stud? What's more, if he did stay in training
would he and Assert ever be allowed to take each other on for a third
time? Most professionals scoffed at that idea and they laughed too
whenever Sangster was interviewed and came up with another of his
standard impersonations of a man whose entire mouth has been
frozen with novocaine. Sadly almost everything associated with the
syndicate was regarded with as much heavy sarcasm about its
commercial motives as it was tinged with admiration for O'Brien's
skill. But at least Assert was allowed to carry on racing. The partners
already had one ace in the hole so why not let the other one keep on
trying to add to his worth? Assert fully justified this decision by
annihilating the opposition in the Benson and Hedges Gold Cup at
York in which Christy Roche, the Irish jockey who had ridden him
to date, had to forfeit the ride through injury. He was replaced by
Pat Eddery who kept the mount for Assert's final two appearances.
In September he achieved his third Group One victory of the year in
the Joe McGrath Memorial Stakes at Leopardstown. His swansong,
the thirteenth race of his career and his eighth as a three-year-old,
was to be the Prix de l'Arc de Triomphe at Longchamp but the Be
My Guest colt, whose astonishing season had made the reputation of
his sire, foundered in the soft going and finished unplaced.

By this time it had been officially announced to an expectant if mocking public that Golden Fleece had been retired. O'Brien had experienced so many genuine problems with the horse but even so it was a decision that still upset the purists and went some way to wiping out the good impression created by the rigorous and competitive policy adopted with Assert. It had always been maintained that the purpose of racing was to improve the breed. How could you do that if all the best horses were retired at three instead of being kept in training the following season to prove themselves against the next generation? How physically sound were these lightly raced Derby winners going to prove as stallions? And what about the race-going public? Didn't they deserve to see the best horses in action more often on the racecourse instead of having to listen to large dollops of hype based on just one or two actual races?

Sangster would talk earnestly about training bills, insurance and veterinary fees, the shortage of decent prize money and so on, but the truth was that in the new order of things the world was being told that a Derby winner was literally too valuable to risk on the track. Assert was syndicated by Windfields Farm in Maryland to join The Minstrel and Northern Dancer. Golden Fleece was retained in Ireland and syndicated to stand at Coolmore. This was a bold and brave commercial decision but it signified the partners' determination, now they had another Derby winner, to build up their own stallion station to rival that of any stud farm in Europe and even America. The two horses were collectively valued at $50 million.

The rise of Coolmore, which was going to be the next stage in the Ballydoyle story, has come as no surprise to anyone familiar with the farm manager, John Magnier. A large, very tall man with a high forehead, longish receding hair and a rather bullying appearance, Magnier is one of those exceptional characters who genuinely merit the clichéd description, 'formidable'. People meeting him for the first time encounter a driven, greying figure who looks less like a racing man and more like a high-intensity, venture capitalist, which is really what he is anyway. They think that he must be in his mid-fifties. In fact at the outset of the 1988 season, Magnier was just thirty-eight years old.

Magnier, Sangster and O'Brien don't personally own all the stallions at Coolmore but it's Magnier's endless, restless energy, his flair and ambition that has always secured a full sale of all the shares in those stallions, as well as a full book of the best quality mares available – not simply those owned by the syndicate partners – to each horse. He is the man who ultimately decides which stallions have failed commercially and should be dispensed with via a judicious sale to New Zealand or Japan and it's usually him who makes the main move when the partners have their eye on an outside horse, like Last Tycoon in 1985, that they think they'd like to buy. In 1987 he was made a senator by the Irish premier, Charles Haughey, who has himself had shares in some of the Ballydoyle horses. This was a national recognition of the invaluable importance of the bloodstock industry to the Irish economy. Horsey images may be a staple ingredient in the Tourist Board, or Bord Fáilte, marketing of Ireland but there's nothing folksy about Coolmore. The electronic gates, the wide straight drive, the American barns and the one-storey modern office block with the Subarus and Range Rovers parked outside, give the place more the feeling of South Fork Ranch than of a traditional ivy-clad and elm-shaded stud.

It is partly Magnier's exclusive use of bright, personable and youthful personnel with the same flair and professionalism as himself – as opposed to relying on hidebound old army officers from a bloodstock agency – that has enabled him to sell the Coolmore stallions and their progeny so successfully in the market-place. It's sometimes a hard sell too. The 1986 Coolmore stallion prospectus was eager to promote their new young sire, Salmon Leap. There was an enticing photograph of him finishing fourth in the 1983 Derby but no mention was made of the fact that the horse with the jockey in the yellow cap, visibly toiling at the rear of the field, was none other than Lomond, the self-same 2,000 Guineas winner that they were busily selling elsewhere in the portfolio. In fact Lomond had failed altogether in the Derby and never won another race after Newmarket.

The promotional copy for that controversial pair Storm Bird and Try My Best was equally careful to avoid mentioning their less than finest hours on the racecourse. Coolmore would argue that a commercial stallion station is a player in a highly competitive market and that it's entitled to sell its wares as aggressively as it can. And besides, without a happy and satisfied buyer none of their videos, brochures and intensive marketing techniques would be worth the cost of producing them. O'Brien would say again that if a horse has the right breeding and conformation, disappointments on the racetrack still may not prevent it from passing on its own sire's qualities to its offspring.

1982 ended on an interesting, indeed an ambiguous note for the syndicate. Once again they produced a champion two-year-old. Once again he was by Northern Dancer, only this time he raced in the colours of Danny Schwartz. His name was Danzatore and, on the strength of two undefeated runs in Ireland, he was hyped up to ante-post favourite for what was fast becoming O'Brien's jinx race, the English 2,000 Guineas at Newmarket. He wasn't sent over to England for that year's Dewhurst Stakes. Either O'Brien had decided that this time he didn't want the opposition to see his hand or he was just worried that the horse might not be good enough.

Another of the syndicate's two-year-olds, yet another Northern Dancer colt named Ballydoyle who ran in the name of Niarchos, proved to be an extremely costly flop. He'd cost no less than $3.5 million at Keeneland in 1981 but in four runs in Ireland in 1982 he could only win one small race at Naas at the very end of the season. He now stands as a stallion in Oklahoma with a covering fee of $5,000.

There was one other Northern Dancer yearling sold for over three million dollars at the 1981 Keeneland sale. But he wasn't bought by the Sangster syndicate. His new owner bought him as a present for one of his brothers. The colt's name was Shareef Dancer and he was entrusted to the care of Michael Stoute at his Beech House Stables in Newmarket. Shareef Dancer made his eagerly awaited début – the most expensive yearling ever put into training in England, as the *Raceform Notebook* observed – at 'headquarters' in August. He managed to win too though only by three-quarters of a length in a field of twenty-four. A few weeks later he was fourth giving weight away in a stakes race at Doncaster. A useful prospect, no doubt, though no one was taking odds-on about him ever doing enough on the racetrack to recoup his enormous purchase price.

Not that his owners only had him to look forward to for 1983. At that 1981 Keeneland sale where they'd 'snapped up' Shareef Dancer they had also bought twenty-eight other yearlings for an overall total of more than $10 million. At Keeneland the following summer they bought no fewer than sixty-one more for an outlay of very nearly $30 million. And in September of 1982, their colt, Touching Wood, who had been the runner up to Golden Fleece at Epsom in June, won the St Leger at Doncaster, giving his owners their first classic victory in England.

For Robert Sangster these were ominous developments and potentially the most serious since the syndicate had commenced operations in 1975. For the first time in seven years there was a whole new game in town.

The Arabs were coming.

6 : Newmarket Heath

It's a few minutes after six o'clock in the morning. A bedside phone is ringing persistently in a small double-room in an average to middle-range but definitely not luxury-class Newmarket hotel. Eventually a gaunt, rather grey-looking man in his late thirties picks up the phone with a bad-tempered howl. 'Good morning, sir,' chirps a bright little voice. 'This is your alarm call. Would you like me to call you a taxi?' The man shakes his head and throws the receiver away miserably. Then he peers at his watch and moans once again. In the bed next to him is the leggy blonde with the rather large nose who he met at the jockeys' disco at Blazers nightclub near Bury St Edmunds. Still caked in her eye make-up from the previous evening, the blonde rolls over heavily and goes back to sleep.

The man fumbles his way out of the tangled bedclothes and immediately trips over his open suitcase which lies sprawled across the floor. He goes into the bathroom and looks at himself in the mirror. It's not a pretty sight. He fills the tooth-mug with water and tips about half a dozen Alka-Seltzer into it. He tries to drink it too quickly and chokes on the bubbles. Then he goes back into the bedroom and puts the kettle on for a cup of tea. He gets the tea-bag in the cup and the boiling water on top of the tea-bag but then he breaks a fingernail trying to tear open the little plastic carton of UHT milk. He ends up shooting his thumb through the top of the carton and squirting milk into his eye. There's no time for a bath. He'll have to leave all that until after breakfast. He looks at his suitcase and wishes that he'd gone out after all and bought a Barbour and some wellies. Then he pulls on his suit trousers and his white shirt with the dried sweat under the armpits from his efforts on the dance-floor at Blazers and he slips into his already scuffed but once smart black leather shoes. He abandons his tie as too formal. He runs a hand through his hair and then remembers that at a moment of passion he left his black velvet-collar overcoat lying on the floor at the foot of the bed. Fully dressed, or as near to it as he's going to get, he tries to open the bedroom door. The night porter has already slipped a *Sporting Life* underneath it but it's wedged so tightly that he can't actually get the door open. By the time he can get it open the front page of the *Life* is in shreds.

He gives up and walks off down the corridor past the 'Do Not Disturb' signs and down the stairs to reception. He spots a few pals hanging around in a similar condition to himself. There's the old booze-hound with the blue anorak and the chicken-wire veins on his purple face and there's that plummy one who wanted to be a gossip columnist and ended up in racing by mistake. The booze-hound is just collecting a couple of aspirin from the porter. The three of them see that awful know-all from the *Daily Telegraph* striding out through the hotel front entrance in his flat cap, Husky and smart green wellingtons. If he's got his car up here, perhaps he can give them all a lift to where the action is? But no. He's disappearing into an assistant trainer's Range Rover. Perhaps a taxi would be a good idea after all. A bit late for that, sir, smirks the porter. The eccentric *Times* bloke with the funny old biddy of a wife with the headscarf and the Barbour, they got the last taxi ten minutes ago. The last taxi? Afraid so, sir. There won't be another one up for half an hour. This is getting serious. It's already past 6.30 and Cumani's meant to be working his Derby horse at seven. They'd better hurry if they want to see it. Looks as if they'll have to walk, but which way? Somebody says Racecourse Side. The overcoat man groans. That's a longish walk. Right the way up by the Rowley Mile racecourse. Wouldn't he be out up Warren Hill? reasons the booze-hound. It's on his doorstep after all. The others look doubtful but it is a hefty walk to Racecourse Side. Too far on a cold damp April morning. Well, all right then, they decide. We'll go up to Warren Hill. Bound to see plenty of horses there. Walk up to 'H's' place and back again. Probably see Luca on his way back down. Get a word in with him then.

So off the three of them go. Out of the warm hotel foyer and turn right on to the chill, grey and deserted early morning High Street of

this generally unremarkable East Anglian town. These gentlemen of
the press. Of the racing press. These hacks. Here in Newmarket on
their expense accounts to cover the Guineas meeting in April 1988.
Man Nowhere Near the Spot. Man Without a Clue and Man in the
Members' Bar. Never mind that the Editor's only ever interested in
about two paragraphs of copy and that's all tips. They've got to see
for themselves. Got to capture that inimitable gallops atmosphere.
What 'headquarters' is all about. If they could only find that bloke
from the *Life*. He's meant to be up at 'H's' chatting with Steve. He'd
put them right.

They carry on slowly to the traffic lights. Past the NatWest branch
on the other side of the street where Lester said he had his only bank
account. Turn right at the top and slip up that narrow road past the
motel and the miserable back entrance of one miserable old stableyard
and suddenly there it is. The Heath. Straight ahead of them. The
road winds its way up the open hillside ascending about one hundred
and fifty yards up to a cluster of trees at the top. They puff on up
this narrow road, up the steep enough hill past one or two parked
cars, a few onlookers with binoculars and yes, incredibly, the jogging
figure of the mighty Bruffscot getting in quite splendid trim for some
impending marathon.

There are at least sixty different training establishments in Newmarket and about 2,300 racehorses. Just now, at a few minutes to
seven on this shivering spring Thursday, it feels as if several hundred
of them have got out of bed at the same time and decided to
converge on Warren Hill. The journalistic trio are impressed. 'It's
just like Custer and the bleeding Indians,' mutters the grey-faced
hero in the crumpled coat. Groups of horses are coming in to the left
and the right of them. Appearing at the foot of the hill in single file.
Well rugged up against the cold and their lads rugged up too. At
regular intervals and in groups of two or three at a time, they break
into a canter, starting off slowly up the hill like a bunch of swimmers
kicking off stiffly from the shallow end. It's as if some signal-box or
traffic control is synchronising the whole thing. All of a sudden a
whole string of horses is streaming up the left-hand side of the road
and then swinging right along the rim of the heath, silhouetted
spectacularly against the skyline. They ease up by the clump of trees
and then wheel around and walk back down again to the foot of the
hill. At closer quarters some of the 'lads' look old enough to be
grandfathers while some of them look as if they've just walked in
from the orphanage scene in *Oliver Twist*. One trainer, a veteran in
years but no longer a serious player in terms of winners, is watching

the action on horseback, positioned half-way up the hill. He's immaculately turned out too with smart tweed cap and spotless jodhpurs tucked into his elegantly polished riding-boots. By contrast Michael Stoute, who guides a team of rather nervous-looking two-year-olds across the road just below Warren Place, is bareheaded and wearing an old pullover and an open-necked shirt. Unlike his trackside manner Stoute has the slightly surprised look of a man who has only recently leaped out of bed.

There's quite a little group of men and women gathered at the top now by the trees. One or two owners. Some journalists. A few touts. The three newcomers, badly out of breath, pause to look around them. One lights up a fag. He puffs out. They see the cigarette smoke and their breath hanging on the damp morning air. They're standing out on the grass now and it's soaking wet and they're ruining their shoes and their heads ache and their cholesterol level is probably way too high, but oh yes. Oh nice. Oh very, very nice. This view is fucking amazing.

Down at the foot of the hill they can see the red-brick walls and the grey rooftops of the town. Away to the left are the trees and lush paddocks of the Arabs' demesne up at Dalham Hall Stud. In the top right-hand corner they can just make out the distant buildings of the Rowley Mile racecourse and down on the right there's the Eastern Counties Omnibus Company's bus garage and the road and the rush-hour traffic beginning to build up on its way to Cambridge. It's still grey and cold but there's a faint sun shining now and the dew on the grass seems to twinkle in the brighter light.

'So where's George, then?' somebody mutters. George, who of course isn't here but up on Racecourse Side, is George Robinson, last of the official gallops-watchers, and a man with a rare and consummate skill that may not survive his own retirement. He can probably identify just about every single horse on the Heath simply from its colouring and its physical characteristics. George has always been a wholly respectable 'Our Man in Newmarket' figure. Not so some of the other work-watchers and touts who lead a somewhat more conspiratorial existence. There are a few of them around this morning. They're not all dapper and eagle-eyed either. Some of them look like bad actors out of a John le Carré dramatisation. Lots of winking and dandruff and hiding behind trees. They may be charged not only with recording the details of sometimes secret gallops but with prising out information about a stable's supposedly confidential running plans or about the well-being of its leading occupants. This may come via a jockey or a stable lad and will usually be reported back to a major bookmaking firm or a big-time professional gambler. The bookies will occasionally issue pious denials that this sort of thing goes on but don't believe a word of it. The world of big bookmaking is a Mafia-like jungle, and survival depends not only on access to good information but on ensuring that at all times you have considerably more information than the ordinary punter. There have probably been times when some major firms have had an unofficial payroll in almost every leading stable in the land. When a fancied horse suddenly takes a walk in the ante-post market for a big race, it's not because the charitable bookie has decided to make the price more attractive for the put-upon gambler. It's because his intelligence service will have told him that this horse has just done two successive pieces of disappointing work or that it hasn't been out of its box for three days or that, contrary to the trainer's public denials, it's highly unlikely to even run in the race at all. Serious gamblers must scrutinise the movements of the market at all times.

There are one or two bookmakers' PR representatives around this morning too. Even if you didn't know them already they're always easy to spot. Nobody else has a pressed trenchcoat and blow-dried hair on the gallops at half-past seven in the morning.

A new string of horses with different-coloured rugs have begun cantering up the hill towards the trees. The onlookers can hear them coming even as they lose sight of them momentarily beneath the crest of the hill. As the first two or three loom up on to the plateau at the top of the gallop the quick-witted newspaper boys spot the trainer's initials on the blankets. L.C.

'Which one's Falco, then?' asks the gossip columnist. 'That's his Derby horse, you know.'

'Not here,' grunts the booze-hound. 'These are the babies.'

'Yes, but Falco's his Derby horse.'

'Not Falco,' corrects the overcoat. 'Kefaah.'

'Isn't Kefaah a two-year-old?' asks the gossip columnist.

'No.'

'These are the two-year-olds,' says the booze-hound.

'Oh,' says the gossip columnist. Pause. 'We're in the wrong place, then.'

But so what if they are really? This has been a good place to be. They've taken a few notes. Recorded a few impressions in the margins of their last Saturday's Sandown racecard. And now they have that good and smug and virtuous feeling of the early riser who has been up and about and done a couple of hours' work before eight. Now they can relax and start to think about the really serious business of the morning. Breakfast. The sun shines down more kindly as the booze-hound spots the Ladbrokes representative who has got his car with him and is about to drive the *Life* man back down the hill into the town. The three lads cadge a lift in the back. And then as they walk back in through the hotel foyer they're talking about how good it is for you to get up in the morning and get a little exercise or, even better, see other people doing the exercise. In they go through the welcoming doors of the Suffolk Carvery or whatever it is the restaurant's been renamed since last year. The sunlight's positively streaming in now through the ruched curtains. The loud carpet is grappling with their hangover but at least the canned muzak, which has just changed ebulliently from 'Love Story' to 'A Walk In The Black Forest', is of a more modest volume than it used to be. They head for their coffee, their little boxes of cereal and their white toast. What shall it be next? Kippers for the gossip columnist? The big-nosed blonde for the overcoat man? Or the full contents of the grill tray for the booze-hound? All over Newmarket many others are hesitating over the same decision.

D. Wayne Lukas may pause for no more than a clutch of vitamin pills and a styrofoam cup of decaff but breakfast in most English racing stables is a major experience. At the humbler or less pretentious establishments everyone mixes in together. At the socially more ambitious yards only actual guests and the leading protagonists will be accommodated in the main kitchen. The other sort will be sweetly escorted by the trainer's wife into the back kitchen or an adjoining room next door. If this sort of trainer is based in Newmarket then he's sure to be entertaining house guests during an actual raceweek. Perhaps another trainer from the Lambourn area and his wife as well as a well-connected journalist or ex-jockey and perhaps a couple of owners too. Other visiting owners may drop by during the morning. They may be a pair of middle-aged Lloyds men kitted out, naturally, in uniform Husky or Barbour, or they may be a rich but cantankerous Arab and his racing manager, kitted out a little too noticeably whatever they're wearing but needing to be fobbed off with stories about their unraced horses having sore shins or needing another winter to mature or some such emollient rubbish. Not that the trainer will be anything less than optimistic about his chances in the races coming up. Adding real glamour to the occasion will be the presence of a famous jockey, still carrying his whip from the gallops, still wearing his black satin Santa Anita or Breeders Cup jacket and swanking around the kitchen table, occasionally fingering a piece of plain brown toast while he glances contemptuously at the afternoon's form in the *Sporting Life*.

For everybody else present, breakfast means lashings of what can best be described as heart attack on a plate. Eggs, sausages, bacon, tomato, mushrooms, fried bread and endless pots of hot, strong coffee. This is particularly necessary for the trainer's friend from Lambourn who is nursing a thumping hangover. He sits at one end of the table, shoulders hunched, little pink eyes staring out of a pale and prickly face, attempting to read a racing paper the wrong way up. He eventually abandons this effort as hopeless and turns instead to the *Mail* or the *Express* in which he hopes that his journalist friend might have given him a mention in the diary. Eventually the portly journalist, attired in a resplendent silk dressing-gown, himself arrives in the kitchen and proceeds to eat an enormous and sumptuous breakfast, all the while mercilessly teasing the drunk trainer about his chances of ever navigating his way back up to the racecourse that afternoon. Let alone of saddling his three intended runners.

In between these bouts of ribaldry everyone keeps congratulating the trainer's simply marvellous wife, Penny or Jilly or Jenny, about the quite splendid breakfast she's prepared for them all. In truth the simply marvellous and exceedingly pretty Penny won't have prepared anything at all. All the cooking will have been done by a stout lady called Mrs Biggs who will afterwards do all the tidying up too. Breakfast over, the chaps all repair back upstairs and then reappear three-quarters of an hour later, shaved, bathed, fully suited and ready for a conference about the afternoon's card. The host trainer confesses that, in spite of what he said to the Arab, his two haven't got a prayer but he's heard that the Neville Callaghan thing is very well fancied in the first. A decision is made to pass this information on to the Arab so that he can back the horse himself and feel slightly appeased. The famous jockey is congratulated about his eldest son having passed his Common Entrance exam for Cranleigh and then the drunk trainer, who now has a smouldering cigar jammed in his mouth, is bundled into his BMW and off they all go for pre-lunch drinks with Timmy across the other side of town.

The main problem for most trainers, when they're not worrying about how to mix the perfect Bloody Mary, is how to deal with that perennial bane of their lives. Owners. During one afternoon of the 1988 Craven meeting at Newmarket a very respectable journalist for a Sunday newspaper approached Henry Cecil with a request for an interview. 'I can't possibly do it this week,' said the harassed-looking Cecil. 'We've got owners.' From the wretched expression on his face you'd have thought he was talking about an infectious disease. Cecil once said that trainers who spend their spare time trawling around night clubs for custom will get the owners they deserve. From a look at Henry's list you certainly couldn't accuse him of scouring any of the shadier night-spots. A Jockey Club reception for the United Arab Emirates maybe, but nothing really insalubrious.

Some trainers have perfected the charming manner and the patient response for dealing with their owners. Others depend on their wives to do it for them and some 'racing wives' do it extremely well. There are still one or two trainers though who are almost paranoid about what they regard as intrusive, interfering outsiders. Even when the outsiders own the bloody horses. If you're not obviously one of them, if you weren't born with the smell of horseshit on your fingers, then you're an immediate object of suspicion.

Margaret Thatcher is not renowned for her visits to either Newmarket or Epsom Downs. Yet she would surely be impressed by the fact that the racing industry survives almost entirely on the patronage of the private citizen be it through the owners' training fees or the punters losing betting slips. Even the most basic training bills at a top-drawer Newmarket stable will be in the region of ten or twelve thousand a year and many owners are paying much more than that for the pleasure and privilege of owning a good racehorse. The relationship of some of these people with their trainers is akin to that of an anxious and ambitious parent with a housemaster at their child's very expensive public school. Rather like a school it is the owners or the parents' money that keeps everything afloat so technically the parent must always be deferred to or well cared for at all times. Actually they are more often simply tolerated or suffered, especially when they ring up out of the blue and want to pop down and see how their little darlings are getting on. Like the top schools you have to have a lot of money and often the right social credentials to get a horse into, say, Cecil's stable or into the yard of the Queen's trainer, the invalided Major Dick Hern. Just as schools will advertise their playing fields, their computers and their laboratories, so some racing stables will get videos made showing off their extensive gallops, their veterinary facilities and their very latest in the line of sophisticated stable accommodation. And just as with a school, the cachet for some non-aristocratic or *nouveaux riches* owners of actually getting their horse into a top people's stable seems to be stronger nowadays than it's ever been. The Arabs of course have gone right in at the top. After some years of not entirely satisfactory service they virtually bought up the top ten trainers and stables in the country. If they ever took their 'children' away then the consequences for the schools would be quite catastrophic. Even the most academic school may sometimes have to accept a complete idiot as a pupil due to the financial or other pressures being exerted on it by the parents. Similarly a trainer may sometimes find himself stuck with an incredibly expensive and blue-blooded yearling who turns out to be completely useless as a racehorse. And sometimes, perish the thought, the horses turn out to be a great deal smarter than the trainers.

At the outset of the 1988 season it was confidently expected that the training tables would be dominated once again by those two great Newmarket rivals Cecil and Stoute with the Italian-born Luca Cumani, third in 1987, mounting an even stronger challenge than before. If Stoute's ultra-competitive approach to issues such as medication and the Breeders Cup has rankled some establishment figures, Cecil's critics tend to come from the other side of the racing tracks and make unkind jokes about his good fortune in being the stepson of one famous trainer, Sir Cecil Boyd-Rochfort, and the son-in-law of another, the late Sir Noel Murless. When 'H' first appeared on the scene in 1969, after a four-year period assisting 'Uncle Cecil', he seemed to fit the standard image of the upper-class drip from the Royal Agricultural College at Cirencester who was now going to train a few horses. Needless to say he's changed and matured a fair bit over the years. Everyone in Newmarket will testify to the fact that his runners always seem to be just that little bit sharper than other stables' horses, to have an advantage of fitness and strength that has enabled him to win all five classic races and to maintain a quite remarkable striking rate, season after season. When the Warren Place team are carrying everything before them, this success seems inevitable, natural, assured. When they suddenly hit a lean spell, some of the old rumblings start up again. Then Cecil's dandified style and laid-back manner, not least his habit of adding a mumbled 'you know?' on to the end of every comment, can start to grate with some of the dourer types in the press-room. Cecil almost always has runners in the two main classic trials at the Craven meeting in April. During one of these races a few years ago, almost all the racing professionals were frantically concentrating their binoculars on the last two furlongs as the contest built towards a climax. All it seemed except Henry. A Cecil-trained Guineas fancy was challenging for the lead but where was her trainer? Standing about fifty yards away at the foot of the terracing. No binoculars. The habitual cigarette in one hand, the other in his overcoat pocket and gazing, apparently unconcernedly, into space.

Great success always seems to lead to some envy and resentment in any sphere as Wayne Lukas has discovered to his cost. You can say that Cecil was lucky to inherit Murless's house and stables as well as some of his staff and a few of his prestigious owners like the nonogenerian Jim Joel, whose father Jack first began privately breeding racehorses in 1897. Yet it was Cecil's successes in his own right in the seventies with horses like Bolkonski, Wollow, Le Moss, Kris and One In A Million that led to him getting the all-important patronage of Sheikh Mohammed. The Arabs may have bought a few used cars in their early dealings with English racehorse trainers, but nowadays they are much warier and much more demanding. It is inconceivable that either the Maktoum brothers or jockeys like Piggott and Steve Cauthen would've chosen to ally themselves with Cecil if he was really just a blue-blooded fool with a silver spoon in his mouth. Some of his critics will still maintain that, as with Lukas, it's easy to be champion trainer when you have unlimited financial resources at your disposal to pick out whatever yearlings you wish. The point remains that the pressures and tensions involved in training a string of hugely valuable and superbly bred horses who are always expected to win classic races are in the end much greater than the pressures on a smaller trainer who may be able to improve an unfashionable or mediocre horse so that it wins a big handicap or lands a nice touch but who never has to contend with having millions of pounds at stake every week. And behind that diffident exterior Cecil feels the tension all right as anyone would've noticed who examined his manner and expression in the paddock at York before the International Stakes in August 1988.

This prestigious Group One prize was the target for his brilliant filly, Indian Skimmer, who had been kept in training as a four-year-old after injury had curtailed her triumphant three-year-old career the previous June. Sheikh Mohammed's American-bred had already been worth a small fortune at that point as a potential brood-mare but after two slightly disappointing runs earlier in the 1988 season her valuation and her reputation were very much on the line at York. Cecil had experienced numerous problems and difficulties in trying to get the filly back to peak fitness and you could see that he was mentally reliving all of those moments as he anxiously watched the grey being led out on to the course. Indian Skimmer didn't win the International but she did run very well in it. Well enough, in fact, to suggest that even bigger things might be expected of her later in the year. Yet the sheer strain of training a horse of this calibre, of not getting it wrong, is incomparably different to the pressure on an average trainer in a thousand-pound handicap at Warwick.

Cecil in his prime has never conformed to the habits of the old-fashioned racecourse martinet. There are no barked commands. No insistence that stable lads should get their hair cut or stand to attention during a trainer's inspection. His enthusiasm for Gucci shoes and American check trousers, or tight-fitting pants as Lukas would call them, and indeed his enjoyment of all kinds of shopping has always been a topic of amusement amongst his fellow trainers. It used to be said that when he went out to Kentucky he spent more time looking around Lexington's men's outfitters than he did looking at yearlings. In the old days he would sometimes turn up at meetings like Goodwood wearing really wonderful-looking banana-yellow suits and outrageous ties. Latterly the more exotic clothes seem to have been kept under lock and key but he still looks stylish enough. Always bareheaded. Usually in a plain blue or black suit with an expensive blue shirt and always with his black hair several inches too long for the liking of the Household Cavalry types in the Jockey Club stand. His wife Julie strikes a more conventional pose with her little twitching nostrils and her sea-shanty hats but she is universally regarded as an outstanding horsewoman and, in view of her background, as an indispensable element in the stable's success.

Luca Cumani, the man who finished third to Cecil and Stoute in the 1987 trainers' championship, actually began his English racing career as Cecil's assistant in 1974 and 1975. From the moment he set up on his own the following year he seemed to be destined for the top but it wasn't until 1984 that he gained his first classic victory when Comanche Run won that year's St Leger at Doncaster. The thirty-nine-year-old Italian and his beautiful 'English rose' wife Sara make a rather more sophisticated combination than some old-school racing partnerships. Small, neat, sharp-faced with a slightly camp manner and walk, Cumani generally favours the Italian Burberry style of dress more familiar in the cafés of the Galleria and the Via Manzoni in Milan than on an English racecourse.

A thoroughly competent amateur rider and the son of a respected trainer, Cumani first established his reputation in Britain with his brilliant placing of improving handicappers in races like the Cambridgeshire and the Extel Handicap at Goodwood. It's a brave man who mentions this to him now as he seems to regard this entire aspect of his career with a mixture of irritation and embarrassment. Some of his stable lads have mischievously nicknamed him 'Lightbulb

Luca' for his enthusiasm for keeping the lights on in his horses' boxes in the hope that this will convince them that whatever the weather or the time of year it's actually a warm summer's day outside. Cumani's list of owners are as wealthy and as socially top-drawer a collection as that of any stable in the country. Included amongst them are two crucial names. Sheikh Mohammed and the Aga Khan. The Aga only has horses with two other English trainers (Michael Stoute is one of them), so when he decided to send a number of yearlings to Cumani in 1986 it was a clear signal to the rest of the racing community of 'Lightbulb's' rapidly rising stock within the industry.

Of course the Newmarket men could expect to face serious competition from their traditional rivals in the other big training centres at Lambourn, Manton, Beckhampton and down in West Sussex. From Hern, Hills and Tree. From John Dunlop and Guy Harwood. Harwood began the new season, as he always does, with an open day for the press at his Combelands Stables near Pulborough. These occasions regularly follow the same pattern. The deserving hacks get all the food and drink they can manage and are then loaded up into a couple of farm wagons and hauled by tractor across the Sussex Downs before being finally dumped near the top of Harwood's gallops like thirty or so inebriated bales of hay. There follows a working parade by Harwood's string and then the next morning 90 per cent of those present tip the same two horses to follow to the general public.

The most noticeable thing about Harwood personally at the start of this 1988 campaign was that his extraordinary haircut seemed to be thicker, greyer and more upwardly sweeping than ever before. The hairstyle and the piercing eyes counteract the otherwise conformist dress and give him a rather thrusting, hunting, skiing, sexually athletic image which is not entirely lost on some of his female patrons. (Indeed there are quite a few dashing white trainers around the country who have managed to pay off a whole year's office bills from the stabling fees incurred by owners' wives so smitten by their deep blue eyes or their hair or the creak of their caramel suede chaps that they insisted on having a horse for themselves.) Only a few seasons ago, Philippa, a still pretty fifty-year-old Sloane Ranger and one-time minor Pinewood star, was trying to persuade her third husband, Roger, a grossly fat City insurance broker with little knowledge of racing, that he should buy her a horse. Hardly renowned for his enthusiasm at parting with money, fatso Roger would consent to no more than a £5,000 purchase price. Barely enough to buy a mediocre novice hurdler these days, let alone a yearling bred for the socially more desirable waters of the flat. None the less the exasperated Philippa set off one day for the Newmarket Highflyer Sales in the company of her horsey friend Tory. And who should they bump into almost immediately but Tory's clean-limbed chum, the exceedingly eligible top trainer . . . Guy Harwood. When Tory explained that her blushing companion with the fluttering eyelashes wanted to buy a horse, the chemistry it seems was immediate. Philippa describes what happened next in her own words. 'Well, Harwood just fixed me with those wonderful eyes of his, darling, and asked me, "What price?" Under the influence of his divine glare I couldn't possibly tell the truth so I just sort of added on a nought . . . just like that.' The businesslike Guy said that he'd see what he could do, tipped them both a wink and then departed on his rounds of the yearling barns leaving the quivering Philippa wondering just exactly what she'd done.

A few weeks later she was reclining alone on her bed in the country one wet afternoon when the telephone rang. 'Hello Philippa,' said a commanding voice. 'Harwood here. I think I've got you that horse.' Philippa panicked and slammed the phone down immediately. A few moments later, the phone rang again. Philippa picked it up nervously. 'Oh hello, Philippa. Harwood here. Now. I think that I've got you that horse! He's got to be a bargain at seventy-five thousand and I think you're going to have a lot of fun. Of course he is a High Line and the family are sometimes a little slow to mature. So we may not see the best of him until he's three. Or even four. But I'm sure that over a distance of ground and when stamina is at a premium he'll be bound to pay his way etc. etc.'

The now-stricken Philippa ended up requiring the best part of a bottle of gin as well as the very best lingerie that Harrods could supply in order to convince the wretched Roger that his £75,000 racehorse was money well spent. And while performing her dance of the seven veils for her fatso husband, there can be no doubt that it was really the splendid Harwood who was uppermost in her thoughts. Unfortunately for all of them – and through no fault of the trainer – the horse never ran as a two-year-old, performed moderately at three and ended up being gelded and running in novice hurdles at Folkestone and Fontwell Park.

Philippa's horse was ridden by a senior jockey. Not that it helped very much. Yet when all the £75,000 or £750,000 yearlings have been bought, be they by Roger or Sheikh Mohammed, and when all the razor-sharp conditioning has been completed, be it by Vincent,

Michael or Guy, the honesty, ability and enthusiasm of the retained jockey can still often make a crucial difference to the fate of the owner's investment.

For the last four years the English jockeys championship has been virtually dominated by two men. Steve Cauthen, stable jockey to Henry Cecil, and Pat Eddery, employed since 1986 on a reputed two million pounds' retainer by the Saudi Arabian, Khalid Abdulla, and also in constant demand when available by all the top trainers in the business.

Eddery had already celebrated his eighth birthday when his rival-to-be was born in Covington, Kentucky in May 1960. Cauthen's mother Myra, formerly Myra Bischoff, was the sister of the racehorse trainer Tommy Bischoff, while his father Tex, a native of the town of Sweetwater in the Lone Star state, had been 'fooling around' with horses since his early teens. He still has the looks and style of the typical cowboy drifter hero of a thousand Country and Western songs.

It didn't take Tex and Myra more than a summer or two to realise that their infant son had a precocious but instinctive gift for horseback riding that was quite out of the ordinary. Steve's skill matured rapidly over the next decade during which time he learned that there are many ways of persuading a horse to run for you other than by just trying to dominate it through brute force.

Cauthen jun. didn't get his first ride in public until the age of sixteen which is the legal limit in America. That year he was champion American apprentice. The following season he was champion jockey with a staggering total of 487 winners. In 1978 Cauthen rode that great racehorse Affirmed to victory in each leg of the American Triple Crown. Each race was a titanic struggle with another great three-year-old colt, Alydar, and the series seemed to establish Cauthen's prowess not only with the railbirds but also with the hard-nosed Emperors of the Blue Grass in Kentucky, and Europe too. Yet when Affirmed was defeated in his first two races as a four-year-old the following January, 'The Six Million Dollar Kid' was summarily sacked by owner Lou Wolfson and Cuban-born trainer Laz Barrera. American trainers don't have retained stable jockeys. They employ whichever top rider they want for a particular horse and a particular race. When you're hot you're really hot but you'd better not go out of fashion or, in the words of that old pro Woody Stephens, 'suddenly it's toilet time'. Starved of the decent rides Cauthen proceeded to go through a 110-runner losing streak. Many handicappers seriously believe that the hardballs in the weighing room, especially on the New York circuit, engaged in a calculated effort to freeze him out of business. Fortunately for The Kid it was at this point that Robert Sangster stepped in and offered him a lucrative contract to cross the Atlantic and ride his English-trained horses based with Barry Hills in Lambourn.

Cauthen's first ride in England was a winning one on a horse called Marquee Universal on a filthy wet afternoon at Salisbury in April. Less than a month later, he won the 2,000 Guineas on Tap On Wood but his final end-of-season tally of fifty-two winners was considered respectable rather than spectacular. It was only to be expected that there would be some English commentators quick to suggest that Cauthen didn't have what it takes to make it in English conditions. What was more extraordinary was that some observers seemed to imagine that Tex and Myra's sweet-faced boy was a cross between James Dean and a hick from the sticks. It was seriously suggested in some quarters that 'little Steve' might be too gauche for the socially complex (i.e. snobbish) world of English flat racing. One newspaper actually described his first appearance in the jockeys' changing room at Salisbury, breaking out a pack of cards and inviting the Limeys to join him in a game, as if he were some caricature pushy 'Yank' from a pre-war comic.

If anyone seriously objected to his manner then, they can have few reservations about it eight years later. Cauthen has turned himself into an immaculately groomed and immaculately polished racing athlete. Like some dedicated visiting American in a Henry James novel, he's almost the perfect young English gentleman. He shoots. He wears the right clothes. His hair is neat and unobtrusive. He's his own man but he's also just deferential enough. And his solidly Republican-Conservative views fit in very happily with the predominant ethos of Newmarket and Lambourn. The *Sporting Life* ran an extensive interview-cum-profile with him on the eve of the 1987 Derby in which he rode the favourite and eventual winner, Reference Point. It was only a week before the General Election and Cauthen allowed himself to be drawn away from racing subjects to express his admiration for Margaret Thatcher's low-taxation, free enterprise policies. He implied that he would find it hard to imagine himself living and working in an England governed by Neil Kinnock. Not that most people who back his mounts in a betting office or go to see him ride on the track could really care less about his politics. His brilliance overrides such partial reactions.

Cauthen has had several well publicised battles with his weight and at one point even checked into a clinic in America in an effort to combat what was not so much a drink problem as a variation on the wasting disease bulimia. In the circumstances The Kid has shown an admirably smiling and outward-looking approach to life and appears to retain an undiminished appetite for the formidable challenge of the European racing circus.

In America, almost all race-tracks are flat, left-handed, dirt ovals of about a mile in length. A complete contrast to the turf racecourses of Britain which come in a variety of differing shapes and sizes, and where working out the many different problems they present is as big a challenge to a young jockey as passing his 'Knowledge' is to a would-be taxi driver in London. Cauthen didn't always find it easy at first but over the years he's continued to adapt and perfect his style to the unique demands of English racing. He's also given English crowds and English jockeys one or two lessons that they'll never forget. Most notably in the American art of riding a race from the front and continually adjusting and dictating the pace. It's a style that was never more evident than in his two brilliant pillar-to-post Derby victories on Slip Anchor and Reference Point in 1985 and 1987. It's not often that you see Cauthen whipping his mounts all the way to the line. He has a touch and feel for a horse that must've been made in heaven. In the colourful words of J. T. Lundy, President of Calumet Farm, the Kentucky home of Cauthen's 1978 Kentucky Derby winner, Affirmed, 'That boy could ride a swamp-hog naked through the Louisiana bayous and still win twenty-five lengths.'

Of course Cauthen isn't the only American to have had a major influence on English jockeyship. The first American invasion of the Turf here occurred around the turn of the century and coincided with the decision by millionaire families like the Whitneys that it would be good sport to race a few horses in Europe. American trainers like John Huggins, who saddled the 1901 Derby winner, Volodyovski, enjoyed highly successful careers in England, although some of Huggins's fellow countrymen were credited with introducing the practice of doping, which was not strictly illegal at the time, into the domestic racing scene. This mostly involved the dextrous use of cocaine to make a horse go faster. George Lambton described it all in *Men and Horses* and memories of this era appear to live on rather erroneously in the minds of some senior Jockey Club members whenever they consider the subject of medication in American racing today.

Along with trainers like Huggins came a whole batch of top-class American jockeys led by Tod Sloan, 'Skeets' Martin, Danny Maher and the brothers, Lester and Johnny Reiff. At first the American style of crouching low over their horses' necks was derided by English racegoers as making them look like 'monkeys up a stick'. Gradually though, as people realised that this new style made the jockeys far less wind-resistant, and enabled their mounts to go faster and win more races, it was the English technique of sitting bolt upright in the saddle and riding with very long leathers that began to look ridiculous. The old English habit (which still persists sometimes today in both England and France) of dawdling for the first three-quarters of a race and then going into a sprint finish in the final two furlongs at least began to be broken as a result of the Americans' example. Races were generally run at a much faster pace and Lester Reiff set a new record time for the Derby on Volodyvoski (or 'Bottle O' Whisky' as the punters called him) in 1901. In spite of their talent (or perhaps because of it, as it takes a clever jockey to lose convincingly) and in spite of Johnny Reiff's smiling, angelic good looks, both he and his brother were apparently heavily involved with the bookmakers and by no means always to be trusted.

Not the least refreshing aspect of Steve Cauthen's conquest of English racing has been his remarkably open and honest manner, especially when questioned by the press about his chances in an upcoming race. It's been welcomed with jubilation by punters and journalists alike. Nothing could be further removed from those old inaudible interviews with Lester or the sometimes equally impenetrable encounters with Pat Eddery. Some professionals would probably put their life on Cauthen if they had to. Not because he'd be certain to win – you can never say that – but because they would be certain that he wouldn't stitch them up.

One of the features of the 1987 flat-racing year was the thrilling duel between Cauthen and Eddery for the jockeys championship which went on right until the final day of the season and which saw Cauthen emerge the narrowest of winners with 197 victories over Eddery's 195. Against that, Eddery had no fewer than 150 more booked rides than the American. That says as much about his astonishing obsession and will to win as it does about his popularity with trainers and his general lack of weight problems.

Of course Pat Eddery had already won the jockeys' title four times before Cauthen even set foot in England. One of twelve children from the Dublin suburb of Blackrock, Eddery's destiny must have seemed inevitable from his earliest childhood. His father Jimmy was an Irish champion jockey and young Pat was riding work for the local trainer, Seamus McGrath, by the time he was nine years old. Pat's drive and ambition, his sometimes ruthless will to win are every bit as emphatic now as they were in the O'Brien era or when he won his first jockeys' title back in 1974. His wife Carolyn is the daughter of one former jockey, the late Manny Mercer who was killed in a fall at Ascot in 1959, and the niece of another, the now retired Joe Mercer who won the championship in 1979 and succeeded Pat as stable jockey to Peter Walwyn in 1980. 'Uncle Joe' is now one of the Maktoum family's racing advisers. The Edderys have two small daughters but, from late March to the beginning of November each year, the jockey sees little of his children. Unless he's injured or suspended he's riding every afternoon and every evening too in summer and on Sundays he's away riding abroad, usually in France. His rides are all booked through his brother-in-law, Terry Ellis, who acts as a sort of combination chauffeur, minder and business manager. You won't get through to Pat unless you speak to Ellis first.

The most distinctive and the most enthralling aspect of Eddery's style as a jockey remains his unflappable nerve. Whether he's riding in the Derby or a selling race at Windsor he remains as cool as a glass of Kentucky iced tea. He's still as strong in a finish and he still has that priceless ability to hold a horse up and wait and wait and then come with a devastating late run. As with Freddie Head it's a style that looks brilliant when he wins but it does lay him open to accusations of poor judgement when it fails to come off. Eddery and Cauthen have each won two Derbys but Cauthen has never won the Arc. This is as much to do with Henry Cecil's strange reluctance to give one of his top three-year-olds a typical Arc preparation as it is with any flaw in Cauthen's ability. Eddery has won the Arc four times as well as just about every other big race in the calendar. Sometimes he keeps his cards so close to his chest that when he gets off one of these classic winners he can be an interviewer's nightmare. On other occasions he's Pat the owner's friend, declaring that his every latest group race success is the best horse he's sat on since Dancing Brave or El Gran Senor, etc.

For men like Cauthen and Eddery, the stakes in the biggest races could scarcely be any higher these days. As well as their stable retainers, they're riding for 10 per cent of the winning prize money as well as the inevitable presents from grateful owners, which have sometimes amounted to as much as all the purse money in a Group One race if the owner has had a breeding jackpot to look forward to in the future. The jockey may also expect a breeding right or stallion share for the rest of that horse's stallion life. It's not so very surprising in the circumstances that Steve and Pat will be clearing at least a seven-figure sum each year. Neither is it surprising, in the wake of the Piggott case, that all their retainers, shares and presents now have to be fully registered with both the racing authorities and the VAT and Inland Revenue inspectors.

All jockeys, be they the best in the business with a Concorde trip each week, or the ordinary day-to-day boys just trying to get by on their basic fee of £39.70 a ride, understandably resent what they regard as ill-informed criticism. Especially from ignorant, losing punters talking through their pockets. You can meet them at any race-meeting or hear them in any betting office on any day of the week. 'That fucking bastard Eddery. My three-year-old son could ride better than that. Don't tell me that race wasn't fixed. Fucking bastards,' etc. Or 'Bleeding Carson. Bleeding Git. He's got less brains than a ventriloquist's dummy,' and so on.

The trouble is that jockeys and trainers aren't all saints with sensible sports jackets, artificial hands and an unswerving belief that virtue will always triumph. Races do sometimes get thrown and favourites pulled but it's not the sort of subject that many racing correspondents choose to raise too often. Journalists, whose daily working lives depend on regular contact with the boys in the weighing room, know that it doesn't do to print too many uncomplimentary stories. Let alone name names or embarrassing incidents. Access to interviews, tips and information can suddenly dry up altogether. The comments of most television paddock analysts can be equally bland. Yet not all small-time punters are foul-mouthed dim-witted morons. They can often tell that the race they've just seen is rather different to the cosy generalisations being bandied about by the TV paddock commentator who is himself often an ex-jockey disinclined to criticise a colleague. 'And there we see the old maestro,' says the BBC's Jimmy Lindley at Ascot or Newbury or Goodwood. 'Ridin' like 'is old self today.' To the ordinary viewer that may translate into 'Oh no! Not that conniving old bastard! Stitching us up yet again.' This alternative commentary would carry on something like this: 'And yes. There we see the old maestro. Unluckily losing a few vital lengths at the start. And, oh dear, the old maestro's run into a few traffic problems trying to get a run through the middle of the field. But yes . . . there goes the old maestro. Running on gently into fifth or sixth place. Too late really to figure in the outcome.'

Now it could be that the old maestro is riding for a particularly wily trainer from North Yorkshire who doesn't want his horse to win today or next time either because he's trying to get it dropped down the weights so that he can get a good price about it for a big handicap in six weeks' time. Or it might be that the old maestro's packing it in at the end of the season and that he pulled this favourite for the bookmakers so as to add a little money to his pension fund. Or he might've just been writing his own formbook. Setting up a gamble for next time out when he can get his punters to back the horse for him. Many jockeys have had punters over the years. It's a way of circumventing the Jockey Club rules that forbid them to bet. The punters put a stake on for themselves and for the jockey too. And the horse in question is not always the jockey's own mount. There's an old joke that some riders never put in a stronger finish than when they're riding against their own money!

A generous slice of villainy, of bold protagonists craftily endeavouring to put one over on the bookies is an essential part of racing's attraction. Nobody seriously wants it to be too cleaned up. Yet there's something faintly ludicrous about the way in which every time any journalist or commentator comes near to mentioning the truth about gambling jockeys some pompous establishment figure, usually an ex-amateur rider in a regimental tie, either leaps up to claim that this is an outrageous calumny and slander on the game or reacts as if the very idea of gambling money on racehorses is a novelty that he'd never considered before in his entire life. These self-appointed ambassadors of the sport are often the type who will applaud the most melodramatic scenarios in a Dick Francis novel but when it comes to the real thing, 'racing's as clean as a whistle, old boy. Never been straighter. Jockeys and trainers all jolly good chaps and stewards doing a splendid job' etc.

The fact is that probably 90 per cent of all racehorse owners, in fact almost everyone other than the Emperors of the Blue Grass, are in racing strictly for fun and for the love of it rather than with any realistic expectations of winning the Derby. To have any hope of also occasionally pulling off a tilt at the ring they need a trainer cunning and skilful enough to lay out their horse for a particular race and they need a jockey who will follow instructions implicitly: to try his hardest to win when the money's down but not to try too hard at all when it isn't; and in particular not to grass up their plan to a bookmaker. Naturally enough the best jockeys at giving a horse a deliberately quiet time are not far off being the best jockeys at winning too. Just like the Americans, Lester and Johnny Reiff, you need artistry and finesse to lose and make it look unavoidable. Only the clumsy ones get caught. Most ordinary punters understand the general situation well enough and don't mind discovering that some clever trainer has pulled off an inspired gamble with a horse with no obvious chance. They do mind when a genuine favourite loses a race after a strangely lazy or inept performance from a leading jockey which then fails to result in an effective investigation by the stewards.

One recent exception to the general blandness of the standard paddock analyst has been John Francome, the brilliant former jump-jockey who joined Channel 4 at the beginning of 1988. Francome's paddock co-commentator is sometimes the admirably succinct Jim McGrath of the *Timeform* organisation. More often it's the remarkably long-winded Lord Oaksey who with each new season makes an ever more spirited attempt to walk off single-handedly with the Edward Fox award for upper-class overacting on television. By comparison Francome's dry, laid-back manner, his simple, acute observations made out of real, recent knowledge of what's involved and his willingness to state the obvious, even if it embarrasses official ears, makes gloriously refreshing viewing. He always sailed close to the wind as a jockey and will no doubt end up on the carpet as a broadcaster one day too if the stuffed shirts have their way. Probably for the length of his hair if not for the artful drift of his remarks.

Francome, Oaksey, Bruffscot. Cecil, Cumani, Stoute. Eddery and Cauthen. Guy Harwood. The booze-hound, the gossip columnist and the crumpled overcoat. All the Philippas and Rogers. All the old bastards and all the old maestros. Every major participant in the racing circus was here in Newmarket for this three-day Guineas meeting beginning on 29 April. For the ante-post gambler these first two classic races would be like the opening rounds of a no-limit card-game. How strong is your hand . . . and your nerve? Who's going to be smart? Who's going to play their best cards early and go out? Who's kept something up their sleeve? And does anybody know the telephone number of the local branch of the Samaritans?

For the big players, for the European Emperors of the Blue Grass and for the Americans too, Guineas week, and the other classic trials that happen around the same time, would be the first serious indication of which of the big battalions might have made the right breeding and yearling choices two or more years before. And of which bloodlines could expect to be dominant in 1988.

Accepted racing wisdom has always said that one of the first places to start looking for a classic winner is in the official ratings of the International Free Handicap compiled by the senior handicappers of England, Ireland and France and published over the winter. The top-rated two-year-old colts of 1987, all three of them unbeaten, were Warning, a bay son of Known Fact out of a Roberto mare; Sanquirico, a son of Lypheor, himself a grandson of Northern

Dancer and Caerwent, who was by the 1983 French Derby winner, Caerleon – a son of Nijinsky – out of the brilliant sprint mare Marwell. Warning was owned and bred by Khalid Abdulla who had owned his sire, was trained by Guy Harwood and would be ridden by Pat Eddery. Sanquirico was owned by that luckiest of racing's lucky gentlemen, the suave and silky-haired Lloyds member, Charles St George, was trained by Cecil and would be ridden by Steve Cauthen. Caerwent was part-owned by Robert Sangster but would run in the colours of his breeder and principal owner, the very traditional Anglo-Irishman, Edmund Loder, whose family's Eyrefield Stud in County Kildare bred the historic mare Pretty Polly. Caerwent was trained by the now seventy-two-year-old Vincent O'Brien and would be ridden by the Ulsterman John Reid, in his first season as contract rider at Ballydoyle.

The top-rated two-year-old fillies of 1987 included what the handicappers believed to be the equal of the very best juveniles of her generation. Her name was Ravinella and she was a bay daughter of Mr Prospector out of the Northern Dancer mare, Really Lucky. Although from the Native Dancer as opposed to the Nearco line, Mr Prospector, with a record of eighty-five stakes winners through to 1987, was indisputably America's leading sire and, now that Northern Dancer was retired from the breeding shed, he was set to replace him as the most dominant as well as the most commercially fashionable stallion in the world.

Ravinella was trained at Chantilly by Criquette Head and owned by Ecurie Aland, the trading name for the celebrated partnership between Criquette's father, Alec, formerly one of the most successful European racehorse trainers since the Second World War, and the Comte Roland de Chambure. The Comte, a silver-haired banker in his early fifties, was a well-established and much liked figure in international as well as French racing circles and as noted for his enjoyment of the gourmet pleasures of life as for his successes in the racing and breeding industry. Ecurie Aland described the partners' racing interests while Société Aland was their breeding operation. Head's Haras du Quesnay stud farm, just outside of Deauville, houses Aland's mares as well as those belonging to his wife. The Comte's stud, Haras D'Etreham, situated, like du Quesnay, in the verdant Normandy countryside, raised the 1979 Arc-winning filly, Three Troikas, who was trained by Criquette.

Ravinella had won three of her four races as a two-year-old including Newmarket's Group One Cheveley Park Stakes over six furlongs of the Guineas course in which she'd revealed the kind of explosive speed and acceleration that had swept Miesque to such thrilling successes in 1987.

Set to take on Ravinella in the 1,000 Guineas were a whole clutch of Arab-owned fillies including Diminuendo trained by Henry Cecil and about half a dozen exposed or less exposed prospects trained by Michael Stoute. Diminuendo, only little but unbeaten in four races and seemingly abundantly strong and brave, was a daughter of a horse called Diesis, himself trained by Cecil, who had been a fine two-year-old in 1982 but who had been prevented from training on due to injury. Already making a major impact as a stallion with only two crops at the races, Diesis had moved from England to that sybaritic haven for equine Lotharios, Gainesway Farm, power-base of the leading Emperor himself. Victories for Diesis colts and fillies in Europe in 1988 would be sweet music to his syndicate of shareholders and Diminuendo seemed certain to be a major factor in the English fillies' classic races.

Cecil had already won the 1,000 three times but for his greatest rival it was rapidly becoming, his excellent place-record notwithstanding, something of a jinx race. In the decade he'd been training, Stoute had saddled five seconds and three thirds in the 1,000 Guineas but never a winner. This time his chief candidate was something of a dark horse, a daughter of Shareef Dancer called Dabaweyaa, who was leased to her Arab owner Mohammed Obaida by the Maktoum family who were standing Shareef Dancer at their Dalham Hall Stud. In view of his princely syndication fee they were extremely anxious to see his first full crop of three-year-olds do well on the racecourse. Dabaweyaa had run just once in 1987 and finished second in the Blue Seal Stakes at Ascot in September, a race traditionally favoured by Stoute as a try-out for his top juvenile fillies.

Of course there could be any number of other potentially outstanding and, like Dabaweyaa, unexposed horses, tucked away further down the Free Handicap ratings. Few of the best trainers would've declared their full strength in advance and the scope for improvement in some dark and lightly raced animals could've been enormous. Yet it was these top-rated thoroughbreds who carried the first big burden of expectation into the new season. By the end of November some of them might be champions. Others might as easily have flopped altogether and been adroitly removed from the stage. Which considering their cost, training bills and financial potential at the start of the year, just further underlines the very high stakes that the big camps are playing for. And there were high stakes too for the leading bookmaking firms who faced a pay-out of over a million pounds if

Warning won the 2,000 Guineas and almost as serious liabilities if Ravinella made it a favourites' double.

The action when it came was to be sudden, dramatic and, in the case of one or two connections and ante-post supporters of these most fancied horses, a painfully disillusioning experience. But amidst all this eager excitement and nervous anticipation the opening of the classic season at Newmarket in 1988 was touched by another rather different set of emotions. Disbelief, sorrow and incredulity that the man who has lived half his life at the headquarters of racing, the man whose very name is synonymous with the sport, should be looking forward to spending this particular championship year behind bars.

Everyone who's ever been in the least bit moved or excited by a great horse-race, let alone the millions of passionate devotees who were brought up on first the television pictures and then their own first-hand impressions of Piggott's genius, was in some way affected by the sight of one of the most gifted sporting achievers of the twentieth century being taken out of Ipswich court as a convicted criminal and led away to the waiting prison bus. The distress was heightened by incomprehension that a man so well able to take care of the kind of financial pressures that have enmeshed other less fortunate creatures to the point of suicide, should have allowed his own affairs ever to reach such a fatal point of no return.

It's difficult to believe that anyone actually welcomes receiving a tax demand. Once you've been on the receiving end of those endless, official investigations you can feel little sympathy for the type of mealy-mouthed bureaucracy that feeds off such harassment as a part of its daily life. None the less, intelligent lovers of horse-racing were quite able to understand if not entirely share the sentiments of those critics who asked why anyone should feel especial sympathy for Piggott when thousands of less famous people, people without access to solicitors and secret bank accounts, not to mention hapless benefit 'scroungers' and rate defaulters, are prosecuted to the full limit of the law every week. The unstated agreement by which everyone pays a part of their income to go towards the desperately needed services and provisions that are used and depended upon by everyone, but by the least well-off most of all, collapses into a ruinous chaos if the richest individual tax-payers decide to lie or play false about their earnings and means.

One of the great myths about Lester is that he was some kind of brilliantly manipulative financial genius. He wasn't anything of the sort. But he was, by anybody's standards, extremely avaricious. At the time of his trial there were many fine, loyal and heartwarming statements from his friends. Some of them, frankly, strained credulity but certainly no more so than the index note in the official Dick Francis biography referring to Lester's 'supposed closeness with money'. Piggott rarely spent any of his fortune. He invested some of it, unsuccessfully, in one or two shaky insurance syndicates but he didn't use it actively to make him any happier or any wiser. He just left most of it sitting around in bank accounts. Untouched, gathering dust and, as he saw it, out of reach of anyone or anything who might try and threaten his achievement or diminish his success. To try and account for Lester's obstinate insularity, people sometimes refer to his speech impediment and his partial deafness which undoubtedly increased his sense of being a loner on the outside of general human activity. Yet what surely compounded Piggott's remoteness and his determination to hang on to every penny he'd earned was his painful awareness, experienced since his earliest childhood, of the brutal vicissitudes of a jockey's existence. And what possibly contributed to his seeming ignorance of the eventual consequences of his actions was that very insularity endemic to Newmarket in particular and to the whole of the racing community in which Lester lived so much of his life.

Newmarket is a strange place. It may be beautiful on the gallops at seven o'clock in the morning but the surrounding countryside is mostly flat and monotonous. If you're driving up from London on a grey or rain-swept spring or autumn day the whole landscape can seem overpoweringly bleak and oppressive. And hanging over everything, there is sometimes a tangibly enclosed and inward-looking atmosphere. Most racing people live in a world of their own. That doesn't mean that they're all mad, weird or fraudulent. Some of them are mad. Some of them are positively barking. Some of them are generous, loyal, brave, talented, humorous and extremely good if eccentric company. Some of them are also pompous, snobbish and stupid and some of them are twisters and crooks. But there are not many members of the Newmarket racing community who come home in the evening after work and sit down to discuss a new play or novel or opera or the contents of a leading article in that morning's *Independent*. The conversation is almost always about horses and the only book being seriously studied is the formbook.

The stories of some jockeys' early lives sometimes sound like a cross between a Dickens novel and a sentimental Ealing melodrama of the post-war years. The hero is always a heroic little midget who has to overcome the unwelcome attentions of a tyrannical Major and a race-fixing gang in loud check suits. Then one day he wins the

Derby for Lord Snooty and ends up retiring to the country with an OBE, a foxhunting wife and a pair of gun dogs in the back garden. Behind the clichés there are one or two genuine facts, harsh but inescapable aspects of a top rider's life, that forge a common link not only between men like Piggott and Eddery but also between them and their earlier predecessors like Morny Canon and Fred Archer. They were almost all born into a close-knit racing family where a skill or talent with horses seems to have been passed down from one generation to the next. At an early age they experienced the long hours and numbing physical grind of hard stable-labour. And they all had to subject themselves to exhausting self-discipline to keep their weight down and relentless concentration to get to the top and stay there. Analysts who are prepared to compliment a track-and-field athlete or a swimmer or a boxer on the phenomenal training routines they put themselves through frequently overlook the equally gruelling demands of body and spirit that go with being a leading jockey. It used to come as quite a shock for an outside observer to catch a glimpse of Piggott through the weighing room door, naked from the waist up, and to see all the pinch-marks and lines left on his body by the years of wasting. It was all too much in the end for Lester's melancholy *alter ego* of the nineteenth century, the great Fred Archer who took his own life at the tragically early age of twenty-nine. Other famous jockeys ended their careers in bankruptcy and alcoholism. And today the pressures on the best of them are greater than ever before.

In the last twenty-five years the increasingly competitive and international face of racing as an industry and no longer just a sport has meant that the top jockeys are riding seven days a week and for nine months a year. This has left little spare time for a lengthy formal education or for much interest in books or music or wider cultural activities. Considering the obsessional nature of this existence it is again not surprising if some riders have slipped off the tightrope of honesty and financial rectitude from time to time. Or if others, having followed in Lester's wake and established themselves as among those handfuls of riders worldwide who can add millions to an owner's bank balance by getting a horse home first in the Derby, or the Kentucky Derby or the Breeders Cup, should end up acting as hard to get and keep as megastars from the movie and entertainment business, which is what the best of them really are anyway.

Robert Sangster may have begun the serious commercialisation of the owner's role in 1975 but the racetrack has always been a milieu awash with speculative ventures from the era of Charles II through to the Prince Regent, the Prince of Wales and Prince Aly Khan. Flat racing in particular has always attracted men with money, men who wanted to make money and men not entirely to be trusted with money. The general level of moral probity, or lack of it, has probably been no worse than, say, that of the City and some would say a lot less hypocritical, but no amount of successfully contested libel cases can detract from the open secret that owners were giving jockeys presents and special inducements from the moment two people realised the competitive possibilities of betting on which of two horses could run faster over a given distance.

In the first great phase of his success in the fifties and early sixties Lester's monetary affairs were 'managed' or kept an eye on by the financier Sir Victor Sassoon, who was the leading owner in the Noel Murless stable that Piggott rode for and for whom he won the Derby twice on Crepello and St Paddy. By the time of his famous Derby victories on Sir Ivor in 1968 and Nijinsky in 1970 and particularly after his devastating short-head triumph on Roberto in 1972, Piggott knew better than anyone the enormous difference to a horse's stud value and to the dreams and bank balance of a big player that a jockey like himself could make. And following the start of the Sangster/O'Brien partnership three years later, all top racing professionals became steadily more aware of their value in the market-place and steadily more determined to protect and preserve it.

Piggott in particular was never a conformist. He was never the establishment's man. In the early days of his career he had to endure regular suspensions and trips to the stewards' room as the authorities, whose attitude was just as heavy-handed with the equally rebellious Francome two decades later, did their best to slap down the precocious upstart. And just as with O'Brien's training methods, and later Sangster's readiness to spend huge sums of money to get his hands on the best horses, there was an implied criticism of anyone's will to win being that single-minded, that highly developed, that disinterested in compromise. In 1954 Lester was banned for six months for supposed rough riding in a race at Royal Ascot in which the principal loser was the veritable headman of the weighing room, Sir Gordon Richards. In 1966 he created a sensational precedent by breaking his retainer with Noel Murless to accept freelance mounts from other trainers, starting with Vincent O'Brien, if he saw them as providing him with a major or a better chance of big-race success. Never before had the jockey called the tune, dictated the terms, stepped out of line. After the notorious Roberto Derby and the jocking off of Bill Williamson in 1972, Piggott was actually booed by some sections of the Epsom crowd as he returned to unsaddle. And twelve years later he did it again. Ousting the American, Darryl McHargue, who hadn't impressed in the highest class, so as to get the ride on Luca Cumani's Comanche Run, owned by his friend Ivan Allen, in the 1984 St Leger. Piggott and Comanche Run won of course. Narrowly ... but brilliantly.

It was part of Lester's genius that, no matter how strange, inscrutable and positively uncharismatic he might seem on the ground, once he got up on to a horse's back he could emanate a genius and a charisma unrivalled by any other flat-racing jockey in the sport's history. And an essential part of that charisma, one of the reasons why you loved him so much, was because he seemed to personify the archetypal role of the laconic, ruthless outsider who could always be relied upon to trump the nice guy's ace. It was a style that suited Vincent O'Brien, and the particular requirements of the highly strung American-bred horses he was training, to perfection.

Lester made very few errors of judgement in a horse-race. His demise came partly from the complete absence of the same kind of judgement, skill and intuitive understanding in the sphere of his personal and financial affairs. He neglected the crucial importance of what Woody Stephens has described as C.Y.A. ('covering your arse'). The actual agent of his downfall was, in keeping with numerous tragic scenarios, not some racing colossus of equal stature to the jockey but a disgruntled bit-player called Melvyn Walters, whose real grudge was not with Lester anyway but with Henry Cecil.

Walters was one of two directors of a bloodstock company called Alchemy International. In 1982 a foal by the stallion Riverman was bought in Kentucky on Alchemy's behalf by Henry Cecil's bloodstock partner 'Tote' Cherry-Downes. The price was $95,000. The foal was raised and prepared for the English yearling sales at Henry and David Cecil's Cliff Stud in North Yorkshire. On the evening of 27 September 1983 at the Tattersalls Highflyer Sales in Newmarket he was apparently knocked down for 430,000 guineas to the Irish gambler James Flood. But then Flood denied making the final bid and claimed that his last offer had been 410,000 guineas. Tattersall's auctioneer Kenneth Watt identified Omar Assi, personal secretary to Maktoum Al Maktoum, as the second-highest bidder at 420,000 guineas. Assi denied going that high and claimed that he'd thrown in his hand at 400,000. The question now was whether or not Tattersalls should resubmit the colt for auction again later that night. Walters was particularly keen that they should. He was worried that the horse might acquire the aura of spoiled goods if it was brought back at a later date. In the end Tattersalls decided that there wasn't time to put the yearling back up for sale in the same session. But when Lot 116 did re-enter the ring two days later, Walters' worst fears were confirmed and he made just 200,000 guineas.

Alchemy decided to sue Tattersalls for 230,000 guineas claiming negligence over their conduct of the sale. After a thirteen-day High Court hearing in 1985, Mr Justice Hirst acquitted Tattersalls of the negligence charge and awarded Alchemy 230,000 guineas damages against James Flood. As almost all of the £250,000 costs of the case were taken up by Alchemy's unsuccessful claim against Tattersalls, neither Walters nor his fellow director the cosmopolitan Maurice Lidchi, a one-time art consultant to the South African government, were exactly delighted by the outcome.

Although it had been demonstrated that Henry Cecil had no personal financial interest in the Riverman colt it was at him that Walters decided to vent his anger. Walters had been involved in a small way in the ownership of one or two of the horses in Cecil's yard and had received a copy of 'H's' notorious letter to his owners stipulating the payments that would be required, over and above the registered retainer, to secure Lester's services in future. At the bottom Henry had unwisely stated that it might be advisable to destroy the letter after studying its contents. Walters had leaked a copy of the letter to the *People* journalist Brian Radford and in due course it came to the attention of a team of VAT and Inland Revenue investigators who'd been after Piggott before and who had just decided to shake racing's branches again and see if any plums fell out. Now they found themselves with an opening beyond their wildest dreams. And Lester, as the most prominent racing figure of all, became, most uncharacteristically, everybody else's fall guy.

There were many bizarre aspects to the Alchemy case that have intrigued regular sales-observers ever since. Anyone with more than a passing knowledge of Irish racing was aware that the flamboyant Jimmy Flood could scarcely have signed a bankable cheque for 4,000 guineas let alone 400,000. Even the judge concluded that Flood was bidding without any intention of actually honouring that bid. The Arabs and their agents were aware that, due to the huge sums they were prepared to pay at the sales, attempts had been made in the past to deliberately run up the bidding against them. So was there any connection between Flood and Walters? Why were the names of the Northern professional gambler Michael Tabor and the subsequently convicted krugerrand smuggler Freddy Thomsett and his brother George mentioned at intervals throughout the trial? And did the Maktoums not suddenly suspect something and pull out of the bidding at the last minute?

Melvyn Walters has been something of a stranger to both Tattersalls and English racecourses ever since. He's probably aware that there are quite a few embittered enthusiasts who would gladly assist him off the grandstand roof.

7 : The Guineas

The race traffic approaching Newmarket from the west and from the M11 up from London has to pull off the main A11 road just before the entrance to the town and swing left down a wide avenue almost half a mile in length. The avenue is lined by tall trees with the open grass of the heath on either side. At the end of the avenue is the Rowley Mile. On really still April and May afternoons the vast green heath seems to literally meet the sky at the horizon's end: one great expanse of green and grey, though rarely blue. Stretching all the way from the Cambridgeshire border to the North Sea at Yarmouth beach. No self-respecting Breeders Cup mogul or NBC television executive would ever dream of staging their showcase spectacular at such a venue. Yet it is precisely the bare, unfettered nature of Newmarket that has helped it to remain, for more than three centuries, every purist's idea of the perfect, natural setting in which to witness the thoroughbred compete.

On Guineas day the build-up of traffic on to the heath becomes steadily more intense from midday onwards. Leading the way are the Daimlers, the Mercs, the Jags and the Roly Polys of the smart high-rollers. And waiting for them by the Members' entrance are the usual absurd car-park attendants, all attempting to lure the flasher wheels into unsuitably squelchy and treacherous areas of bog. As the car doors slam shut behind you, you can immediately hear the rat-a-tat sound of helicopter blades bringing in the grandest of the big shots from London, France, Ireland and the Isle of Man. The

114

breakfast-time sunshine has faded altogether and it's now a grey and misty, slightly overcast spring day. A far from mild day with the possibility of rain. A light breeze flaps the flags flying high over the grandstand and snaps against the white-tented walls of the hospitality suites and the sponsors' marquees. The raucous cries of the *Sporting Life* salesmen stand out above the general soundtrack of background noise, and from all sides come the enticing smells of crushed grass, cigars and horses.

Walking back into Newmarket on 1,000 Guineas day you can feel that old tense, trembling excitement beginning to well up again in the pit of your stomach. This is one of the élite moments of English flat racing. In a few hours' time you will witness the dramatic gladiatorial confrontation of one or two potentially great racehorses. You will also have a ringside seat should the fortunes of one or two of their already rich owners suddenly go into a spectacular climb or decline. Even the racecourse buildings seem to reflect the sense of occasion, to look smarter, sharper and better-presented than on an ordinary afternoon. Everyone who is anyone in the industry is present. The leading bookmakers are all wearing their sleekest made-to-measure suits and their best signet-rings while the Members' Enclosure and the private boxes appear to be dominated by a whole host of suave, rich, upper-class men and women who look as they've been assembled for a company photocall by *Harpers & Queen*.

In direct contrast to countries like France, Australia and America, English racecourses are still divided up into separate enclosures with differing facilities and differing rates of admission. This is supposedly in the interests of choice, offering the public competitive amenities at a contrasting price, etc. It would be more accurate to say that the exorbitant cost of going racing in England is largely a reflection of the poor deal the racecourses are getting from the big bookmaking firms who make enormous profits from off-course betting in particular but are required to reinvest only a small amount of those profits back into racing itself. Countries like France which operate a state-run tote monopoly may lack the atmosphere of the betting ring but they also enjoy healthy tax revenues from gambling while still having a substantial surplus to keep the cost of racecourse admission much lower than in England and the level of facilities and prize money far higher.

There is also something about the compartmentalising of English racecourses that smacks of racing's ruling body, the Jockey Club, attempting to hang on for as long as they possibly can to some absurd idea of the class system that would've seemed outdated in

1945 let alone in the last twelve years of the twentieth century. The cheapest enclosure is the Silver Ring which is often up to two furlongs from the winning-post. You get no view whatsoever of the paddock and the unsaddling enclosure and only an incomprehensible rear view of the finish. Catering is likely to be a cheese sandwich and a brown ale served on a formica-top table in a Nissen hut bar, or evil-smelling burgers and Kentucky Fried Chicken dished out from the back of a van. At Newmarket on Guineas day the Silver Ring costs £3.50 to enter.

Next up is the Grandstand or Tattersalls enclosure which at Newmarket costs £7.50 on their five major racedays. Tatts is where the principal cash-only course bookmakers – for many the most colourful attraction on the course and not to be confused with the villainous big four – ply their trade from their pitches in the ring. At right angles to the course and along the rails separating Tattersalls from the Members' enclosure will be the major credit bookmakers, including the big four, most of whose clients will be wealthy and smartly dressed punters from the Members' next door. The idea of these pitches on the rails seems originally to have been designed to enable gentlemen to stroll over and conduct a little private transaction with their bookie without actually having to set foot amongst the unrefined plebs to get the business done. Tatts racegoers will have at least one large covered self-service restaurant and bar which will be about as tasty as an average station buffet but not a lot more so. The food will range from soup and sandwiches to a few knife-and-fork dishes like sausage and chips or 'fried fillet of plaice with lemon wedge and tartare sauce', etc. The Tatts patrons get a stand of their own and access to the paddock and unsaddling enclosure but not to the best and technically most spacious viewing areas opposite the finishing line.

The most expensive enclosure available on the day to the general public is the Club or Members'. This is where serious racing people of any background automatically head for. On Guineas day the Members' Enclosure at Newmarket costs £15 a head. Jeans are out and a jacket and tie is essential. The day members get unlimited access to the paddock, pre-parade and unsaddling areas, to all the main viewing terraces and stands at the top of the course and to a range of bars where champagne will be as readily obtainable as gin and tonic, and to a restaurant where a three-course lunch with waitress service will be available as a contrast to the hot beef rolls, steak sandwiches and bite-size helpings of Peking Duck available from the fast-food stands outside. Annual members, boxholders,

Miesque and Freddie Head annihilate the opposition in the 1987 Breeders Cup Mile. Some English racegoers remain convinced that Freddie would be better employed riding a donkey on the beach at Deauville.

Luca Cumani, Sheikh Mohammed and Sheikh Hamdan conduct a post-mortem with jockey Rae Guest in the unsaddling enclosure at Newmarket. Guest is wondering where Hamdan got that tie.

Stavros Niarchos. The man who broke the bank at Monte Carlo.

The Hungry Stoute.

Vincent O'Brien. The Lion in Winter.

His Highness, Prince Karim Aga Khan. The consummate racehorse owner.

Sheikh Mohammed steps out . . .
into the slop at Churchill Downs.

The Foppish Cecil. This was
Henry's front-of-house photo when
he appeared as Prince Charming,
opposite Bruffscot as Buttons, in the
pantomime at the Arts Theatre,
Cambridge, in 1974.

The Aga Khan gratefully accepts his
Derby loot from the oldest swinger
in town, Sir Gordon White.

The Wily Cumani.

Only a matter of inches separates Kahyasi and Insan at the finish of the 1988 Budweiser Irish Derby. Insan's jockey, Richard Quinn, dropped his whip in the last few yards. Insan's owner, Fahd Salman, dropped Quinn for the colt's next race.

Eugene V. Klein. Biggest of the 'Big Rich'.

Barney Curley. Britain's most successful professional gambler and Lord Vestey's choice as the next chairman of the Jockey Club Disciplinary Committee.

Mr and Mrs Robert Sangster (mark III). A poker-faced mumble and a
wide-brimmed hat.

D. Wayne Lukas auditions for the Steve McQueen role in the remake of *The
Magnificent Seven.* Lord Oaksey would simply love the fact that he is not
wearing a hat. And . . . D. Wayne Lukas again, the most famous shades in
racing.

The Ageless Willie the Shoe.

Steve Cauthen. The Immaculate
Racing Ambassador.

The Inimitable Angel Cordero Jr in full flow at Saratoga. Note the distinctive
periscope whip action.

'Come racing. Come racing.' Payout time after the Derby.

'Marshal Mike Dillon' of Ladbrokes. The shrewdest bookmaker's man in the business.

The Grand Finale. Alysheba and Seeking The Gold charging out of the night at the climax of Breeders Cup Five, Churchill Downs, Kentucky. 'America's Horse has done it!'

Sheikh Mohammed, in tasty flared trousers, leads in Steve Cauthen and Indian Skimmer after the brilliant grey filly has defeated Miesque and Little Freddie in the 1987 Prix de Diane at Chantilly.

sponsors and their guests, and members of the Jockey Club will have further amenities all to themselves.

On occasions like 1,000 and 2,000 Guineas day the official racecard will have a map of these various restaurants and bars and will generally make them sound a lot more inviting than they actually turn out to be on closer inspection. Whereas one or two brave provincial tracks have held out for local firms, most large-scale racecourse catering is in the hands of one of two companies. Ring and Brymer and Letheby and Christopher. And make no mistake about it, most racecourse catering is excruciating, serving mediocre food at often extortionate prices. The menus usually revolve around a sort of school-dinner roast with overcooked vegetables and the odd prawn cocktail and Ogen melon thrown in at the beginning. Mark-ups on quite ordinary bottles of wine are of an order that require little change from serious bank-notes, while standard brands of champagne that retail for about twelve quid in most wine merchants will be value all the way at more than £20 or £25 a time.

The quality of service is not the fault of the hard-pressed staff, least of all the tireless and seemingly ageless all-star ladies of the champagne bars at Sandown and Newbury, or of the hapless and rather wan-looking kids who get drafted in for long hours and low wages at the extra special meetings like Cheltenham and Royal Ascot. The top management are usually too smart to be around in person to get cornered by the luckless diners. Intermediaries do the job instead. At Newmarket on 1,000 Guineas day the old Members' restaurant (as opposed to the hideous new Guineas room where prices are even higher still) is presided over by a sort of cut-price Lord Carrington figure in pin-stripe trousers with black silk jacket and tie. This elegant gent, smiling nonchalantly, is waiting in the doorway to take your cheque or credit card number in advance before escorting you to a distant table facing the wall where, in view of the imminent draconian drinks and extras bill, he might as well relieve you of your shirt, trousers, wallet, car keys and mortgage at the same time.

At least one side of the Newmarket restaurant does face on to the racecourse. Cheltenham's execrable Prestbury Suite is sited in an ugly modern building behind the stands. There is only one television set, the curtains are kept drawn at all times and the general ambience is about as inviting as being in the functions room of a Crest Motor Hotel somewhere off the M5. And Cheltenham charge upwards of £24 at the Gold Cup meeting, just for the basic meal. Even Kempton Park down near suburban Sunbury-on-Thames sticks you for £15 or

more on an average day when the chances are that the Wraysbury
Suite or the River Room will be redolent with its usual tangy aroma
of incinerated lamb cutlets. Diners popping out to bet on the first
race leave in the unmistakable knowledge that if they arrived at the
course in a cloud of expensive scent and aftershave lotion they now
smell as if they've spent the entire morning sitting in a grill tray.

About a decade ago one or two enterprising courses started letting
in a fishmonger from Kent, a large and jovial gentleman called Barrie
Cope, who began serving generous portions of cold seafood – fresh
salmon, lobster, crab claws, etc. – with mayonnaise and brown bread
and butter. Initially priced at around five or six pounds a platter with
bottles of white wine at two or three quid, Cope's refreshing menu
was quickly in huge demand. Outsize trouser fittings and new and
even larger wallet encasements must have been equally in demand
for Mr Cope, who began to look bigger and richer each week. It may
not have been easy trying to eat his goodies while standing up in a
crowded space with lettuce trickling down your dress and seafood
sauce splashing your tie but the price was still an absolute snip
compared with the opportunist demands of the catering companies.
Of course the really exclusive place to eat and drink at the races,
especially on occasions like 1,000 and 2,000 Guineas day, is as a
guest in the comfort of a private box. At top courses like Newmarket
these cost thousands of pounds a year to rent out and are monopolised
by big-race sponsors, the major bookmakers and the likes of the
Maktoum family and their entourage.

The 1,000 Guineas is the fourth race on the card and the preceding
three are all conditions events for three-year-olds only and they act as
a kind of ascending prelude to the great race itself. In the first of
them, Nail Don, the 25-1 outsider in a field of four turns over the
favourite, Shehiyr, ridden by Steve Cauthen and owned by the Aga
Khan. The second is the £8,000 Miesque Stakes, a three-year-old
maiden over the Guineas mile, named in honour of the 1987 1,000
winner. Some of the twenty horses engaged in the Miesque are
regally bred but, alas for their owners, they matured much too late to
be candidates for the first two classics themselves. Sheikh Mohammed
is represented by no fewer than three runners who proceed to finish
first, third and fourth. In the correct order too with Luca Cumani's
Polar Gap, the 15-8 favourite, winning by five lengths with Crossed
Swords, an Alydar colt trained by Michael Stoute, in third and
Cumani's dark horse, Falco, making a promising début back in
fourth. On paper this looks to have been quite a high-class contest
and some of these Newmarket maiden races are often up to Group

Three standard at this time of the year. What the form would amount to in another three or four or six months' time was entirely open to question but for now the *Timeform* men and the readers for the *Raceform Notebook* are busily marking their cards for the future.

The second placed horse is a colt called Busted Rock trained, in lieu of Lester, by Susan Piggott who looks smart, tough and like someone pretending to have grown used to a walking nightmare as she talks briskly to her jockey Tony Ives in the unsaddling enclosure. The winning trainer, Luca Cumani, is at his super-smooth Milanese best as he chats to the press and then watches the Sheikh receiving his trophy from Niarchos' daughter Maria. It seems as if every single racing member of the Maktoum family is present here today on the heath. All of them undoubtedly waiting to see if their nap hand of Diminuendo, Dabaweyaa and Diminuendo's Nell Gwynn Stakes conqueror, Ghariba, can topple the heir presumptive to the throne of Chantilly at 3.25. *En masse* at the races in England or France the Maktoums make a palpably rich though not especially elegant group. They seem to have kitted themselves out in the kind of clothes that they think are expected of them as men of substance on a Western racecourse. Yet these rather shiny-coloured suit-jackets, often worn with clashing flared trousers and shiny leather slip-on shoes, do nothing for their natural dignity and style that is so much more visibly apparent when you see them in a formal Middle Eastern setting.

The watching crowd around the winners circle manages a brief ripple of polite applause as England's leading racehorse owner displays his prize for the photographers. Then the Arabs and their retinue troop off towards the paddock for the third race and presumably the confident expectation of yet more saturation-level success. The departure of the principal players seems to be the cue for everybody else to move off in the same direction. In fact the top people seem to flow backwards and forwards almost impassively, all afternoon long. Paddock, bookies, stands, unsaddling enclosure, bar, box, paddock, etc. Always the same pattern and it will be repeated over and over again throughout the summer. At times this English flat-racing cycle can seem as smooth, as hard and as impenetrable as a glistening sheet of reinforced glass. The races are over so quickly but, whatever the excitement, whatever the result, the people, these Newmarket 'headquarters' people, remain so tight-lipped and self-contained. Visible displays of emotion are as alien as they are welcome and rejoiced over at a jumping meeting such as Cheltenham or Punchestown.

The third race, a ten-furlong listed event for fillies, is won not by the Arabs but by a filly called La Vie En Primrose who is trained locally by the jaunty Clive Brittain – a man whose trousers are even more flared than those of the Maktoum brothers – and owned by Steve Cauthen's landlord, the rather eccentric property developer Mr Bill Gredley, who looks like Michael Winner on a good day. The happy formalities surrounding this victory are ignored by many industry professionals and by the keenest *aficionados* who are already on their way to the saddling-up area beyond the pre-parade ring. At Newmarket this is reached via a small arch at the south-eastern edge of the paddock. On the other side of the arch are the racecourse stable saddling-up boxes facing each other neatly across a small grass oval. It is in this confined and compact space, this inner sanctum, that the combatants for the 1,000 Guineas – which will be worth £88,000 to the winner in 1988 and several million more in stud value – are now being made ready for the most important race of their lives to date.

The top trainers pass through. Cecil, heavier in the face than he used to be, slopes neurotically past, a fag in one hand and Diminuendo's saddle in the other. Julie follows on behind, sea-shanty hat, nose twitching and sucking a boiled sweet. Then comes the splendidly fruity Jeremy Tree, his bulldog jowls larger than ever; the patrician John Dunlop, as upright and ramrod straight as an unflappable paratroop commander at Arnhem Bridge; Michael Stoute, bareheaded like Cecil and once again the hungry professional; and Alec Stewart, once of Gordonstoun and a merchant bank and now possessed of the permanently anxious frown of the most promising boy in the class who knows that he's been singled out for promotion by the Arab owners. Stewart, unlike any others, is wearing a coat – an unsuitably thick green cape, that's making him perspire in the cramped space. As the crowd press closer towards the horses, you can smell not only human sweat but also expensive perfumes and colognes as well as the pungent odour of horseshit. The officials try to push the onlookers back while the pocket-sized clerk of the course, Captain Nicholas Lees, all trilby hat and no chin, nervously asserts his authority and insists that the stable lads and their charges are not allowed too many walk-rounds. It's Lees' job to get these animals out into the main parade ring so that the ordinary public can catch a fleeting glimpse of them before the jockeys mount up. The insiders know that the saddling-up area is the place to see them, especially if they still want time to have a last bet and then get a good position for the race.

Back on the lawn the photogenic Bruffscot hurries past importantly on his way to his Channel 4 camera position just inside the parade ring itself. The BBC's link man Julian Wilson, here merely as an ordinary racegoer, strides away equally purposefully in the opposite direction. Ears flapping, hair slicked back severely and with the most doleful and humourless expression on his face, the greying Wislon looks more than ever like some haunted character out of a Bram Stoker novel. He rightfully regards himself as a highly experienced journalist, cruelly underestimated by comparison with his more charismatic colleagues, but it would still be fair to say that he will never enjoy a thriving alternative career as a stand-up comedian.

Before the 1,000 there would be a parade of the whole field in front of the stands. These parades are not loved by some trainers who fear that the combination of the prolonged delay, the noise and size of the crowd and the rising tension may spook their horses and cause them to start to sweat and fret and worry away their chances before the race begins. (This never seems to be a huge problem in America where parades happen before every race although paddock inspection is much less important there and much less understood.) Yet to any lover of romanticism and theatre the parade before an historic classic or Group One race at Newmarket is a matchless spectacle. The horses pass out one by one through the gate on to the huge, wide Newmarket course and as they walk – some tense, some relaxed, some about to boil over – up towards the furlong marker it's like the moment when the Indians first appear in a Western, strung out in single file and moving slowly along the horizon. The experienced eye can often spot a classic winner or loser at this moment. A tense and nervous horse can win. So can a relaxed horse or a horse on its toes. Beware, though, unnaturally sweating flanks and rolling eyes or an animal too light and skinny or too docile and dull in its coat.

For many of the thousands watching, this is their first chance to see these classic horses, this season's élite crop, actually walking out live and it's not entirely fanciful to say that the best horses already have an aura about them, an air every bit as intense, competitive and self-aware as, say, the star contestants in the Olympic 1500 metres final as they arrive at the holding area at the back of the stadium before the big race. Why should horses be so very different from human athletes? Will they look each other in the eye these equine rivals, seeing their known enemies in the flesh at last, or will they contemptuously ignore one another or attempt to psych each other out?

At Newmarket now on this 1,000 Guineas afternoon, Ravinella, last but one in the procession of eleven, has a sheen about her, a dancing, coiled power and beauty that seems to stamp her every inch the winner. While the eyes of the English racing community were focused on the second day of the Grand National meeting at Aintree at the beginning of the month, the Head family had taken the winter cotton wool wrapping off Ravinella and reintroduced her in the seven-furlong Prix Imprudence at Maisons Laffitte racecourse down near the river Seine in Paris. Maisons is one of the most delicious racing venues in the world, not simply for its park and its château or the mouth-watering *pâtisseries* and charcuterie shops on its main street but because right there next to them all is a weathered old racing bar called the Café de Paris which is mentioned in Hemingway's celebrated short story 'My Old Man'. The walls of the backroom of the Café, which is always filled with local jockeys, lads, touts and faces, are still decorated with signed caricatures of some of the great turfistes of the twenties and thirties. Characters like Zuzu, Didi, Jo le Camiche and Bob le Flambeur. The Café de Paris is a wise and well lubricated racing school and the latter-day descendants of Didi and Jo were rendered almost speechless by the ease with which Ravinella won the Imprudence on 2 April. They were all of them emphatically convinced that she would go on to win at Newmarket too as Miesque had done twelve months before her.

And back at the Rowley Mile three and a half weeks later, with less than fifteen minutes to go before her greatest test, the English professional gamblers appear to have unanimously picked up the hint. Opening up at 5-4 against and drifting briefly to 11-8 against she has been backed massively right back to 5-4 on. Almost everything else is on the slide. Diminuendo, who has herself made a quite satisfactory reappearance when second to Ghariba over seven furlongs of the Guineas course in the Nell Gwynn, is out to 6-1 from 9-2. Ghariba, not seriously fancied to confirm the form at level weights, is 8-1 from sevens and Dabaweyaa, impressive winner of a maiden race on the same day as the Nell Gwynn is out to 14-1 from tens.

The terraces and stands in the Members' and Tattersalls enclosures are all packed to the limit now. Many of these spectators will be bitterly disappointed once the race begins. The ones who have been here before know what to expect but you can always tell the racegoers visiting Newmarket for the first time. They're the ones training their binoculars on the mile start as soon as the stalls open whereas you can actually barely make sense of anything until the runners are about three and a half furlongs from home. In fact the best place on the course to watch the last quarter of a mile of the

1,000 and 2,000 Guineas used to be a small patch of raised ground on the opposite side of the track from the stands just beyond the runners and riders board about fifty yards before the winning-post. No less a man than the dashing Guy Harwood came out there to watch Lear Fan take on El Gran Senor in the 2,000 in 1984. When the final stages of the race are in progress, as the runners charge down into the dip and then meet the rising ground, the sight and sound of those classic horses stretched out and at full power with the packed stands and the wall of noise behind them is an unforgettably intense and intoxicating experience. Sadly in 1988 the mound had gone. Razed utterly to clear a space for the omnipresent sponsors' chalets and marquees.

English racing has gained hugely from private sponsorship over the last ten or fifteen years . . . but at a price. No big race day is now complete without its tented village filled with plump, smooth-faced young executives keeping the fire of Thatcherite corporate hospitality ablaze in the land. Most of the time they rarely step one foot outside of their tents. The television sets flicker in the background. The hostess girls keep coming with the Laurent Perrier or the bittermints or the selection of teatime savouries and, as the real enthusiasts huddle together in the enclosures, some credit card, insurance or double-glazing king is busy telling Gerry from personnel that they ought to get out in the fresh air like this more often. The saddest casualties of all are the proper names of the oldest and most famous races. Where's the history and emotion in a clumsy title like the Ever Ready Derby, the Holsten Pils St Leger and the General Accident 1,000 Guineas?

The race when it finally happens is over exceedingly quickly. All the speculation, anticipation, worry and tension comes down to less than two minutes of proper action. Just one minute and 44.8 seconds in which the owners involved get to discover which of them correctly bought or bred what has now to be considered the leading three-year-old filly over a mile in England and possibly Europe too in 1988. When the stalls open it's Diminuendo who goes quickly to the front. Cauthen and Cecil reckon that their filly will definitely stay further than a mile. They know that Ravinella's trump card is her speed but Mr Prospector hasn't had a classic winner in Europe before and it could be that Ravinella won't stay the stiff Newmarket mile. So Cauthen and Diminuendo head out into the lead on their own and hang in there for a full five furlongs. At that point Robert Sangster's outsider Obeah trained by Barry Hills and Niarchos' Magic of Life trained by Jeremy Tree are starting to go backwards.

Jungle Gold, the outsider from the North, has a chance if she's good enough but Ghariba has a lot to do and Ravinella, who has been held up in the rear and is only just starting to enter the race seriously, has an awful lot to do. Then two furlongs from home Walter Swinburn and Dabaweyaa, who have been moving along sweetly on the outside, suddenly dash into a clear lead and as they race past the bushes Swinburn's filly is looking top-class, all the doubts about the quality of her maiden win dispelled and surely Michael Stoute's first ever 1,000 Guineas victory only fifteen seconds away. Except that Ravinella, this hugely gambled-on French filly, is definitely beginning to pick up ground now too, although as they race down into the dip it's still Dabaweyaa who holds a vital two-length advantage. These are the moments in a classic horse-race that you will always remember. One courageous filly making her break for the line and another beautiful and even more celebrated thoroughbred, her whole much-vaunted reputation at stake now, pulling out of the pack and going after her. Coming to the rising ground Ravinella changes her legs, her jockey Gary Moore hits her for the first time in her life and, whatever your views on the appropriateness of a jockey using a whip in a horse race, the response is undeniable. Demonstrating a quite thrilling change of gear this magnificent filly surges past Dabaweyaa in the last half-furlong and her speed takes her a full length and a half clear at the line. Moore raises his fist in the air in triumph. Dabaweyaa is beaten and the Michael Stoute stable have, quite astonishingly, come second yet again. Diminuendo, who rallies again bravely up the hill, finishes the same distance away third and Ghariba is a running-on fourth.

The runners flash on up the hill towards the edge of the heath and then seem to be caught there in arrested motion for one brief moment; outlined dramatically against the sky and as timeless and as unchanged in their integration with the heath and its landscape as so many others have been in reality and on canvas for generations before them.

So there it is. The Maktoum family and their representatives have finished second, third and fourth in the 1988 1,000 Guineas but they are not the winners. The real victors, aside from Ravinella and Gary Moore, are Ecurie and Société Aland which means the beaming Comte Roland, Alec Head and of course Alec's daughter Criquette. Ravinella is led back into the unsaddling enclosure by a pair of General Accident personality girls who for some strange reason are dressed up in tartan caps, tartan scarves and yes, long heather-mix evening dresses which make them look like a couple of old British

Caledonian air hostesses on their way to a St Andrew's night ball. The victorious horse and jockey are greeted by a tremendous round of applause in the winners circle. Everyone it seems is genuinely excited and delighted by the result. This is partly because the press have almost unanimously tipped her – well, they had to really – and also because even at odds as low as 5-2 they've been backing her all winter long. Now it's time for much authentic Gallic kissing and embracing and for a lot of English racing hacks to try and get in on the act. Maktoum Al Maktoum gives Criquette an affectionate embrace and she apologises for beating his and his brother's fillies. *Daily Mail* racing correspondent, the porcine-featured 'Jolly Jim' Stanford, a man who has done for Distillers shares what Wyatt Earp did for sales of the Colt ·45, thinks he'll give Criquette a kiss too. Clearly his invaluable advice was a key element in her success. Peter O'Sullevan, still the peerless voice of racing even if he is unable to do justice to Newmarket as it's not a course covered by the BBC, much more stylishly and unobtrusively pats Alec Head on the shoulder. These two have memories of shared victories going right back to Head's English classic raids of the early fifties when legend has it that 'Pedro' used to organise their commissions with the bookmakers. M. Head, tucked up in a sort of smart French anorak to protect him from the cold, is wearing glasses and a small green square trilby hat but the beautifully cut hair and the tan are still noticeable. As is the fact that he seems ageless, looking forever like not only one of the great racehorse trainers but also like one of the great chefs of Europe, with his beloved wife, the now grey-haired but still so smart and chic Ghislaine, at his side.

The unsaddling enclosure is overflowing with people now. All of them wanting to associate themselves with the aura of a winner. The press boys from the gallops are there. All shampooed and combed since the early morn. John McCririck wobbles up in his customary guise as a cross between Stanley Baxter and William McGonagle. There's Michael Seely of *The Times* and Peter Scott of the *Telegraph*. The French trainer Olivier Douieb, (who would sadly die of cancer the following summer) looking, as always, the archetypal turfiste with his flat nose, Boston haircut and zee very good accent. Even the Queen's racing manager, Lord Carnarvon, is slipping in for a kiss. And now the working journalists are crowding in close for the story even as the smiling Bruffscot commandeers Criquette for a live Channel 4 interview barely six inches away from Ravinella's tail. Geoff Lester, chief reporter for the *Sporting Life*, is pushing into shot to get the details, mouth half-open and pencil at the ready. Corals' rep, the grey-suited Wally Pyrah, gawps from the back of the crowd. Wally and his sports-loving chums must now frame – wonderful word that – their prices on the Guineas runners-up for the Oaks. Ravinella will definitely stick to a mile and go for the English/French double accomplished by Miesque in 1987. Michael Stoute, laughingly dismissing the idea that the 1,000 Guineas is an unlucky race for him – we just keep coming up against a better filly, he says – confirms that Dabaweyaa definitely goes to Epsom and, as a daughter of Shareef Dancer, he expects her to be well suited by a mile and a half. 'Gucci Shoes' declares that Diminuendo will probably also go for the Oaks but that she may run first in the ten-furlong Musidora Stakes at York in May.

Surveying it all from the edge of the weighing room area is the bluff, rough, *Sporting Life* editor, Monty Court, the man who was brought in by Robert Maxwell to beef up the paper's content and to put the boot into the Maktoum-owned opposition publication, the *Racing Post*. Monty has a column in the *Sporting Life* each Saturday, imaginatively entitled the 'Court Circular'. They sensibly print his photograph above the copy as 90 per cent of all racegoers probably have no idea who he really is. Bluff, rough Monty turns out to look like the fifties English comedy star Ronald Shiner, complete with the grin and the fashionable National Serviceman's hairstyle. For Guineas day he appears to be favouring a sensible green coat and a pork-pie hat. Not so much 'Man On The Spot' as 'Our Man Taking The Jack Russell Round For A Quick Light Ale At The British Legion Club In Purley'.

Ravinella's victory means that Monty and his sub-editors will not be short of imaginative headlines on the morrow. It's the brave, courageous English against the low-down, flighty French again: 'Saucy French Miss Dances Can Can Across Newmarket Heath' etc.

There are no classic races on the second day of the Guineas meeting but Friday does see a magnificent classic trial, the ten-furlong Newmarket Stakes in which Lady Beaverbrook's Minster Son, a colt actually bred by his jockey, Willie Carson, scores a length victory over Geoff Wragg's lightly raced son of Kalaglow, Red Glow, running in the colours of the veteran Hong Kong-based owner, Eric Moller. Both horses instantly go into the smart boys' notebooks as possibles for the Derby at Epsom.

Saturday is a cold but sunny day with some blue sky and a lot of grey cloud. The crowd is bigger than on Thursday but it's a less intimate and a less professional atmosphere. All the same suave, smart people are around but there are a lot more occasional racegoers present too. And back in that traffic build-up bumper to bumper with the grander motors and the regular *Timeform* subscribers, there is a whole plethora of coach parties. Some of them innocent and cheerful: groups of senior citizens, social clubs from as far away as the Midlands and the south coast and clerical staff outings from the offices of the sponsors, General Accident. Then there are the other kind: Executive Travel of Chelmsford, Barry's Coaches from Leighton Buzzard, Tour World of Epping, most of them filled with loud, well-lagered lads, the new kind of Liverpool Street commuters so beloved by passengers and staff alike. Yet how many racecourse managements at the start of the 1988 flat racing season were being brave enough to turn away these lads and turn away the extra revenue too?

2,000 Guineas day is hardly a traditional black spot in the racing calendar. The worst trouble would come in the high summer months and on the big brewery-sponsored racedays during the football close season. The Jockey Club, for all its attempts to put a high wall up around the Turf in Britain and insulate it from the outside world, have slowly begun to realise that racing, like any other industry or sport, is not magically immune to what else is going on in the society in which it takes place. They're also having to wrestle with that distressing problem so acutely understood by soccer boards through-out the land. Why us? Why here? In a supposedly more violent society like America, why is it that families and rival bands of partisan fans watch the NFL gridiron maulings week after week and still leave the ground unaffected by any apparent desire to attack one another. And American racing crowds are the same. Hialeah race-track in North Central Miami is one of the lushest and most beautiful racing venues anywhere in the world. Outside the gates it's heavy, major-league Cuban-Hispanic 'Give me the coke, you motherfucker, or I'll blow your fucking head off' country. But inside you can walk freely around the tropical setting, apparently safe from any threat of attack or molestation. And yet on the edges of the coach-park at Newmarket or York on a hot boozy July afternoon you can sometimes feel the aggression rumbling towards you like an impending migraine.

Unlike the States, a day at the races in England has always been for many people primarily a social occasion, i.e. a day's boozing. Each enclosure at a British race-track has its named bars and drinking places, welcoming new and regular clients all afternoon long, at every meeting throughout the year. At the end of the 1987 season the Jockey Club decided that what was needed was a curfew that would mean no more orders after half an hour after the last race. Yet the irony is that many of the characters who've been drinking themselves silly in Tatts' and Members' watering holes over the years have never shown the slightest inclination to stick a punch on anyone. It's the familiar and repellent psychology of lad-land that seems to have made the difference.

Of course the Hooray classes do their best to add a few ghastly characters of their own to balance things out. As well as the London society Hoorays, the 2,000 Guineas is a regular outing for the young bloods of the Cambridge University Conservative Association all dressed up in their identikit Hackett corduroy trousers and striped shirts. And then there is that special class of authentic public schoolboys: the Marks, Willies and Toms who are all the younger brothers of Hamish, Rory and Alistair who are generally assistant trainers or junior bloodstock agents or assistant Arab racing managers to the likes of Angus Gold, the Honourable Robert Acton and Pasty Face Stroud. The Marks, Willies and Toms usually have the odd Sophie, Tatty and Camilla hanging around too. Some already a clone of Mummy in blue tights, buttoned-up blouses and black coats. Some going wild with lots of exposed leg and nightclub eyeshadow.

One sober little Willie is without his Henrietta and it's tough on them both as they were only married a fortnight ago. But Willie's learning the trade with the BBA (British Bloodstock Agency) and Henry's had to stay behind in South Ken' to help Tickie get on with the cooking for her special twenty-fourth birthday dinner party that's taking place later this evening. The restrained Willie chats to a rather grand old Dowager Duchess type, a dry old stick in a Robin Hood hat, who's cornered him down by the saddling-up boxes. The Dowager did want to be at the wedding, only then she and Johnny decided to stay on in Cape Town for an extra weekend. 'Was it super?' she asks Willie. 'I heard it was super.' Willie mumbles politely. 'And everything went so well?' Willie mumbles again. 'You love her, don't you?' What a wise old bird she is. 'She is a splendid girl.' Willie nods obediently. 'And will you be happy?' A mumble. 'Go on. Be happy.' A nod. The Dowager dismisses Willie with a smile and then heads for the Tote windows while Willie looks round again for Robin or Rory or Hamish or Alistair or whoever it is he's meant to be carrying the bags for.

The big racing news this Saturday 30 April concerns Henry Cecil's Sanquirico who was once upon a time one of the leading ante-post fancies for the 2,000 Guineas itself. Only then he flopped completely in his reappearance race, the Craven Stakes over the Rowley Mile earlier in the month, and was withdrawn from the 2,000 betting altogether. But now it seems he's done a sensational piece of work this very morning, finishing twenty lengths clear of his galloping companions and some big punters are clamouring to get on him for the Derby like crazed investors chasing rising stock in a bull market.

The 2,000 Guineas is to be the fourth race on this Saturday Newmarket card but the first three contests are a lot less interesting than on 1,000 afternoon. In the second of them though, a mile-and-a-quarter handicap for four-year-olds and upwards, there's quite a plunge on the favourite, Merce Cunningham, who, like Minster Son, is trained by Major Dick Hern and ridden by Willie Carson. The owner this time is a rich young Ivy League polo-playing American called Mr Peter Brant. He just happens to be a major newsprint and magazine king back in America as well as a leading shareholder in the Fasig Tipton sales agency which is Keeneland's only serious American-based rival. The beautifully named Merce Cunningham, who is a son of Nijinsky, had been a major disappointment as a three-year-old and could be said to owe a few to his connections. He'd begun to repay that sum by winning a small race at Bath on the Monday of Guineas week and is running again so quickly because Hern's assistant, Alex Scott, thinks that they might as well strike while the iron is hot.

In the race those punters who have piled over fifty grand in on-course bets on Merce Cunningham's elegant bay nose rarely have an anxious moment. He takes up the running two out, soon goes clear and wins unextended by a length and a half. After the race respectful members of the racing press attend on his trainer in the unsaddling enclosure.

1988 would be Major Dick Hern's thirty-first season as a licensed trainer. For almost half that time he's been principal private trainer to the Queen, working from the West Illsley racing stables in Berkshire that he leases directly from the palace. His other owners range from Lady Beaverbrook on the one hand through a whole host of staunchly traditional Jockey Club members to all four Maktoum brothers on the other. Hern's achievements over nearly three decades as the conditioner of such outstanding racehorses as Troy, Bustino and Brigadier Gerard speak eloquently enough for themselves. This is probably just as well as he's often reacted to quite innocent enquiries from the general press as to the well-being or running plans of his stable inmates as if they were outrageous interference by upstarts and bounders of the most reptilian complexion. Any aspiring tout or bookie's mole who has had to spy from behind a bush on the

Major's gallops has earned his money the very hardest way. In December 1984, the former Cavalry officer and coach to the British Olympic equestrian team suffered a grievous injury while out fox-hunting. He's been virtually confined to a wheelchair ever since.

In good times and bad the Major's number one stable jockey since 1977 has remained the diminutive Scotsman, William Hunter Carson. Carson has won the jockeys championship five times in the past but he's tended to be somewhat overshadowed in recent years by the Cauthen/Eddery axis. This is not a situation that Carson, now in his mid-forties but still looking like the Clitheroe Kid of the weighing room, particularly enjoys. In spite of his cheekie chappie unsaddling enclosure act, little Willie has been pretty much a solidly establishment figure for the best part of a decade now, which is what you might expect of a man retained by the Major. Carson's greatest assets as a jockey are perceived to be his light riding weight and his prodigious strength which he used to such telling effect on horses like Troy, Henbit, and Ela Mana Mou in the late seventies and early eighties. His biggest fans tend to be the television viewers and casual racing enthusiasts who see him as a humorous, likeable personality and a battler. Yet his style and manner, not least that grating laugh, have not always been to everybody's taste. Some professional observers, and they're not all disgruntled gamblers, feel that the drawback in Carson's head-down and elbows-pumping technique is that sometimes he doesn't seem to notice where he's going in a race and that he gets himself pocketed more easily than other jockeys or ends up riding his mounts into the backs of the horses in front of him.

Carson suffered an appalling injury in 1981 when Silken Knot, a filly he was riding in the Yorkshire Oaks, fell suddenly and fatally in the middle of the race. He made a remarkably successful recovery from this horrendous-looking accident and was back undiminished the following season. None the less the sight of his apparently lifeless form being scraped off the turf by the York emergency services was a grim reminder to the huge and festive crowd that it's not only steeplechase jockeys who take grave physical risks for the punters' pleasure. Immediately after Dick Hern's accident in 1984 the fortunes of both the West Illsley horses and their retained rider seemed, not surprisingly, to wane rather than prosper. For a while the Major imposed an embargo on all interviews with the voluble Carson. This was a painful experience for little Willie and somehow added to the impression that he was no longer quite the force of five years before. Then at the end of the 1987 season, Emmson, a West Illsley two-year-old colt, won the Group One Futurity at Doncaster and, along with such promising young horses as Unfuwain, Charmer and Minster Son, suggested that 1988 could see a return to the premier stages for that eccentric double act, 'Willie and the Major'.

Carson's spare-time passion in the close season months is fox-hunting. He lives in rural splendour in the beautiful Cotswold village of Barnsley which is about four miles from Cirencester and on the western edge of the Vale of the White Horse country. Willie's interest, though, lies further afield. There is actually a clause in his contract with West Illsley that allows him to spend a couple of months each winter hunting in Southern Ireland in County Limerick and County Tipperary. He takes all these things very seriously and, like an English character in an American soap opera, has the right wardrobe for every occasion. One freezing grey February day in 1987 he turned up for a sponsored race-meeting at Thurles in Tipperary where he was a guest of the Irish cattle exporters and racehorse owners, the Purcell brothers, who were sponsoring one of the races. Some of the racegoers, including the local stewards, were kitted out in their warmest, though not necessarily most fashionable, apparel. Not Willie. He arrived in an immaculate brown tweed suit and a rather close-fitting overcoat with a little chiseled-out brown trilby hat perched impeccably on his head. Everything was so sharp and smart though that somehow he looked less like a typical Anglo-Irish country gentleman and more like James Cagney in a suit one size too small for him.

Back in the unsaddling enclosure at Newmarket on 30 April, the Major chats with Willie and then Willie departs for the weighing room. The Major surveys Merce Cunningham one more time to make sure that everything is to his liking. Very slowly, yes, they're going to try it, one or two journalists tentatively approach. Hern royalists Scott and Seely are to the fore. The Major senses their presence. Scott congratulates him. The Major starts expostulating about the horse's problems the previous year. To hear what he's saying the grubbier hacks and bookmakers men have to bend forward from the waist like respectful courtiers. This appears to be a state of affairs that the Major finds entirely satisfactory.

The serious professionals ignore the next race which is a two-bit affair for maiden two-year-olds over five furlongs. The big action is starting to develop now down by the saddling-up boxes. The pre-race atmosphere leading up to this 2,000 Guineas is nowhere near as tangible or intense as before the 1,000. This is partly because it's such a small field. Just nine runners. Just nine out of the many thousands of colts born in 1985 who have made it all the way from the foaling shed and the sales ring through training disappointments, not to mention training incompetence, injury and loss of form, to Newmarket racetrack on this last Saturday in April.

The crucial race for the serious 2,000 Guineas aspirants has been the Craven Stakes run over the full Guineas mile on 14 April. Each of the last three runnings of the Craven has featured the Guineas winner himself. Shadeed and Dancing Brave had won both races in 1985 and 1986 and in 1987 Don't Forget Me had finished runner-up to Ajdal and then gone on to reverse the form a fortnight later. Five runners went to post for the 1988 reunion and they were headed by the odds-on favourite, Warning, who was already down to 6-4 for the 2,000 itself and confidently expected to stamp himself on the classic picture by winning decisively. Also in the field was Sanquirico, 7-1 second favourite for the Guineas at the time, and an intriguing colt of the Aga Khan's called Doyoun who was trained by Michael Stoute.

Doyoun was superbly bred being a son of the great 1971 Derby winner and champion sire, Mill Reef, out of a mare by the 1966 2,000 Guineas winner, Kashmir II. He had run just once as a two-year-old, running out the impressive winner of a well contested maiden race at Newmarket in October. Over the winter Doyoun had been built up into the unenviable status of a major talking horse. On the morning of the Craven he stood at 12-1 for the Guineas, although some punters were already backing him for the Derby over half a mile further, even though his breeding didn't guarantee that he would stay the extra distance.

Sanquirico led the field for the first five furlongs of the Craven but the Newmarket dogs had been barking against him all morning. He'd opened at 9-4 and then drifted out to 11-2, the kind of market slide that says a horse can't possibly win. The story of the Craven betting was the huge confidence in Warning. Harwood's horse who opened up at even money went briefly to 11-10 before being pushed back to 8-15 and 4-7 at the off. For his backers the race was to be a chilling experience. Sanquirico dropped away tamely with over three furlongs to run and at that point Doyoun quickened into the lead and Pat Eddery asked Warning to go with him. Running down into the dip, there was only a length between them but although Eddery, not wanting to leave the classic behind in the Craven, never once touched his mount with the whip, Warning couldn't go past. Swinburn gave his horse two smacks and Doyoun went clear for an impressive four-length victory.

Doyoun was receiving four pounds in weight from Warning but he'd won in a good time and suddenly looked a horse with a big future. The reaction of the leading bookmaking firms was instantaneous and all of them except Corals installed him as their new 2,000 Guineas favourite at 2-1 pushing Warning out to threes. City Index laid him to lose more than £100,000 at 3-1, minutes after his victory, and were forced to cut his price right down to 7-4. The Craven was a splendid result for the bookies. The *Sporting Life*'s starting price correspondents recorded more than £140,000 worth of bets on Warning in the ring. If the Warning punters caught a cold in the Craven, one or two of them could begin to sense a positive gale blowing in the direction of their ante-post vouchers for the Guineas itself.

At first Pat Eddery insisted that he was not despondent. He pointed out that he'd never hit Warning and both he and Guy Harwood tried to take comfort in the fact that their horse had blown hard after the Craven and that they had sixteen days before the Guineas when Doyoun wouldn't be getting any weight allowance at all. Then, exactly one week after the Craven Stakes and with over a week still to go before the big race, came the announcement that the Warning punters had been dreading. Harwood admitted that he was unhappy with the colt and considered it doubtful that he would run in the classic. Doyoun was shortened again to 4-7 favourite with Caerwent, who had won unimpressively on his reappearance at Phoenix Park, next best at 6-1. Four days later came the final confirmation of Warning's definite non-participation.

Nothing could more vividly demonstrate the risky and ruthless business of ante-post betting on big classic races. The bookmakers had faced a possible seven-figure pay-out if Warning had won the Guineas. Corals alone had liabilities of £380,000 while Ladbrokes had laid the colt to lose more than a quarter of a million. The son of Known Fact had been put up as 10-1 long-range favourite as far back as the previous September and had been backed down to 3-1 over the winter and to as low as 10-11 on the eve of the Craven. Doyoun, a 25-1 shot ten days before the Craven, was now himself odds-on. When an ante-post bet goes down because a horse is injured or doesn't run, there's no part-refund. The bookmakers keep all the money.

In the absence of both Warning and Sanquirico this 1988 2,000 Guineas has a slightly substandard look about it. Only Doyoun has pretensions to star quality. From the way he won the Craven he could really be an outstanding colt and perhaps one good enough to go all the way and take the Derby too. It is the real or supposed charisma of this only twice-raced horse that is the main drawing power for almost everyone here at Newmarket on this chilly April

Saturday. And the tension and strain involved in this almost ridiculous situation where a three-year-old colt who has won only two races in his life is already worth three or four million pounds provided he wins this classic race now in forty minutes time, is beginning to be visible on the face of Michael Stoute. Hair a little more bouffant than on Thursday. Still crisp, still hungry, still professional but pale too and a lot less smiling and talkative as the big moment draws closer. Stoute knows better than anyone that even in a nine-horse race against supposedly inferior opposition it could still easily go wrong, be it through his colt's inexperience or as a result of that extra gallop he gave him or because of the extra gallop he didn't give him. All of these thoughts, these problems and worries are churning around inside Stoute's mind now. The bookies for one don't share them. Opening at 8-13 Doyoun's price does go out but only by the smallest two points to an equally unattractive 4-5. There's a little money for Caerwent at 4-1 from fives and for Clive Brittain's Free Handicap winner, Lapierre, at 9-1 from tens. Same price 9-1 is the Free Handicap runner-up, Charmer, the mount of Willie Carson, while Luca Cumani's Italian import, Tibullo, is out to 12-1. Common Grounds trained by François Boutin and running in the colours of Stavros Niarchos is in to 16-1 from 33-1 and that's the same price as for Clive Brittain's other runner, Intimidate, who, for all that breeding operation and for all the money spent two years ago, is Sheikh Mohammed's sole representative. The French rag Aiglefin is a 66-1 shot and the English maiden, Bellefella, the rank outsider at 100-1.

Some but by no means all of the Coolmore set are present: Timmy Hyde, David Nagle of Barronstown Stud, a Horgan brother, Gerry Gallagher – Vincent O'Brien's famous travelling head lad. You can tell by the looks on their faces though that there's no way that Caerwent is going to win. There's nothing like the same buzz or aura as there was before El Gran Senor four years earlier. Gallagher, in a smart black suit walks through under the arch carrying Caerwent's saddle and preparing the way for his master like Oddjob in *Goldfinger*. Behind him a short, self-effacing man in a grey suit and a brown trilby hat is very quietly and politely trying to squeeze his way through the crowd of Dowagers and Marks, Willies and Toms who are gathered around the entrance. A gateman recognises him. 'Keep back please,' he shouts. 'Keep back.' Dr Vincent O'Brien gratefully slips in through the gap created for him. Close up, the famous trainer is beginning to look old. The rather pinched face, like ET. The folds of loose skin now around the neck. He raises his hat courteously to Edmund Loder and his very Anglo-Irish family and explains charmingly in a soft voice what he thinks of Caerwent's prospects.

François Boutin swaggers in under the arch, a cigar in one hand, a saddle in the other. In his wake comes the super-smooth Parisian art dealer, M. Daniel Wildenstein, who would be unlikely to come near the top of a poll to discover the most popular racehorse owner in Europe. Wildenstein is the fellow who once described Pat Eddery as a mere boy and it was his rage at not getting the services of Lester Piggott to ride his filly All Along in the 1983 Arc that led to the severing of Piggott's partnership with Henry Cecil and hastened Lester's eventual retirement from the saddle. The unloved monsieur in his glasses and blue raincoat is followed by a batch of senior Riviera millionaires with mottled skin and sun-tans, expensive trenchcoats and a lot of glinting Cartier watchstrap to match. At the rear comes Olivier Douieb, also in a trenchcoat today, and looking more like a flattened Belmondo than ever. They are followed through by a *très snob* and *très* drippy young French racing correspondent, sporting a Chirac Presidential Election badge on the Barbour that he's wearing over his Hackett-style striped shirt and corduroy trousers.

Finally the Aga Khan, in a white raincoat worn over a dark suit, comes waddling through to join Michael Stoute. The Aga, or 'K' as his friends refer to him, causes almost as many gasps as his horse, Doyoun. For underneath that mack, there can be no doubt whatsoever that he's putting up several pounds in overweight. Gone is the lithe tennis-playing athlete who led in Shergar after the 1981 Derby. In his place is a purring, silky, well-fed, indeed extremely well-fed, chappie.

The rug is pulled off Doyoun. The Aga's face betrays nothing, but as a serious judge of a racehorse he must be excited. Doyoun, this son of Mill Reef out of the French 1,000 Guineas winner Dumka, is a handsome and sturdy bay colt who has clearly been honed to a physical peak by his trainer; though, as he walks out towards the paddock, he shies a little at the pressing attentions of the crowd and there is a distinct possibility that this inexperienced three-year-old may be finding the highly charged atmosphere just a little trying.

Out beyond the saddling-up boxes stands another candidate for the role of the silkiest man in racing. The purring former Coldstream Guards officer, Charles Anthony Barbaro St George, who has managed to pad softly away from the huge losses incurred by two Lloyds insurance syndicates associated with his name as well as from the scandal surrounding the downfall of his great friend, L. Piggott. Earlier today St George has been hosting his annual Guineas day lunch at his house in Newmarket and one man who didn't stint himself at the buffet table was that noted gourmand, imbiber and raconteur, Charles 'Fatty' Benson, one-time 'Scout' of the *Daily Express* and long-time chum of Robert Sangster. Benson, whose working tasks since leaving the *Express* have mostly been onerous special features for the likes of *Pacemaker* magazine as 'Our Man In The Champagne Bar' at Ascot, York, Churchill Downs, etc., is bareheaded as always and kitted out in a sort of silvery grey suit. There is a perplexed look on his face as he stares towards the runners and then back at his racecard. This is like Pooh just setting out for Rabbit's house and wondering if he should first take the precaution of tucking into another jar of honey. Benson, boxbound to watch the big race, is trying to decide whether to rush towards the rails and take out another few precautionary wagers with William Hill before he does so.

The bookies are watching the parade in front of the stands. Doyoun is definitely getting a little nervous which helps to explain the slight easing in his price. For Michael Stoute this is a genuinely worrying moment. In 1985 he feared that Shadeed might go over the top through the long preliminaries and gave Lester instructions to break out of the parade and canter on down. It was a tactic that paid off as Shadeed did win the 2,000 although only by the narrowest of margins. Stoute was fined afterwards by the Jockey Club and some people accused him of cynical gamesmanship. Others just saw it as another instance of the trainer's exemplary professionalism at the highest level. Doyoun does not break the parade but it's a relieved Stoute none the less when they all start to canter away into the distance up the long straight mile.

Everyone is running and scrambling frantically to get a good position to watch the race. For the unlucky mob in Tatts this means being herded through the grisly tunnel, thick with the aroma of rancid hamburgers, that connects the paddock area with the ring. The top people are pouring up the narrow escalators that lead to the terraces at the top of the Members' stand. The people who are already up on the terraces are not very smart. Instead of moving down to the front of this balcony enclosure they all cram together at the highest point by the escalators. So as each new load of toffs push on up, they ride hopelessly into the group already there like a train crashing into the back of another stationary train in the rush hour. The upshot of it all is that many of these smartly dressed society ladies and their smooth-cheeked Cecil Parkinson husbands, with their velvet-collar coats and monogrammed shirts, end up catching only the barest glimpse of the 1988 2,000 Guineas but get a detailed close-up of the well-barbered necks, smelling of money and Trumpers hair oil, of the trilby-hatted men in front of them.

The build-up to this 2,000 may have suggested that there was only one good horse in the field but the race when at last it happens is in no way lacking in drama. The early leader is Tibullo, reverting to the tactics that he used to employ in Italy as a two-year-old. Charmer and Caerwent are tracking Tibullo with Lapierre tracking them, but there on their left on the outside of the group and right up close to the leaders is Doyoun. This is an immediate surprise. Surely the favourite would've been held up in the rear and ridden more for speed near the crucial stages of the race? The fact is that Walter Swinburn has a problem. Doyoun has been drawn nine on the outside of this small field and out there in the middle of this great bare heath his jockey has no opportunity to cover him up. The horse is seeing too much daylight. He's striding out too freely. Unless Swinburn is careful, he may run his race out in six furlongs.

At the three-furlong marker Charmer seems to be the first to be struggling. Then Common Grounds, who has refused to settle, begins to drop out and Tibullo starts very rapidly to head in the same direction. From the stands the big danger to Doyoun looks to be Caerwent who is going ominously well in behind with his jockey John Reid yet to move and riding the perfect waiting race. Two and a half furlongs from home Swinburn makes a crucial decision. He kicks Doyoun on into the lead and tries to win his battle here with a decisive change of pace that he hopes might leave his rivals struggling. And at first it works. Lapierre's fading. Intimidate can make no impression and Caerwent is keeping on but not going any faster. Then suddenly the unconsidered outsider, Bellefella, is beginning to run on strongly from the rear and then even more threateningly the seemingly beaten Charmer unleashes a sterling run as they come up the hill out of the dip. It's classic 'little Willie' stuff too. Head down and elbows pumping all the way towards the line. Yet the supposedly weaker Swinburn gives nothing away in strength and power. Never once losing his balance or his rhythm he drives and pushes and holds Doyoun together and pushes him and pushes him and drives him all the way up the hill to the winning-post. They get there half a length in front of Charmer with Bellefella two lengths away third and the other rank long-shot, Aiglefin, a running-on head away fourth. Caerwent, who perhaps didn't quite stay the distance and may be a sprinter like his dam, Marwell, finishes another three-quarters of a length away fifth.

The time is slower than for Ravinella's victory on the Thursday and the close-up presence of Bellefella and Aiglefin in third and fourth place casts an immediate question mark over the value of the form. All the same the 'expected' horse has won and so now Doyoun is escorted back into the unsaddling enclosure by the same pair of Scots air stewardesses as the French filly. And while there is no more than polite applause for the Aga, there is a real, loud and long ovation for Stoute and in particular for Walter Swinburn whose true grit at the climax of the race kept the favourite going and saved both the Aga and the favourite-backers their money. The press crowd round the winning connections. 'It was only his guts and class that got him home,' says Walter, confirming that his horse saw too much daylight early on. The big question in everybody's mind now is will he go on to the Derby for which he's already been substantially backed. The owner purrs silkily and won't be drawn. Mike Dillon of Ladbrokes, while quoting him at 5-1 with a run for Epsom, thinks he won't. 'The Aga is so commercially minded,' he says. 'He wouldn't go to Epsom just for the glory.' Stoute, who knows the horse best, is equivocal. Looking immensely pleased to have just got a Group One classic success into this colt who was no better than a 25-1 chance over the winter, he will say only this: 'There are contradictions in the dam's side of his pedigree but I take heart that he had a three-parts brother by Riverman who got a mile and a quarter and the Mill Reefs ought to stay that bit better.'

There are two more races to come at Newmarket this Saturday afternoon but effectively Guineas week is over. Willie and the Major could be on their way back, but for the Maktoum family, for Vincent O'Brien and Robert Sangster, it's been a mixed start. And for Khalid Abdulla, Guy Harwood and Pat Eddery, who must have really fancied their chances in the 2,000 after the way the race developed, it's been a bitter disappointment. Two outstanding sires, Mill Reef and Mr Prospector have further cemented their reputations, especially the American stallion with his first European classic winner. The Heads, Comte Roland de Chambure, Michael Stoute and the Aga Khan are all most definitely winners, and as for the horses it's Doyoun who has captured the first colts' classic but Ravinella who has captured the imagination. For all of them, Newmarket's premier racing occasion is finished with for another twelve months. The only big race that counts now is the next one: the Derby.

8 : Wheel of Fortune

There are four of them: Maktoum, Hamdan, Mohammed and Ahmed. In America they call them the Dubai Brothers. Many of the people who watch them in action in the sales ring or on the track in Europe and America have little or no idea where Dubai actually is. Some of them imagine it to be a vast oil-rich kingdom surrounded by palm trees and sand. In fact, Dubai is minute. A tiny city-state in the Persian Gulf, barely discernible on the map. In 1971 it joined with six other neighbouring states to form a new nation, the United Arab Emirates.

The UAE is indeed an oil-rich power, albeit one situated in just about the most politically sensitive region of the world, right across the Straits of Hormuz from Iran's revolutionary guards. It may be a rich man's country, it has an annual undeclared income that in terms of interest alone is said to stretch into stratospheric billions, but it would not be everyone's idea of a paradise. It's extremely flat. It has a proliferation of concrete and glass modern buildings including an American-style Galleria shopping mall, a Gucci shop, a Hyatt Regency hotel and lots of flats, apartments and office blocks for Western engineering and construction companies, computer firms and banks. It also has a specially laid golf course built mainly for the expatriates and featuring imported grass and trees, home-made bunkers and a mock Mediterranean-style clubhouse with its own not quite top-line resident professionals to coach and instruct. 'Have you seen the golf course?' everybody asks. 'Isn't it wonderful?'

Dubai is not a democracy. There are no taxes. For the fortunate majority the standard of living is exceptionally high and there are huge American, Japanese and European cars as well as glitteringly modern European-built hospitals, roads and sports stadiums. Yet there is no elected government. As with Saudi Arabia it is the royal family, in this case the Maktoums, who are the government, and working visitors have learnt when to compliment their hosts and when to keep silent. (The *Sporting Life* was actually banned in Dubai for three weeks at the end of 1988 for running a big article which suggested that the Maktoums' influence on English racing had started to become harmful and suffocating as opposed to beneficial.) The actual head of state is the boys' ageing father Rashid but the real power resides with the brothers. Eldest son Maktoum is Deputy Prime Minister, Hamdan is Finance Minister and Opec representative and Sheikh Mohammed, the third and most important son in both Dubai's affairs and in the world of international horse-racing, is the official Defence Minister of the UAE.

Like the rest of his siblings the forty-year-old Sheikh, a handsome, black-bearded man, about five foot ten inches tall, was educated in England, and the most influential stage of that process seems to have been his period at Sandhurst. He's a crack shot, a weapons expert and an accomplished flyer, and many of his closest advisers seem to be Englishmen with a decidedly military stamp about them. The Sheikh has a genuinely commanding presence which is never more apparent than when he's wearing his full-dress ministerial uniform of officer's khaki and burnous. Apart from the horses his other great passions are falconry and camel-racing and if to Western eyes he may seem to slightly miss the mark in his Roger Moore gear in the paddock at Newmarket, some Newmarket racehorse trainers cut an even more incongruous figure loafing around at a camel meet in Dubai, squinting at the sunshine, laying illicit bets with one another and dreaming longingly of a gigantic gin and tonic.

It should've been no great surprise to the English, the Irish and the French when the Maktoums and other Arab families like them decided to take an interest in European racing in the late seventies. It wasn't just a question of all those petrodollars washing around and needing to be reinvested somewhere. Almost every Derby winner and classic racehorse on the European turf is descended from three Arab stallions who were 'imported' into England in the eighteenth century. Their names were the Byerley Turk and the Darley and Godolphin Arabian. If English horse-racing in the last decade of the twentieth century is beginning to sink ever more emphatically into the dominating grip of a small group of Arab owners then that could be said to represent no more than the wheel of fortune coming full circle, the irony of which is not lost on the Sheikh himself. Residents of Dubai prefer to see it all in less grandiose terms, pointing to the unbearable humidity there in July and August and suggesting that their rulers can only be expected to take their summertime pleasures elsewhere.

The Maktoum racing operation is structured like an American Football team with Sheikh Mohammed as the quarterback. He's surrounded by blockers and guards. Professional whitemen most of them too. As well as Pasty Face Stroud there's the silver-haired John Leat who was once in the Merchant Navy and who acts as a sort of family tour manager. He still looks more like a cheerful purser on the Dover–Calais run than a typical racing *eminence grise*. Managing the Sheikh's Dalham Hall Stud at Newmarket is the fair-haired Honourable Robert Acton who came to England in 1964 from what then used to be described as Southern Rhodesia. With his tall slightly stooping frame, his fair to gingerish look and his sticking-out bottom, the Honourable Acton has all the makings of a gauche William Boyd hero stranded in some English consulate in the land of the white man's burden. Acton's right-hand man at Dalham Hall is the sixty-one-year-old Scotsman, Alec Notman, a rather terrifying and choleric looking ex-army officer. And then there's the forty-three-year-old former jump-jockey, Bill Smith, who used to ride for the Queen Mother's trainer, Fulke Walwyn. Towards the end of his career in the saddle 'Smithie' was felt to have quite understandably fallen out of love with the more dangerous aspects of a steeplechase rider's life; which makes it all the stranger that he should now be employed as a sort of combination Maktoum minder and bodyguard, supposedly even armed on occasions with a Smith and Wesson .38 calibre special to underline the potentially lethal nature of his task.

The Maktoums are not the first exotic foreign owners to wade heavily into British racing. The 'old Aga Khan', as he's still described, took the turf by storm in 1921 when the eight yearlings bought for him by George Lambton at that year's Doncaster sales averaged 3,065 guineas each, compared with a 649 guinea average for all the other yearlings in the sale. The Dubai Brothers initial purchases were somewhat less spectacular. In 1977 a filly called Hatta, who had been bought for a mere 6,200 guineas as a yearling and who was a daughter of the unremarkable stallion Realm, won four races for Sheikh Mohammed including the Group Three Molecomb Stakes at Goodwood in which she defeated the odds-on favourite Amaranda.

England's first glimpse inside the possibly cavernous depths of the brothers' wallets came in 1979 when Hamdan paid 625,000 guineas, more than twice the previous domestic record, for a yearling son of Lyphard, one of the few to be sold in this country. Though not for the last time in the Arabs' experience of high-priced purchases, the colt hardly developed into a champion. He was sent to the Newmarket stable of Harry Thomson-Jones, a former jumping trainer and an old India hand and fox-hunting enthusiast who was soon to be nicknamed 'Big Spender' by his neighbours. The Lyphard yearling's most notable achievement was to win one Group Three race in Italy in October 1981. Yet this record didn't deter Hamdan from buying a horse already in Jones's yard, a four-year-old called Princes Gate, at the end of that year. He was rewarded this time with his first Group race win in England when Princes Gate collected the Group Three Westbury Stakes at Sandown in April 1982.

That same spring Sheikh Mohammed won the Lingfield Derby Trial with Jalmood and by the end of that season he'd won thirty races which was a big improvement on the twenty-eight he'd won over the previous five years. It was his brother Maktoum, though, who pulled off their biggest triumph of 1982 when Touching Wood, the colt who'd been second to Golden Fleece in the Derby and who was trained by Tom Jones, won both the English and the Irish St Legers in the autumn.

Of course the Maktoums weren't the only Arabs already involved in the English game. Crown Prince Khalid Abdulla of Saudi Arabia, a very rich and self-effacing man who prefers to be known as plain Mr Abdulla in Britain, had picked up what should've been Nureyev's 2,000 Guineas with Known Fact. Known Fact, a much more economical Keeneland purchase than the Niarchos colt, went on to win two further Group One mile races before being retired to Abdulla's own stud, Juddmonte Farms, near Wargrave. Other players in the market were the younger Saudi Arabian Prince, Yazid Saud and his cousin, Ahmed Salman, who were involved in the 1982 Guy Harwood-trained two-year-old winners, Hays and Kafu. These two raced some of their horses as a partnership under the name of Yazid and Ahmed Ltd. This sort of title amused some English racegoers no end. Yazid and Ahmed sounded like a cowboy house-painting firm or Dubai's favourite late-night plumbers. Sniggering and overtly offensive racist remarks were very much one of the problems that confronted the Maktoums and some of the other Arab owners at the outset of their investment. And they came as much from racing's upper-middle classes as they did from the ignorant masses in Tatts and the Silver

Ring. Women who used to joke about there being tents in the foyer at the Dorchester and at Harrods now smirked about there being magic carpets over Newbury and one or two little minor public schoolboy ex-junior army officer bloodstock agents, especially the ones devouring fat fees and commissions from these new big rich suckers, laughed openly behind their clients' backs about camels' and sheeps' eyes being the staple ingredients of a good Lambourn party these days. And for all manner of racing personalities, ex-jockeys looking for a job, trainers on the way down and trying to conceal it or trainers on the way up and trying to promote it, these oil-rich Arabs did indeed seem to represent a magic carpet ride to easy money.

The rash of jokes and the big spending sprees that weren't exactly yielding spectacular results were preventing the Maktoums in particular from being taken as seriously as they wanted. They were hooked all right. They liked the respectable and traditional set-up of the sport in England with the Jockey Club enforcing the rules and in charge of discipline and they wanted to invest a lot more money but Sheikh Mohammed quickly decided that they weren't going to be played for a soft touch.

At the 1982 Keeneland July yearling sales Robert Sangster was once again the top bidder paying $4.25 million for a son of Nijinsky who would be called Empire Glory. It was the Maktoums though who emerged as leading overall buyers spending a total of $29.6 million on no fewer than sixty-one yearlings. Earlier that year representatives of Sheikh Mohammed had tried to contact Sangster to suggest some kind of partnership or at least an arrangement whereby the two camps would carve up the Keeneland catalogue in advance and agree not to bid against each other on certain horses. Sangster wasn't interested. He was enjoying himself at the time anyway and hardly surprisingly as he'd just done a runner from his second wife, the shrill Australian, Susan Peacock, and was partying it up in LA in the ravishing company of Jerry Hall. He welcomed the presence of the Arab competition partly because he could see it as only benefiting and assisting the whole purpose of the syndicate's operations. At the time he was also convinced that they could never beat him either on the race-track or in the sales ring. For all the money at their disposal he was sure that his people, the genius of Vincent O'Brien and his inspired assistants, would always be a match for their people like 'Big Spender' Jones and the white-suited Colonel Dick Warden.

This rebuttal seemed to be a decisive catalyst as far as Sheikh

Mohammed was concerned. If they couldn't get Vincent O'Brien, then they'd do the next best thing. From now on the massive financial investment would be spread right across the board. Hamdan would continue his enormous stake with the Tom Jones stable but the brothers would also place their yearlings in every top-drawer yard in Britain: Henry Cecil, Michael Stoute, Guy Harwood, John Dunlop, Barry Hills, Dick Hern; and John Oxx and David O'Brien in Ireland; and Criquette Head and later André Fabre in France. They'd go for such depth in quality and quantity that their rivals simply wouldn't stand a chance.

The first part of the 1983 season seemed to split the honours pretty evenly between the two big camps. The winter favourite for the 2,000 Guineas had been yet another son of Northern Dancer trained by Vincent O'Brien. The colt's name was Danzatore. He raced in Danny Schwartz's colours and he was unbeaten as a two-year-old. Come the spring though, he performed only moderately, scoring a narrow win in his reappearance race at Phoenix Park and suddenly the old tune started up once again. Danzatore had been well backed ante-post for the Guineas (didn't they ever learn?) but now there were rumours that he was wrong, that he'd worked badly and that he might not even run. Some bookies took him out of their lists. Some extended his odds. And some actually shortened them up. Contradictory statements kept coming out of Ballydoyle but when one apparently authoritative report insisted that he'd worked well and that he was definitely coming over to Newmarket and when even Sangster himself admitted having backed him his price shortened again everywhere. Within a week he was confirmed as a definite non-runner. Once more the press were furious and O'Brien was accused of contemptuous disregard for the betting public.

The situation didn't improve when the Irish trainer still went ahead and won the 2,000 Guineas anyway with a horse called Lomond who, mistakenly regarded as the stable second string, was allowed to start at 11-1. Just like Danzatore, Lomond was by Northern Dancer, only he was running in Sangster's own colours not Schwartz's. He'd been an impressive winner of his first race as a two-year-old but then had flopped when favourite and ridden by Pat Eddery for O'Brien's preferred Irish two-year-old race, the National Stakes at The Curragh. Afterwards he was discovered to have been suffering from a severe throat infection at the time. He easily won his three-year-old reappearance race back at the same track and obviously commended himself to his handler as a far speedier type than the hard-pulling, long-striding Danzatore, and as therefore a much likelier winner of the Guineas.

Lomond won well at Newmarket showing a high-class turn of foot to go away from his rivals in the final furlong. It was probably a substandard Guineas field but it was still Vincent's first winner of the race since The Minstrel and the predictably fickle racing press were all over him afterwards in the unsaddling enclosure. Lomond wasn't an obvious Derby horse as there were too many doubts about his stamina but the syndicate were extremely confident that he would carry off the Irish Guineas too at The Curragh. It therefore came as a most unwelcome surprise to them when the Newmarket form was dramatically reversed in Ireland and Lomond finished second to a horse called Wassl who had been only seventh to him on the heath. Wassl, whose name is the ancient Arabic word for Dubai, was trained by John Dunlop and he raced in the colours of Sheikh Ahmed who had been presented with the horse as a gift by his older brother, Sheikh Mohammed.

Wassl was the Maktoum's second classic winner of the year as a truly outstanding French filly, Ma Biche, who was trained by Criquette Head and who had been bought off the Head family by Maktoum Al Maktoum over the winter, had won the 1,000 Guineas at Newmarket. There were still some expensive embarrassments too. The top-rated English two-year-old colt of 1982 had been a horse called Dunbeath who was trained by Henry Cecil and owned at the time by an American, Michael Doyle Riordan. Over the winter Dunbeath was bought by Sheikh Mohammed, seemingly at the instigation of his then principal racing adviser, the very pukka Colonel Dick Warden, for a sum rumoured to be in the region of ten million pounds. This appeared to be a staggeringly high price as the horse would virtually have to win the Derby to make such a short-odds investment worthwhile. He ran a promising second on his first outing as a three-year-old but then failed dismally in the Dante Stakes at York, leaving Cecil hanging around the weighing room afterwards looking as sick as a Gucci-attired parrot. And he didn't manage to do any better when he was shipped out for an abortive campaign in America later in the year.

Episodes like the Dunbeath affair hardly increased Sangster's respect for the opposition. The Arabs didn't have a horse in the first four in the 1983 Derby in which runners bearing Sangster's colours finished third and fourth. The Sunday after Epsom, Sangster's Nijinsky colt, Caerleon, trained by the senior O'Brien, won him the French Derby for the second year in succession. And later that

summer Caerleon gamely defeated the older horses in the Benson
and Hedges Gold Cup at York. Ballydoyle also triumphed in the
Eclipse Stakes at Sandown Park with Solford but the Maktoums had
their great day too.

The 1983 Irish Sweeps Derby looked on paper to be a showdown
between the English Derby winner Teenoso and Sangster's French
winner Caerleon who had missed Epsom altogether. The Ballydoyle
staff seemed very confident beforehand that their horse would swamp
Teenoso for speed. Caerleon did beat Teenoso at The Curragh but he
could still only finish second. The winner was none other than the
once-derided Michael Stoute-trained Shareef Dancer. The same
Shareef Dancer who Sheikh Mohammed had paid $3.3 million for at
Keeneland in 1981. When he was beaten in his first English three-
year-old race, a handicap at Sandown, many professionals were
prepared to laugh him into oblivion. Then he suddenly came out and
won a Group Two race over a mile and a half at Royal Ascot but he
was still one of the outsiders at The Curragh. Only Stoute and
Walter Swinburn knew his true ability.

Shareef Dancer won the Irish Derby convincingly, passing both
Teenoso and Caerleon in the last two furlongs and showing that he'd
inherited plenty of his father's famous speed. For once Sangster and
O'Brien had occasion to rue not having bid more for a yearling in the
sales ring. The Curragh classic was the sheikhs' finest hour to date.
Some English establishment types were prepared to welcome them
now as honorary gentlemen; not to elect them to full membership of
the Jockey Club of course, but to let them carry the banner of
sportsmanship into battle against the detested entrepreneur, Sangster.
If they thought that the Arabs were really that different from the man
and the commercial operation that they had decided to emulate then
they were soon to be disappointed. Shareef Dancer never raced
again. He was syndicated for a massive forty million pounds, not
dollars, and became simply too valuable to run. American breeders
who had seen Sangster and the Arabs going to three and four million
dollars for Northern Dancer yearlings in the ring at Keeneland were
quite happy to pay a million dollars for a fortieth share in a new
young Northern Dancer stallion, even if he was going to stand at
Sheikh Mohammed's own new stud acquisition, Dalham Hall, which
he'd actually purchased two years before. American commercial
breeders, the greedy and the shrewd, could see no end as yet to the
spiralling prices, and events at Keeneland that July proved just how
right they were.

If the Ballydoyle syndicate's successes with The Minstrel and

Alleged in 1977 and 1978 had sent them back to Kentucky with renewed resolve then the syndication of Shareef Dancer sent Sheikh Mohammed into battle as never before. There were twenty-nine yearlings that sold for a million or more at Keeneland in 1983 and the two big camps accounted for twenty-one of them. Over one yearling in particular they locked arms in single combat. The breeding was no surprise. Northern Dancer out of a mare called My Bupers. No surprise that Vincent O'Brien wanted him. No surprise that Sheikh Mohammed wanted him too. They went at it bid for bid to the awe and astonishment of the merely mortal rich who were watching from the ring.

You have to try and imagine what it's like to be at Keeneland in July. In the town of Lexington, Kentucky in the heart of the Blue Grass. Where 'Fast Eddie' Felson came to shoot straight pool with Findlay the playboy in *The Hustler*. Lexington has changed a fair bit since Eddie's time. The skyline nowadays is dominated by tall modern hotels, banks and finance houses, the symbols of wealth and success that horses and foreign money have brought to the Blue Grass. The continuing significance of the annual Keeneland Select Yearling Sale is a powerful reminder of the debt that the Old Kentucky Home owes to Vincent O'Brien and the Maktoum family. There may be other big yearling sales in the world but none can compare with this one. This is for the élite. This is for the chosen brethren. To be at Keeneland in July, even if you are amongst the most junior Marks, Willies and Toms, means that you've got the racing and breeding industry's equivalent of a seat at the post-war nuclear negotiating table. And to spend big money here, wisely or unwisely, is the ultimate indication of an owner's status in the game.

The Select Sale usually begins on the third Monday in July and lasts for just two days. There are generally some 330 to 350 yearlings consigned to be sold and no more than fifty to sixty sires will be represented in the catalogue. That catalogue is drawn up by the sales company's vets and bloodstock advisers who travel around the stud farms each spring to inspect their possible products. Needless to say it's as important to the big commercial studs to be represented at Keeneland as it is to the major players to come away with a batch of quality purchases. Not all the yearlings will make their reserve but the 300 or more deals that will go through will tell everyone in the industry which stallions are hot, which stallions are really hot, who is solid, who is on the way up, on the way down, too old or newly emerging and something to get your money into now, etc. It all depends on what the market wants. It's the American capitalist game applied to the bloodstock business and acted out with spectacular panache.

The Association buildings are actually located some five miles out of town at number 4201 Versailles Road, opposite the turn-off to Blue Grass airport. Driving up to the front entrance you feel as if you could be arriving at a very sleek and exclusive private golf course or country club. It's something to do with all the serene green trees, the huge car-park, the almost silent, gliding, power-steered automobiles and the large squares of grey stone with which the offices and pavilion have been constructed. Young, tee-shirted employees of the company are waiting to valet-park your car and then it's in through the cool, businesslike and air-conditioned foyer and on towards the main auditorium beyond.

The forty or so barns, which is where the yearlings are housed during the sale, are in an attractive landscaped area at the back of the pavilion. Everybody comes out to view the yearlings during the two or three days leading up to the sale. All the stud farms have their grooms and sales managers kitted out in shades and matching baseball caps and shirts. The yearlings are identified with their catalogue or hip number and pedigree above or in front of their box, while in the tackroom at the end of each barn you can go and see a video of the farm's consignment and of their parents' past achievements, genealogy and breeding history.

You sit out on long green benches under a green and white awning, sipping cans of frozen Tab and cartons of iced tea, and watching as the yearlings are led out into the brilliant sunshine and walked up and down for your inspection. When it comes to the sale, the horses are taken up to the holding area behind the pavilion and then, as their turn arrives, they are led theatrically into the main ring.

More than three hundred of the game's very biggest players are all gathered in the modern bidding theatre, with its little green seats with the names of the players on the back. Outside it's a sweltering 97°F and the humidity's suffocating. Chances are you can hear hot rain falling on the roof. Inside the arena you're hypnotised by the seductive patter of the auctioneer, the whirr of the air-conditioning and the theatrical shouts and gestures of the bid-spotters. The bidding is relayed by closed circuit television to the barns out back, to the holding areas and to the adjoining bars and restaurants where the Good Old Boys are enjoying their mint juleps and their bourbon whiskey sours and their delicious platters of iced shrimp, chicken and crab.

Around the edges of the auditorium there's a huge crowd of onlookers watching the auction: humungous women in knee-length shorts; cowboys in high-heeled boots; bank officials; creditors; conmen. Down in the main seating area the pink-faced Honourable Acton and Pasty Face Stroud and the sweating colonels try to take their eyes off a bevy of taut and silky Southern ladies with lots of hair and leg and eyeliner, not to mention a string of husbands, lovers, chequebooks and toy boys in tow.

The Sheikh and his men are usually centre-front. Right under the auctioneer's eye. Sangster, Magnier and O'Brien generally prefer to be behind the podium at the back. And the actual yearling, the object of all this concentration, he stands up there on his wood-chip stage, sleek, muscular, calm and resplendent. Every few minutes a black groom in a green Keeneland Association jacket steps forward to sweep away the horseshit from beneath the yearling's feet.

That was roughly how it was, that night at Keeneland in 1982, although for once both camps were seated in the main auditorium, wearing jackets and ties as it was a formal evening session; not that this affected their bidding duel. Five million. Six million. Seven million. Eight. Nine. Ten. As the two rivals smashed the ten-million-dollar mark, half of their audience stood up and applauded and whooped and hollered and waved their catalogues and their straw hats in the air. One English bloodstock correspondent covering the sale for a racing paper would describe it as a bizarre and faintly nauseating tribute to the intoxicating power of money. Finally at $10.2 million, Sangster and O'Brien gave way. Sheikh Mohammed had got his horse. Was this a mere macho virility symbol or a serious pointer of where the ultimate victory would reside? 'Sheikh Mohammed. Lord of ten thousand years.' The Maktoum purchasing power at least seemed never-ending.

The Sheikh called his new pet Snaafi Dancer, which means Elegant Dancer in Arabic, and put him in training with John Dunlop. And over three full seasons he never once set foot on a racecourse. The truth was that Snaafi Dancer turned out to be plumb useless. And when they tried to salvage some of their money by launching him as a stallion, the results were just as bad. His fertility level was almost zero. The only thing this luckless horse would ever be remembered for was his record-breaking purchase price.

One or two people speculated wildly that Sangster had run the Arabs up on purpose. Certainly there was a widespread belief that some Keeneland consignors were employing fake bidders to help push the prices up once they knew that Sangster or the Maktoums were interested.

Even while the Sheikh was still contemplating Snaafi Dancer's two-year-old début his rivals came back at him on the race-track with another embryonic champion of their own. In the autumn of 1983 El Gran Senor became Vincent O'Brien's seventh winner of the Dewhurst Stakes, his fifth for Robert Sangster and his sixth with a son of Northern Dancer.

From the very beginning El Gran Senor seemed to have everything required to turn him into a superstar. He was a full brother to the controversial Try My Best and O'Brien and Sangster had actually bought a two-thirds share in the dam Sex Appeal after Try My Best's Dewhurst win in 1977. El Gran Senor was very like his father, not overly large but all quality. A strikingly handsome dark bay with strong shoulders, an intelligent head, and a lovely calm temperament. Named after the man who trained Northern Dancer, the flamboyant Argentinian, Horatio Luro, the Senor was unbeaten in three races as a two-year-old and in the Dewhurst he was undeniably impressive, winning in a fast time from a good young horse of Khalid Abdulla's called Rainbow Quest who was a son of The Minstrel's 1977 Derby victim, Blushing Groom. Many of the English racing press had come ready to jeer but the headline in the following morning's *Sporting Life* reflected their grudging admiration. 'Si, si, Senor,' it read. 'You're smart.' But then winning the Dewhurst was one thing. The syndicate were supremely good at doing that. It made a young horse as a stallion prospect, launching it almost inevitably to the top of the International two-year-old Free Handicap ratings . . . but if necessary the Dewhurst could be enough. After Storm Bird, Monteverdi and Danzatore, who could be sure that El Gran Senor would even show up again at Newmarket the following spring.

The point was a fair one. This imposing and beautifully bred creature was unbeaten and, well, everybody knew that the syndicate liked to keep things that way. In fact El Gran Senor won his prep race easily in April 1984 and for once it looked as if the top juvenile of one year was definitely going to contest the next season's 2,000 Guineas. And what a race that was shaping up to be. As well as the Senor there would be another unbeaten American-bred colt called Lear Fan, owned by Ahmed Salman, trained by Guy Harwood and to be ridden by the syndicate's old adversary, Greville Starkey. In his Guineas trial, the Craven Stakes at Newmarket, Lear Fan had come out on top after a fierce battle with Rainbow Quest who was also reopposing in the classic itself. As well as these three, there would be two other exciting candidates: Keen, a chestnut son of Sharpen Up, trained by Henry Cecil and ridden by Lester Piggott, and a massive bay called Chief Singer who was trained by the unfashionable Ron Sheather and who had won the Coventry Stakes at Royal Ascot as a two-year-old.

The 1984 2,000 Guineas was run on one of those still, blue-green, early May days that show off the great, flat, eerie expanse of Newmarket Heath at its most hauntingly beautiful and atmospheric best. Guy Harwood suggested beforehand that whatever beat his horse would win. And if you knew how to read them, all the signs were there that the O'Brien stable were convinced that they were going to do just that. All the most important figures in the line-up were present: Sangster, the shrill 'Sheila' (who had been temporarily reunited with her husband), Jacqueline O'Brien, John Magnier, Niarchos, grey-haired and spry and looking around for approbation in his sleek overcoat, and Niarchos's daughter, Maria. But also in attendance were some of the most popular and best-connected figures in Irish racing: men like Timmy Hyde, David Nagle, J. P. McManus and 'Mouse' Morris as well as a trio of outstanding current and former jumping personalities made up of Tommy Stack, Jimmy Fitzgerald and the beloved Jonjo O'Neill. They all, it seemed, had been tipped the wink that this time Vincent was going to play a very special card indeed. And if they came with drama and emotion in mind, then the race itself certainly didn't let them down.

Lear Fan made the running in his customary way for the first four furlongs but he could never set up a really commanding lead. El Gran Senor, Chief Singer and Rainbow Quest were all closing on him with about three furlongs to run, but when Pat Eddery and the Senor accelerated alongside Chief Singer with just under a quarter of a mile to go, the race looked over. At precisely that point Chief Singer's jockey, Ray Cochrane, really hurled his mount into battle and for a few electrifying moments, as he took a definite advantage on the stands-side rail, a sensational outcome seemed possible. It was now though, with so much on the line, that El Gran Senor demonstrated just what a truly high-class horse he was. He'd already quickened once in the race but now, when Pat asked him a second, most urgent question, he quickened again. And this time Chief Singer had no answer. El Gran Senor galloped on brilliantly up the hill and swept past the finishing post the decisive victor. Lear Fan hung on to third place and Rainbow Quest, outpaced at the end, finished back in fourth.

This looked to be a way above average 2,000 Guineas and the

below average time confirmed it. Chief Singer went on to become a champion miler and completed a high-summer big-race hat trick that included the Sussex Stakes and the six-furlong July Cup at Newmarket. Lear Fan won the Group One Prix Jacques Le Marois at Deauville in August and Rainbow Quest eventually won the following year's Prix de l'Arc de Triomphe. O'Brien, the embarrassment of Lomond and Danzatore and the fiasco of Try My Best all forgotten now, was mobbed and fêted in the unsaddling enclosure. It had to be the Derby for El Gran Senor now, surely? But would he stay? A top-class mile and mile-and-a-quarter horse with that kind of speed can always stay the extra distance if he relaxes, if he has the right kind of temperament, avowed Vincent. And the temperament of this horse was clearly beyond reproach.

The build-up to the 1984 Derby seemed to be about little else other than the imminent coronation of El Gran Senor as one of the great racehorses of the post-war years. The form of the other runners was barely mentioned. Even the normally shy and cautious O'Brien was smiling and confident this time. In a touching interview with Bruffscot in the *Sunday Times* he seemed to suggest that he genuinely believed that if the Senor won the Derby he might not only deserve to be ranked with Nijinsky and Sir Ivor but that he could just conceivably be the best he'd ever trained. To hear him even hint at such a thing about one specific horse was almost unbelievable, although the Ballydoyle staff still say that El Gran Senor's final piece of work before the Derby was as impressive a demonstration of class and speed as that of any animal they'd ever prepared for a classic race. The result seemed to be such a foregone conclusion that nobody was seriously discussing the opposition at all.

El Gran Senor came through the Epsom preliminaries – the paddock, the parade and the long walk across the downs to the mile-and-a-half start – with the minimum of fuss. Once out of the stalls Eddery quickly settled him in an ideal position just to the rear of the leading group and they held that position with ease as they raced uphill and then along the flat part of the course at the top of the downs before swinging left-handed and starting downhill towards Tattenham Corner and the turn into the straight. At the three-furlong marker a horse called Claude Monet, trained by Henry Cecil and ridden by Steve Cauthen, was still in the lead. Then quite suddenly Claude Monet stopped virtually to a standstill. It later transpired that he had choked on a mouthful of turf but as a result of this mishap Pat Eddery found himself in front. It was almost certainly earlier than he'd expected and sooner than he'd wanted. To everyone in the stands and to the millions watching on television, El Gran Senor seemed to be going quite breathtakingly easily. It looked as if Pat only had to shake the reins at him and he'd pull away to go five, ten, even fifteen lengths clear of his pedestrian rivals. This again was the kind of moment that all true lovers of a great racehorse, no matter what they've backed themselves, cherish and remember for the rest of their lives. To see a field of classic thoroughbreds all struggling and stretched and all off the bit and then to see this favourite, this star, still cruising on the bridle and contemptuously waiting, waiting and waiting to strike. It was like Lester on Nijinsky in the 1970 King George at Ascot and like Johnny Francome on Sea Pigeon in the Champion Hurdle. Except that in this 1984 Derby, there seemed to be one other horse who was determined to ruin the picture. Pat actually looked over at him for a moment. He was called Secreto. He too was a son of Northern Dancer. He was owned by the South American businessman, Luigi Miglitti, who'd paid $340,000 for him at Keeneland in 1982. He was being ridden by the Irish jockey Christy Roche and, best joke of all, he was trained down in Tipperary by the thirty-two-year-old David O'Brien ... son of Vincent.

Eddery may have given Secreto a dismissive look but he had a fight on his hands. This horse had class. He'd been placed in the Irish 2,000 Guineas. And that very morning the *Sporting Life*'s breeding correspondent had rated him a slightly likelier chance to last the mile and a half than his illustrious blood-brother. The stunned amazement in the stands at the apparent ease with which the Senor was travelling changed in a manner of seconds to distressed incredulity. Secreto was not only on terms he was going hard for the line and the favourite's response was almost non-existent. El Gran Senor seemed to go from cantering to walking in a count of three. Seriously, then anxiously, then desperately, Pat Eddery tried to pick his horse up, regain his momentum and drive him to the finish. Fifty yards out he seemed to have the edge but Christy Roche would not be denied. Riding with a power and a whip-cracking fury that would've landed him in front of the stewards in image-conscious 1989, Roche ensured that Secreto's head was in front when it counted, even if it was only by the skinniest of short heads. The Judge called for a photograph but the result was quickly declared in Secreto's favour. Then the stewards announced an enquiry. The two horses had after all come very close together in the final one hundred yards. Pat Eddery, perhaps frantic to redeem his reputation and the owners' millions, lodged an objection to the winner for taking his ground. But nothing was to come to either Pat's or the syndicate's rescue. The objection was thrown out and the result was upheld. It was Secreto by a whisker and a third Derby win for Northern Dancer who had also achieved the unprecedented feat of siring the first two.

David O'Brien was jubilant. His father, though obviously and genuinely moved for his son, looked shattered. How could his great hope have possibly been defeated? Sangster was even more tight-lipped than usual and all colour seemed to drain from his face. Before the Derby there'd been talk of American stud farms offering sixty or even eighty million dollars for El Gran Senor as a stallion. If he won at Epsom. He'd hardly been disgraced but if he was genuinely a non-stayer, a miler who couldn't win further out, even over the Americans' favoured distance of ten furlongs, then that valuation would have to be revised downwards. There was one uncomfortable but unavoidable question that had to be asked. Had Pat Eddery been too cocky? Should he have kicked on for home instead of allowing himself an indulgent look round two out? And then the most painful question of all. Would the horse have lost if Piggott had been riding it? Remember now those unforgettable finishes on The Minstrel and Roberto. But the two runners-up, Hot Grove and Rheingold – how many people remember them? And how many dollars was anybody paying for their progeny?

The big question for the Ballydoyle syndicate now was whether to run El Gran Senor again or not. Many members of the press and public were already sceptical of ever seeing much more of him. The past record of, say, Golden Fleece was hardly encouraging. If he did run, the most likely race seemed to be the Eclipse Stakes at the beginning of July. Crucially the distance was two lengths shorter than the Derby. Only then O'Brien and his staff discussed it all and looked back at Epsom and continued to see their horse thrive and eventually decided that he should be given one more chance to prove whether he could win a top-class race over a mile and a half. They decided to run him in the Irish Derby. The field for the 1984 running of Ireland's premier classic was not exactly of legendary quality but as well as the Senor it did include Rainbow Quest who since Newmarket had finished third in the French Derby at Chantilly.

Pat Eddery made no mistakes at The Curragh. No contemptuous looks or sashaying around this time. He was right on the heels of the leaders turning into the straight and he used the Senor's speed to drive powerfully to the front a good furlong from home and bury the race there. Like so many Northern Dancer colts the Senor didn't do more than he had to once he hit the front and his race was won but there was no way that Rainbow Quest was ever going to catch him. The cynics still sneered at the form but after the runner-up's victory in the Arc in 1985, admittedly achieved via the disqualification of the first past the post, Sagace, it became harder to knock the performance. You could hardly say after this that El Gran Senor did not stay a mile and a half.

El Gran Senor never raced again. He'd partially redeemed his Derby failure by winning another classic, so the syndicate swiftly decided to cash in their chips. He was retired for a rumoured fifty million dollars and flown out to join his father at Windfields Farm in Maryland. This era was the absolute nadir for the traditional concept of rigorously testing good horses over three or four seasons of full competition. If it was felt that their stud value was too great to risk further exposure on the track, then premature retirement was the smart thing to do. Shareef Dancer had gone quickly after his Irish Derby win the year before and Secreto too never raced again after his dramatic Epsom victory. He was sold for $28 million to join Affirmed and Alydar at Calumet Farm in the heart of the Blue Grass.

Robert Sangster was not without other conspicuous successes in 1984. Sadlers Wells, one more son of the prodigious Northern Dancer, won three Group One races for him including the Eclipse and the Phoenix Champion Stakes in Ireland. What's more, he raced with the utmost gameness and consistency no fewer than ten times which was otherwise unheard of for an O'Brien/Sangster horse. Not surprisingly this earned him a degree of public affection and respect not always enjoyed by some of his glitzy but not exactly overworked stable companions. There was one big irony about Sadlers Wells. In the 1984 King George VI at Ascot he'd finished a very genuine but well-beaten second to the 1983 Derby winner, Teenoso, who, unlike Golden Fleece or El Gran Senor, had been kept in training as a four-year-old. Yet at the season's end Sadlers Wells was retired to Coolmore with a stud fee of some £75,000 while Teenoso, an authentic classic winner, went off to less glamorous quarters at about a quarter the price. The reason was that Sadlers Wells enjoyed the most fashionable breeding in the world and all the smooth hype of the Coolmore organisation to ensure he got a first-class book of mares. Even though Teenoso had beaten him fair and square on the track, the market forces that Sangster and his partners had largely created deemed him not to be a speed-horse but a stayer and therefore nowhere near as commercially viable. His owners would struggle hard to get mares of the same quality. Not surprisingly old-time racing men and a lot of Jockey Club members banged on indignantly. The really envious could take malign satisfaction in the fact that Coolmore had itself suffered a disastrous reversal earlier in the year. Golden Fleece, the hero of the 1982 Derby, had died that February of cancer. The horse had become ill twelve months before but at first had fought off the disease and staged a courageous recovery. In July 1983 he was reinsured. By February 1984 he was dead.

Aside from the pain of losing a brilliant racehorse and a potentially brilliant stallion so young, there were also the economic consequences to consider. The young Derby winner, the first real champion that the syndicate had not sold to the Americans, was to have been the flagship of the Coolmore empire, alongside Be My Guest and Kings Lake and then later Lomond, Caerleon and Sadlers Wells. One Derby winner was lost and the other horse who should've been one had lost the Derby. There was only one thing for it. They would have to try and buy a yearling successor to them both. And with the El Gran Senor syndication money in the pipeline and the Arabs in the ring too that could mean only one thing. This time, if necessary, the sky would be the limit. But were they in danger of becoming financially overstretched, perhaps fatally? One man thought so.

Wing-Commander Tim Vigors is one of those bizarre and rather dotty characters who could somehow only exist to their full, colourful extent in the loopy world of horse-racing. An Old Etonian, a former Battle of Britain pilot, and an enthusiastic man to hounds, Vigors is the bloodstock agent who originally owned Coolmore Stud. Vincent O'Brien was his first partner in the farm in the early seventies before he sensibly sold up his share to the serious men and let the new Mafia get on with it. One of Vigors's favourite maxims about the racing and breeding industry, delivered in alternately gruff and chortling tones, is that nearly every bloodstock empire, no matter how invincible it may seem at its height, falls more quickly than you might expect. But there's always another big buyer waiting around expectantly to grab his turn in the limelight, from the old Aga Khan to Marcel Boussac and from the first Americans, Whitney and Mellon on to Engelhard and Bunker Hunt and then on to England's Robert Sangster. The pattern has always been the same. And, incredible as it might have seemed on the eve of El Gran Senor's Derby, within two years of his retirement, there were ominous signs that the Ballydoyle syndicate had passed their own high-water mark.

At the beginning of the 1985 season in England, the Arab owners and the Maktoums in particular seemed to be winning everything in sight. From Newmarket to The Curragh to Epsom Downs it was continually Sheikh Mohammed, or one of his brothers (plus their ever-increasing army of retainers) who was filing into the winners enclosure. The quarterback's great Cecil-trained filly, Oh So Sharp, won the Triple Crown of 1,000 Guineas, Oaks and St Leger while another filly, Pebbles, not only won the Breeders Cup Turf at the end of the year but defeated the Derby winner, Slip Anchor, in the Champion Stakes at Newmarket. 1985 was also the year in which Shadeed won the 2,000 Guineas for Maktoum Al Maktoum (with Sheikh Mohammed's Bairn in second place) and in which Al Bahathri, runner-up to Oh So Sharp in the 1,000 Guineas, went on to win the Irish equivalent at The Curragh for Sheikh Hamdan and 'Big Spender' Jones.

By contrast the Ballydoyle stable only had one really high-class three-year-old and that was the Alleged colt, Law Society, who ran in the Niarchos colours and finished second in the Epsom Derby and then went on to win the Irish Derby three and a half weeks later. But he could only finish fourth behind Lady Beaverbrook's Petoski and Oh So Sharp in the King George VI and was subsequently retired to Coolmore without further racing. Another son of Alleged, Leading Counsel, ended up winning a substandard Irish St Leger in October but this was only mild consolation as so much more had been expected of him earlier in the year. These disappointments didn't prevent the syndicate from continuing to go in hard in the sales ring. In 1984 they and the Maktoums between them had bought the nine top lots at the Keeneland Select Sale. These comprised the second to sixth highest prices ever paid for a yearling at public auction and, all in all, that summer and autumn the Maktoums bought ninety different yearlings in America for a total outlay of more than $70 million. In 1985 they bought seventy-seven for over $55 million but they did let Sangster come away with the Keeneland top lot. This was a Nijinsky colt out of a mare called My Charmer who was also the dam of the 1977 American Triple Crown winner, Seattle Slew. Sangster and O'Brien went to a staggering $13,100,000 to purchase the horse and the Arabs were not the underbidders. That distinction fell to the formidable American triumvirate of Gene Klein, L. R. French and D. Wayne Lukas. It was Seattle Slew's historic achievements in American racing and his influence as a sire of top American dirt-track horses such as Slew O' Gold that interested Lukas just as much as the Northern Dancer blood. From Sangster's point of view it was a simple matter of O'Brien assuring him that in terms of conformation the bay yearling was one of the best he'd ever seen in a public sales ring. And when Vincent said that, you just had to pay.

There were no wild cheers this time when the bidding went over ten million dollars. In 1982 the number board had been unable to accommodate the extra digit. Since then it had been modernised so as to be able to indicate eight figures if necessary. As far as Ballydoyle were concerned the logic of it all was simple enough. The machismo display of financial power may have been partly designed to prove that the Arabs had not yet got them on the run but it was also a straightforward economic decision. They needed another champion. This is where they'd always found the embryonic product in the past. Why should the factory fail them now?

The fact that the Maktoums had apparently not bid on the Nijinsky colt encouraged speculation that a truce had been agreed between the two camps. Particularly in view of a much publicised visit to Dubai by Sangster, O'Brien and Magnier (with 'Fatty' Benson along to break the ice and tell the funny stories), as guests of Sheikh Mohammed in the early part of that year. The visit yielded a lot of cosy photographs of them all getting along famously over the fruit cocktails and the resulting communiqués were mostly full of benign statements about how they weren't enemies at all but friendly rivals and about how each side welcomed the competitive presence of the other for the sake of the market and so on. If Sangster really had harboured any thoughts of floating back to the Sheikh the tentative partnership proposals that the Sheikh had tried to make to him three years before, they would've stood little chance of success. Sheikh Mohammed did come in as a shareholder in a couple of O'Brien's 1984 Keeneland yearlings, including an $8,250,000 Northern Dancer colt called Imperial Falcon, who won two small races in Ireland in 1986 before being whisked away to stud. And Ballydoyle's good miler, Fair Judgement, would run in the Sheikh's colours in 1987 and 1988. But in all seriousness, the Maktoums had no need of partners or syndicates by now. They could buy all the horses they wanted to, straight out and in their own right.

And besides, the results of the 1986 flat-racing season were a poor reflection of O'Brien's genius as a trainer. A virus swept through the Tipperary yard with devastating results. Seattle Dancer, the thirteen-million-dollar yearling, was unable to run as a two-year-old. The 2,000 Guineas colt Tate Gallery was a washout at Newmarket and then Wise Counsellor, another son of Alleged, running in the name of Stavros Niarchos, finished last of all in the Derby. As Pat Eddery dismounted afterwards he was wearing that ominous look of restless disenchantment reminiscent of Piggott after the Monteverdi fiasco in 1980.

The Maktoum Brothers gained yet more big-race successes in 1986 with Sure Blade, Sonic Lady, Ajdal and Green Desert but the season belonged to the Saudi Arabian, Khalid Abdulla, and to his brilliant bay three-year-old colt, Dancing Brave, who won every big European race he contested except, sadly, the one that still counted the most, the Derby. In spite of his Breeders Cup defeat he retired to stud at the end of the year in a blaze of glory and at a comparatively modest valuation of fourteen million pounds. As he was a grandson of Northern Dancer it was perceived to be an outstanding coup of Abdulla's to have beaten off the syndication offers from America and kept him as a potential flagship stallion for the European breeding industry into the 1990s. The situation was made that much more poignant for the Ballydoyle and Coolmore team in that the stud which bought him was the Sheikh's now rapidly expanding Dalham Hall at Newmarket.

For Robert Sangster, still rueing the loss of Golden Fleece, there were problems too with the stud career of El Gran Senor. He had apparently experienced great difficulties in getting his mares in foal at Windfields Farm. The situation got so bad that a majority of the American shareholders in the horse decided to cut their losses and take the insurance money. The 1984 2,000 Guineas winner, now primarily the property of Sangster, O'Brien, Magnier and the insurance companies, left Windfields to try and redeem himself under the Coolmore banner at their American base, Ashford Stud, Kentucky. Of course El Gran Senor had never gone through the sales ring but the chances of being able to outbid the Maktoums to buy another like him, yet alone another as costly as Seattle Dancer, in the near future, did not look promising. Stavros Niarchos had decided that he wanted out of the Ballydoyle syndicate. Officially this was just because he wanted to concentrate on the yearlings he could breed from his own broodmares and had decided to confine his racing interests to France as it was easier for him to get there to see his horses run. Unofficially it was implied that Niarchos, disgruntled at not having had an English classic winner yet in his own colours, believed that the heyday of the O'Brien/Sangster set-up was over and that in the sales ring at least the Arabs were unbeatable.

Pat Eddery had clearly decided the same thing. In the wake of his triumphant association with Dancing Brave it was announced that he was leaving Sangster to take up a thumping new two-million-pound contract to ride all of Khalid Abdulla's horses in England and, when available, in Ireland and France too. As if all of these reversals weren't enough there was one other massive overreaching disaster that threatened to engulf the Pools magnate in 1986: Manton.

It was in 1983 that the then thirty-two-year-old Michael Dickinson, an astonishingly gifted young steeplechaser trainer from Yorkshire, trained the first five horses home in the Gold Cup at Cheltenham. It was an unprecedented achievement that not even Vincent O'Brien had been able to pull off and nobody who was there ever expects to see it happen again. Most top trainers would consider themselves lucky if they were able to keep even two horses sound long enough to just run in the Gold Cup let alone dominate jump-racing's premier event so emphatically.

Towards the end of the 1983 National Hunt season, the racing world was stunned, enthralled and in the case of some of the more diehard jumping enthusiasts, bitterly disappointed, to hear that Dickinson had accepted a spectacular offer from Sangster to become his new private trainer on the flat in Britain. Sangster's principal representative in that area up to this point had been the Lambourn-based Barry Hills, one of the few really successful trainers to have begun his career as a stable lad.

What Sangster proposed for Dickinson was a new dream training establishment to be built around the old racing centre at Whatcombe in Berkshire. When the Whatcombe deal didn't quite work out, Sangster turned his attention instead to the equally famous Manton estate in Wiltshire not far from the town of Marlborough. Dickinson would have the pick of Sangster's Swettenham Stud Company's homebred yearlings to train and the very best facilities and staff that money could buy. Even though he'd never trained flat racehorses in his life before, Sangster appeared convinced that this tanned, neurotic perfectionist, with his gauche smile like a kid in an Anchor butter advert, was already the next Vincent O'Brien. Dickinson was to have two and a half seasons to break himself in during which time he would travel round the world, observing and learning from famous and experienced masters of the craft like O'Brien, Charlie Whittingham and Sangster's greatly respected Australian man, Colin Hayes.

By the time the supremely modern stables, gallops and staff accommodation had been completed at Manton, the original budget of some £4–8 million had swollen to over £14 million. But when the whole complex was finally unveiled in the spring of 1986, even the most beery and boorish members of the racing press were left gasping with admiration. The training grounds alone, complete with two all-weather gallops and miles of different exercise runs, were like those of no other stable in Britain. And the uniform high-tech approach to everything from veterinary care to stable security seemed to be taking racehorse training into the Space Age. Not surprisingly, Dickinson looked like a child let loose in Hamleys with £5,000 worth of gift vouchers. Why fear the Arabs now? Michael Dickinson and Manton would surely be Robert Sangster's ace in the hole?

What actually happened at Manton over the next seven months was a scenario of truly tragic proportions. Dickinson managed to train just four winners, and at the end of the season Sangster terminated his contract. The Manton dream appeared to be in ruins. Over-budget, over-ambitious and now just four winners. How do you explain that to the bank manager? The merely envious revelled in the whole débâcle. Dickinson, it was said, had been trying to run before he could walk. All kinds of fancy forensic tests and theories of training had been indulged in but to little effect. Whatever their value to third-season steeplechasers their application to highly strung thoroughbred two-year-olds seemed to have been disastrous. Horses had broken down. Promising and potentially immensely valuable juveniles were running once and then deteriorating instead of going forward. It had begun with Dickinson not attending in person to see his very first two-year-old runner, Veryan Bay, fail to deliver, up at Sangster's local meeting at Chester in May. Then in June, the four-year-old middle-distance colt, Kirmann, bought to give the yard some ammunition in the older horses' pattern events, finished tailed off at Royal Ascot. Finally at the back end of the year, seven horses all ran most disappointingly at far-flung but mainly lowly destinations such as Hamilton Park. Sangster decided that he could wait no longer.

It was suggested that Dickinson had become almost pathologically impossible to communicate with, that even Sangster, who was paying all the bills, had been left in the dark as to what was going on and that the young trainer had shrouded his stable and everyone who worked there in an unnecessary blanket of security. There was also the implication that there had been a fundamental gulf if not clash between the personalities of the two men. That Dickinson, intense, private and early to bed had been out of step with the high-rolling, high-octane life-style of his boss. Not everybody, including some observers not usually hostile to Sangster's operation, quite saw it that way.

There were plenty of racing professionals, especially in the North of England, who had developed considerable respect and even affection for Dickinson during his phenomenally successful career over the sticks. They felt no inclination to sneer at him now for his fascination with pioneering training methods or for his personal desire to eschew the social merry-go-round of many less intelligent and less successful trainers. They also felt that Dickinson had been put in an impossible position. Vincent O'Brien had been nearly sixty, and with four Derby winners and a more than thirty-year training career behind him, when he was first entrusted with Sangster's million-dollar investments. To expect Dickinson to come up a winner first time round with a bunch of beautifully bred but backward two-year-olds by largely new and unproven stallions like Golden Fleece, was surely asking too much. And if Sangster was really such a clued-up commercial operator, why hadn't he considered Dickinson's character and temperament more carefully before he'd set him up in business in the first place? Why hadn't he employed an older and more experienced hand to help see him through the first few years and a full-time personal assistant of the kind John Leat is to Sheikh Mohammed, to deal with communications with both the owner himself and the media? As for the life-style gap, that seemed the most improbable problem of all. Surely you didn't spend more than £14 million on a new dream training centre and then sack the trainer because he didn't have a bottle of vintage Krug on ice every time you called? What were you looking for anyway? A gifted horseman or a barman?

The eventual terms on which the two men parted company were financially generous to Dickinson but there was plenty of pain involved none the less. For both protagonists the whole experience was something of a humiliation. Dickinson, the youthful genius, had fallen on his face. Sadly he turned his back on Britain and with some bitterness left for a new training career in America. As for Sangster he'd played the big shot, the Hollywood producer, the Irving Thalberg of the turf. He'd made the grand financial gesture and it had blown up in his face.

One name mentioned as a possible replacement for Dickinson was his Australian mentor, Colin Hayes. Only then Hayes won the Melbourne Cup for, guess, Hamdan Al Maktoum. Jolly old Hamdan sent him a new batch of yearlings and after that there could be no question of his leaving the southern hemisphere for Wiltshire. Sangster's eventual choice brought him full circle. It was to be Barry Hills, the man who'd already trained for him for more than fourteen years and who might have been seriously upstaged if Dickinson had actually pulled it off. Hills, a hard but extremely professional little man with plenty of energy for the late nights and considerable enthusiasm for the betting ring, was a million miles away from his predecessor in temperament and style.

If Sangster had a new trainer at Manton in 1987, Vincent O'Brien had a new jockey at Ballydoyle. Pat Eddery's replacement was the twenty-five-year-old Texan, Cash Asmussen, who had been riding in France since 1983. In that time he'd won the Cravache D'Or, the French jockeys' championship, twice, on the first occasion for François Boutin whose principal patron was of course Niarchos. Boutin had been largely instrumental in bringing the American over to Europe and had not exactly been delighted when Asmussen left him for rival George Mikhalides in 1986. Now he was moving again. The jockey's view of that was that he was entirely entitled to do so. Asmussen, Cash by name and Cash by nature, had a very confident, you might say too confident, view of his worth and his ability and was remarkably articulate in a frankly self-centred sort of way. This self-possessed character seemed unlikely to be the perfect foil to the quiet but considerable O'Brien, himself not used to being contradicted.

Asmussen's year at Ballydoyle was as in and out as O'Brien's year in general. Entitled, a son of Mill Reef out of a Sangster mare, was placed in two classics and finished second to Triptych in the Phoenix Champion Stakes but he was unable to win a Group One race himself. Seattle Dancer ran five times, winning two small classic trials in Ireland and running unplaced in the French Derby before going out with a second in the Grand Prix de Paris at Longchamp where he finished in front of the subsequent Arc winner, Trempolino. Only nobody appreciated the value of the form at the time and Seattle Dancer never raced again. He's now at stud in America. Bluebird's victory in the King's Stand Stakes at Royal Ascot in June was O'Brien's first in an English Group One contest since 1984. And of course at the end of the season, Caerwent, the two-year-old son of Caerleon in whom Sangster had a share, won the National Stakes at The Curragh, thus becoming a genuine 2,000 Guineas possibility for 1988. But not everyone was happy with Cash's riding.

Although it was apparent that the syndicate were possibly suffering from their lack of success, compared with the Maktoums, at the 1985 and 1986 yearling sales, there was still a feeling that the Texan wasn't quite up to it. He had an abundance of style and finesse but it was considered that he frequently misjudged the pace of English and Irish races and, most crucially of all, that he was insufficiently effective in a finish. There can be no more demanding audience than a large crowd of Irish racegoers who have stuffed their punts on a short-priced favourite and who expect to see it win even if some of them seem prepared for it to be thrashed and filleted in the process. That wasn't Asmussen's style at all. But his consideration and tenderness with some horses looked like an unfortunate tendency to come down on the wrong side of a carefully balanced margin of error, when he'd get beaten for the second or third time on some expensively bred animal for whom the syndicate desperately needed a little black type for the stud book.

At the end of the year Asmussen was out. The official explanation was that both parties had decided not to take up the second year of the contract. It was said that the Texan felt that the travelling schedule between Ballydoyle, London, Paris and back again was more onerous than he'd expected or desired. Privately O'Brien admitted to a personality clash. A majority of the Irish racing public scarcely seemed heartbroken to see the American leave, particularly the ones who'd been singing 'California Here I Come' around the unsaddling enclosure after he'd ridden three losing favourites in one afternoon at Phoenix Park. In fact Cash returned to Paris to ride for André Fabre, his fourth contract in five years. Meanwhile Ballydoyle had its third rider in three years. But there was to be no question of Steve Cauthen leaving Henry Cecil as Pat Eddery had left Basil Fawlty. The new man was to be the quietly professional Ulsterman, John Reid, a jockey worth every cent of his retainer, but hardly a megastar like the previous three glamorous occupants of the job. Was the syndicate's lustre diminishing in the eyes of the top international riders of the world? There were certainly a few rumblings that the genius of the trainer could conceivably be on the wane.

If the verdict was still out on any revival of Ballydoyle's fortunes, the revival that Manton experienced, under just one season of Hills' stewardship, was a real triumph. From four winners in Dickinson's year they shot up to 101 in 1987. By no means all of these victories were credited to Sangster as Hills brought a fair number of horses and owners with him from his old yard at South Bank and there was a much better mixture than before of older horses, handicappers and early two-year-olds to balance the top home-breds.

The original big three in the Ballydoyle syndicate were also buoyed up by the achievements of the young Coolmore stallions, Lomond and Caerleon, whose first crop did so well on the racecourse that the pair of them ended up first and second in the first-season sires table.

The truth was though, that whatever attempts the men from Ballydoyle were making to re-establish themselves on something like their old scale they kept bumping into the Arabs around every corner. They'd been there first or quicker or in greater numbers and most particularly with more, with never-ending sums of money. Could Sangster keep abreast any longer? Some whispers, that were becoming loud rumbles in the financial markets, suggested that he couldn't. In September of 1987 an article appeared in *Business* magazine implying that Sangster was on a losing streak. That he'd run down the family business and borrowed hugely to try and compete against the Maktoums, that he'd become desperately overstretched and that now that bloodstock prices had declined since the early and mid-eighties he was going to have to sell Vernons just to stay afloat. The man himself strenuously denied such a fundamental weakness but he did sell Vernons none the less.

In January of 1988, Thompson T. Line, a sort of mini Hanson Trust, bought the pools company for ninety million pounds. Some city sages reckoned that Sangster had got himself a good deal. Some suggested that any business with that kind of regular guaranteed cashflow had to be worth more, especially perhaps to a bookmaking firm. As he'd become an Isle of Man resident since the late seventies, Sangster had no capital gains tax to pay on his money. It was said that ten million was going into trust for his children and no less than forty million pounds to settle bloodstock loans that had been secured against Vernons. Sangster insisted that the two sides of his business had never been interlinked and that the sale had no connection with the strength or otherwise of his racing operation. He pointed to his continuing huge investments in racing worldwide, especially in Australia, and insisted that he'd been bowing out of the sales ring anyway due to his home-breds coming on tap. So in that case why had he sold? He and his sons, he said, no longer wished to continue running Vernons as a family concern based in Liverpool. The timing had seemed right and his son Guy, who worked as an investment analyst for Thompson, believed it was a good offer. No more to it than that. So what of the fifty million left out of the deal? Was this perhaps to be used for one final stake, for one last desperate bid to wrest control back from the Arabs?

The idea, popular in the late seventies and early eighties, that

Sangster was just some sort of ruthless businessman, an ice-cold manipulator of the bloodstock market only in it for profit, had never quite squared with his cavalier lifestyle and relish for the sociable accompaniments to big-time racing. For if the fourteen years of the Ballydoyle syndicate have proved anything it has to be that Robert Edmund Sangster is quite some gambler. A man in the grip, albeit willingly and not so far with really fatal or destructive consequences, of a glorious obsession. It was only due to the genius of Vincent O'Brien that he walked away from the table a winner so many times in those first nine years but it's the kind of luck that rarely holds for ever. The really hard-headed big-business dogs of the world, fully aware of fiascos like the Snaafi Dancer purchase, just don't invest their money in racehorses because it's far too risky a proposition. (The smart ones, like Cyril Stein, become bookmakers.) O'Brien made it work better than anyone could have imagined possible just as Wayne Lukas has been making it work for Gene Klein but both Paulson and the Maktoums have discovered on numerous occasions that you can plough in millions and still get a turkey. The Arabs, and particularly the Maktoums, are so rich that racing as a luxury pastime need hold no limits for them, and that's why they'll always win in the end and why they'll always outpoint the gambler whose capital is mortgaged three times over and whose cash must eventually run out. But for 1988 at least, Sangster did have a new stake to play with, even though he couldn't keep it all to himself. And it was one which seemed as if it just might inspire Vincent O'Brien – now awarded an honorary doctorate by the National University of Ireland – to a late-career flourish every bit as productive as that associated with W. B. Yeats in the mid to late 1930s.

Classic Thoroughbreds is a public company and was formed during 1987. It was largely devised by the thirty-six-year-old Dermot Desmond, a partner in Dillon and Waldron, Chairman of the National and City brokers group and the star skills player of the Dublin stockbroking world. With so many new capitalist endeavours seeking institutional finance, Desmond thought it was the ideal moment to try the same thing with racehorses. He approached O'Brien with the idea, and the trainer was immediately impressed.

Vincent, as befits the sole trainer of the horses, is the company chairman and owns 12.3 per cent of the share capital. Sangster, John Magnier and the immensely successful Irish businessman, Michael Smurfit (who chairs the company's finance committee), own 7.8 per cent each and the Cork cattle baron, John Horgan, has 3.2 per cent. Between them these five sank three million Irish punts into the new project. On the strength of their involvement, especially Smurfit's and O'Brien's, Desmond was able to raise a further seven million Irish punts from the institutions on the condition that the company go public to make the shares readily marketable and to provide a broad base for the equity. There are now some 2,500 shareholders and the vast majority of them have invested less than £700. The first share issue price in October 1987 was 30p. The company is liable to the same brutal mechanisms of the stock market as any other quoted stock and, unless those shares appreciate by about 60 per cent in the next four years, it will probably go out of business. To succeed, it is depending on Vincent O'Brien buying quality yearlings at the right price and turning a sufficient number of them into Group or even classic race-winning horses with breeding potential. The same old story but with a new cover. Whether the scheme would even have seen the light of day if Niarchos hadn't pulled out of the old syndicate is impossible to say.

At Keeneland in July 1987, O'Brien bought four yearlings for the new business, including two by Northern Dancer, one of them a full brother to Secreto, for a grand total of $3,204,000. Interests in five more were purchased at the Fasig Tipton sale at Saratoga in August and by the end of the sale season in October some £7,500,000 of the original capital had gone, topping up the shopping list to thirty-eight yearlings in all. This would mean the trainer starting the 1988 season with a string of seventy horses of which forty would be two-year-olds, many more than in the past. It was all a long way from the Ballydoyle paradise of twelve years before. In place of that élite syndicate of owners, O'Brien now had two and a half thousand people, including lots of little people, to whom he was technically responsible. And he was going to be particularly responsible to the stockmarket and to the new company's accountants. Every shareholder had the right to subscribe for one share, for every two they held, at the original offer price of 30p. This right was due to expire on 30 June 1988. But no shareholder would be interested in taking up that right if the market value of the shares was less than 30p. To avoid that happening might not the financial advisers start pressurising O'Brien to get a few early season two-year-old winners on the board before the deadline? But how could the maestro, famously patient and unhurried with his horses, ever tolerate that? In the past decade most of his classic-winning colts hadn't even set foot on a racecourse before the end of July.

There were certainly enormous financial pressures for O'Brien to make the new company a success. He had an option to take up three million shares at 40p at any time before 30 September 1992. The other four had similar options at 50p. Down in the Golden Vale, there was a feeling that in spite of his traditional eagerness to have a piece of the action, the great trainer was quite motivated enough to make a success of this new venture, if only to prove that he was not yet a back-number and that there was still one priceless racing brain that the Maktoums had failed to acquire.

It was a rich irony that Sangster and O'Brien, once so resented by the establishment for being too successful, were now being willed on by the same observers to take back a share of racing's spoils from the Arabs. Those same Arabs who in turn had been welcomed as Sangster's nemesis five years before, but were now perceived to be so all-embracing in their designs that it was they who had become the enemy. Certainly by the outset of 1988 the vast juggernaut that these latest Blue Grass Emperors had constructed was beginning to display such an insatiable appetite that it would surely eventually consume everything in its path.

From the lowliest Grade Four track to Ascot, Newmarket and York there would be at least one Arab-owned runner on every card throughout the 1988 British flat-racing season and it wouldn't be more than a 3-1 shot against any one of them being a winner. In 1977 Tom 'Big Spender' Jones had forty-three horses in training of which more than twenty were older horses and jumpers and most of his owners were British and American. For the 1988 season Jones would have 106 horses in training, none of them jumpers and 85 per cent of them owned by Hamdan Al Maktoum. Jeremy Tree and Paul Cole (whose Whatcombe yard is owned by the Saudi Arabian, Fahd Salman) would have a ratio of three Arab-owned horses to the rest, while for Michael Stoute and Big Spender's one-time assistant, Alec Stewart, the balance would be roughly fifty-fifty. One third of Cecil's string would be Arab-owned and one quarter of Dunlop's and Dick Hern's. All told, fourteen trainers – eight of them in the top twelve for prize money won in 1987 – would be training roughly 1,500 horses between them, of which 630, or 40 per cent, would be Arab-owned, and owned too by only about a dozen different personalities. In 1987 the five leading Arab owners won about £2.4 million worth of prize money in Britain out of a total pool of £12 million. Yet considering they owned around 20 per cent of the horses in training, most of them aimed at the best and best endowed races, a prize money scoop of less than 20 per cent was the least they might have hoped for.

In truth, the big Arab players have as much as anything proved what Sangster and O'Brien knew all too well from the outset, that in thoroughbred flat racing, money alone cannot guarantee you success. It's not as if Snaafi Dancer has been their only expensive failure. Whatever happened to Lahab ($1 million in 1981), Hidden Destiny ($2.2 million in 1982), Gallant Archer ($4.1 million in 1983), Amjaad ($6.5 million in 1984), Laa Etaab ($7 million in 1985) and Northern State ($3.6 million in 1986)? Sheikh Mohammed bought all of them except for Laa Etaab who was technically knocked down to Sheikh Ahmed. $24.6 million for that bunch and about one win between them.

The Maktoums may have won numerous prestigious races but they've done surprisingly badly in the classics themselves. Up to the start of the 1988 season Sheikh Mohammed's four English classic victories had all been with fillies and three of them had been recorded by the same horse, Oh So Sharp, in 1985. Maktoum Al Maktoum had enjoyed just three classic wins, Ahmed none and Hamdan, in spite of a consistently huge investment with 'Big Spender', still had only that one second place to show for it with Al Bahathri in 1985.

Khalid Abdulla, though still with just the two classic winners, Known Fact and Dancing Brave, had carried off many other top Group races, some of them with horses he'd bought into during their racing careers. Abdulla's purchases had been generally more careful and less expensive than the Maktoums – he paid $950,000 for Rainbow Quest but only $200,000 for Dancing Brave – but even so these Arab buyers between them, coming in on top of the commercial trends initiated by Sangster, had caused a considerable inflation of bloodstock prices worldwide with the middle- to lower-range owners and trainers finding it very hard to keep up. Few of the Arab purchases were going to Northern stables, and Northern trainers were beginning to bitterly resent the fact that the scale of the Arabs' operations meant that they were often coming up against million-dollar yearlings from some of the big Southern yards in even small maiden races at Hamilton Park and Carlisle. New races, special auction and claiming races, were having to be framed to exclude the most expensive horses. But what of the small commercial breeders? They were finding that they had virtually no market left any more at all.

The fat cats amongst the American Blue Grass Emperors and

chief sales consignors to Keeneland and elsewhere in America knew that it was now the Maktoums who virtually dominated their sales market. Their acquisitions accounted for some 30 per cent of the gross at Keeneland in 1986 and 1987 when they bought the most expensive yearlings of the year both in Kentucky and at Tattersalls in Europe. This relentless appetite was helping in real terms to maintain prices on a par with the spectacularly high levels of the early eighties. But there were still many Americans who had spent massively in the boom era to breed their mares to the most fashionable stallions when those stallions' covering fees and yearling sales' averages were at record levels. Only now the progeny of some of those matings were coming on to the market several years later when yearling prices had dipped considerably and in some cases, and unless their lot's conformation was as impressive as its pedigree, the consigners were taking a bath.

It was exactly their fear over what would happen if the Arabs should ever pull out that had convinced even the most initially reluctant Emperors, like Seth Hancock, of the importance of new market-stimulating events like the Breeders Cup. And although it seemed a sure bet that the Maktoums would always be in the market, up to a point, for the very best yearlings on offer, it was also abundantly clear that their own private breeding plans were now equally important to them. And as the home-breds increased so, like Sangster, the sales purchases would presumably decline.

In 1979, two years after Sheikh Mohammed's colours were first registered with Weatherby's, racing's civil service, the Sheikh bought Aston Upthorpe Stud in Oxfordshire. This is now the base for Maktoum Al Maktoum's dual Leger winner, Touching Wood, who comes under the management of Maktoum's Gainsborough Stud near Newbury, which was the family's second stud purchase in 1981. Gainsborough's American farm at Versailles, Kentucky is the stud base of Shadeed.

It was in 1982 that Sheikh Mohammed bought Dalham Hall from Jim Phillips. The bloodstock that went with the deal, fifteen mares, their yearlings and foals, included Oh So Fair, dam of Oh So Sharp. Phillips's veteran stallion Great Nephew, sire of Grundy and Shergar, was already *in situ* at Dalham Hall. Touching Wood joined him for a season and then the controversial Shareef Dancer went there in 1984. The next acquisition was the Aga Khan's 1979 French Derby winner, Top Ville, who was to have been sold to the Americans and who had produced four Group One winners in his first four crops. Then at the end of 1986 came Dancing Brave, a remarkably modest syndication at £14 million and an appropriate amalgamation 'Mafia'-style of the two most powerful Arab interests, Abdulla and the Maktoums'. In 1987 they acquired the Derby winner Reference Point who had been owned by a senior Jockey Club member, Louis Freedman, in partnership with the Derby sponsor, Sir Gordon White. As a son of the most favoured of all European stallions, Mill Reef, Reference Point would give Dalham Hall an invaluable balance to the Northern Dancer horses, Shareef Dancer, and 1987's champion sprinter, Adjal, who had joined this select band at the end of the 1987 campaign.

In 1983 Hamdan Al Maktoum acquired Derrinstown Stud in County Kildare in Ireland which had formerly been the property of Arkle's owner, the Duchess of Westminster. Wassl was installed as Derrinstown's first resident stallion. In 1984 Sheikh Mohammed added Woodpark Stud in County Meath and the Rutland Stud in Newmarket. In 1985 Hamdan bought Shadwell Stud in Norfolk and made it the home of his July Cup winner Green Desert who was by Northern Dancer's sensational American-based son, Danzig. Finally, for now at least, Sheikh Mohammed acquired Kildangan Stud in Kildare in 1986 and put in his Group Two mile winner, Sure Blade, as the resident stallion there. But the Maktoum interests don't end with these nine stallions. There are a further eleven wholly or partly run by the family's management teams. This is the ironic aspect of so much big-race prize money going into so few hands, as those hands are exactly the ones that need it the least, as for them it is the breeding side of racing that represents the real target and the big pay-off.

Khalid Abdulla, who to date has raced more frequently and more successfully in America than the Maktoums, has two English stud bases. Juddmonte Farms in Berkshire is the home of his fifty European-based brood-mares and the 360-acre Banstead Manor Stud near Newmarket is the home of Rainbow Quest. Abdulla and the Maktoums have both steadily built up a heady collection of brood-mares with both impeccable breeding as well as Group One-winning form on the track. Many of them, such as Pebbles, were bought from other owners during their racing careers, although the 1986 1,000 Guineas and Oaks winner, Midway Lady, bought for $3.3 million by Hamdan in November of that year, was purchased after she had retired.

The ultimate implication of these dynastic monopolies is that although men like Sangster and the Sheikh will always be interested in the very best yearlings in the commercial sales ring, more and more of their battles on the track in future will be fought out with home-bred horses. In that context the Coolmore and Dalham Hall stallions are the new generation of modernised weapons in flat racing's theatre of war. For the ordinary racing public the spectacle should be thrilling while it lasts but between Sangster and the sheikhs, mutually complimentary but deadly serious rivals, and the other top guns, like Abdulla and the Aga Khan, big-time flat racing in Britain, Ireland, France and America will continue as a decorous game to discover and test the best horses in the world at a ruthlessly high level of competition; with the strong surviving and the weak ending up with a little operation and a new career running over hurdles at Fontwell Park.

It may be eleven years since The Minstrel's Derby victory set the Ballydoyle syndicate on their way, but the character of his principal owner, the man who initiated racing's revolution, remains something of an enigma, even to his friends. Some of Sangster's public utterances on turf matters have made him seem thunderingly dull and unimaginative. Comparing making money out of owning racehorses with trying to achieve the same ends from building office-blocks was hardly reminiscent of the immortal spirit of the great George Lambton. Neither did it sound like the manifesto of a man daring enough to challenge the generations-old orthodoxy of the Jockey Club, of which he was even elected a member in the end.

Shy and naturally reticent, Sangster has never been the type of owner to gush effusively with Channel 4's Derek Thompson as his classic winners jog back to the unsaddling enclosure. Even so, his alternately mumbled and tight-lipped comments, worlds away from the thoughtful, analytical observations of a D. Wayne Lukas, have scarcely done justice to the scale and *élan* of his empire-building or to the many famous men and horses who've been involved in its creation. And Sangster's own generous, expansive life-style, encompassing three wives, five children, houses in Barbados and Australia as well as the Isle of Man, and many famous parties, heavy sessions and long nights from Las Vegas to Mayfair – with a constant supporting cast of 'celebrities' from all walks of life, some grand, some tacky, but all of them a gossip columnist's dream – has always marked him out as a rather different kind of Blue Grass Emperor from the older generation of hard-boiled turf plutocrats like Engelhard and Bunker Hunt.

If there is indeed a touch of Gatsby's book on etiquette and manners in Wayne Lukas's 'Daily Dozen' pinned up on his office wall, it would be a fine, romantic notion to see in Sangster just a hint of Gatsby the social swell and party-giver who occasionally retreats from the centre of the action to brood on a private dream. Only the green light shining for him is not at the end of Daisy Buchanan's dock. It's the metaphorical light of Vincent O'Brien's Ballydoyle stable and of the Coolmore stallion barns out there across the Irish Sea. Can either the eternal seventy-one-year-old Tipperary genius or the twenty-years-younger Barry Hills, training the home-bred colts at Manton, somehow provide him with just one more winner of the most important horse-race of them all. The one at Epsom Downs?

9 : The Big Touch

The young men (well, no longer quite so young actually, in fact, hovering on the grey and fattening stage) in the beat-up old Ford Sierra, glide up on to level five of the multi-storey car-park behind Purley station. So far it's been a dull and rather cold June morning but the sun begins to shine as these two well-coiffeured and well-groomed gents check their belongings, lock up their car and then head for the lift and the Exit signs for British Rail. Unfortunately they go down a level too far and have to make an unscheduled detour via the take-away sandwiches department of an adjoining supermarket. Heads turn and eyes flicker in their direction. It's not just their shades and their smart shirts and ties that attract attention. It's the grey morning-coats, waistcoats and trousers coupled with the grey top-hats carried, necessarily, due to the high embarrassment factor, somewhere down behind the right shin. 'We're just a couple of prats/In a couple of hired top-hats.' This would not be entirely fair as at least one of the fellows owns every inch of his kit although he has had to adjust the buttons on his waistcoat to cope with his expanding girth.

The two chaps turn right on to the High Street past the Abbey National and make a quick raid on a NatWest cash dispenser, gratefully pocketing the notes before alarm bells ring in head office and a top team of managerial hitmen descend from the skies to tear up their Access cards on the spot. They then cut back along an insalubrious footpath that leads to a quiet back-street of thirties pebble-dash villas at the end of which can be seen the welcoming red and white signs for BR Purley. A train is rattling into the station even as they arrive. The tickets are soon bought and before they can even get the words out, 'Excuse me. Can you tell us the time of the next service to . . .' a scruffy and unsavoury-looking porter is bundling them towards the underpass. 'This way, guv. Platform Three. Just leaving.' The signal's green, the whistle blows but they dash up the steps in the nick of time and are helped, or rather propelled, by another British Rail official through an open carriage-door. They cannon into the one hundred or so other standing passengers who have already been piled in on to the completely filled seats. Then as the train gathers pace they look back sheepishly at their predominantly, not to say exclusively, proletarian fellow travellers. ''Ere, mate,' smirks a crop-haired youth with a scar above his eye. 'Are you going to the races?' The low-bellied laughter of the lads with their designer cardies and their lager cans swirls cruelly around the carriage. The chaps, wondering whether they will arrive at the course with their hats and their trousers intact, blush, curse inwardly and wish that they'd gone by helicopter. 'I bet Robert Sangster doesn't arrive by train,' mutters one of them bitterly.

As the special proceeds to stop at a succession of improbably suburban halts with names like Smitham and Reedham Junction, the misery is compounded. The complicated ruse of driving from London down to Purley was supposed to have avoided all this. Cut out the waiting. Get there in comfort. For whether or not the Derby is still the greatest race in the world, just getting there before tea-time is still one of the biggest headaches of the smart man's racing year. There has been a nine-mile tailback on the M25 since 9.15. Yet how on earth can British Railways, with months of advanced knowledge that up to a quarter of a million people will be heading for Epsom Downs on the first Wednesday in June, run no direct trains, expresses or big-race specials, but only the normal stopping service of superannuated cattle-trucks into which the passengers are jammed in a mid-morning replay of commuter horror.

On arriving at Tattenham Corner, which is literally the end of the line, the fellows discover that the station has been decked out like a scene from *Thomas The Tank Engine*. Incredible though it may seem to those racegoers who are just disembarking from the 11.20 slow from London Bridge, no less a top racing person than Her Majesty the Queen is also arriving at the 109th Derby by train. Royal train naturally. And no stopping at Purley for her. In a moment of magnanimity she probably pencilled down a tip for the big one and tossed it through the window on to the platform at Smitham for the benefit of her devoted followers. At Tattenham Corner one whole platform, admittedly there are only four of them, has been laid aside for her convenience. There's a red carpet, lots of policemen and numerous British Rail officials, some in old-fashioned braided railwaymen's jackets that they must have borrowed from the Orient Express and one, a Mr Smee from Network SouthEast, in a bowlerhat and a pin-stripe suit. The Queen, no doubt anxious to fill in her jackpot tickets, wastes little time over handshakes and prolonged chats with her loyal NUR-member subjects. A little less than two and a half minutes after arriving, she and her mother and daughter are on their way down to the racecourse in an enormously comfortable-looking black state limousine.

For all the other punters – toffs and spivs, proles and swells – a short walk is now required. About fifty yards if they're heading straight for the downs and about four and a half furlongs if they're off to the Members' entrance. But all of them, the moment that they leave the confines of the station forecourt, have to take a deep breath and then plunge into a shimmering flock of arriving cars and coaches and taxis and open-top buses, some filled with wine-bar Sloanes, some with lads or Hoorays and some with old South London pub regulars. There are mounted policemen and gypsy caravans and gypsies selling sprigs of heather and sideshows and picnics and tottering heels and tottering hats and nearly blown-away top-hats and rows of touts and scalpers and even one or two pretenders to the throne of the late great Prince Monolulu, selling tips and selections in a closed envelope. The air is permeated with the smell of frying hot-dogs and hamburgers. Away to the right, adjacent to the local Berni Inn, the wild hurdy-gurdy atmosphere of the funfair is in full swing. Rick Astley's voice, turned up and amplified badly at full decibel, cuts across the sound of the car horns, of the shouting souvenir-sellers and of the hundreds and thousands of excited and expectant conversations taking place on all sides. And out there somewhere in the middle is the quite extraordinary switchback racetrack itself. The actual historic grass of Epsom Downs. You can't see much of it now because of the virtual army of beer tents and marquees that will obscure any view of almost half the race unless you're watching it from high up in the top of the stands. Epsom town is out of sight. So is Lord Derby's old house, The Oaks, at Woodmansterne. In the distance are the blue-green hills of Surrey. London is some eleven miles away to the north-east.

This largest of all racing crowds, this 'sea of humanity', which is what even the most original sports-reporter will be calling them by the end of the afternoon, is here to take part in a vast populist tradition that has managed to retain an almost pre-war, belt-loosening, let-yourself-go, bank-holiday, end-of-the-pier atmosphere right on into the era of Next and home computers and Perrier water and low-cholesterol vegetable burgers and safe sex. Modern British flat racing may be hard and rich and dominated by the Maktoums and their million-dollar yearlings but they are only one part of the picture at Epsom on Derby Day. It's a world away from Newmarket and the 1,000 Guineas. Seven-eighths of the punters present barely know or understand the first thing about the horses running in the big race but they do know one thing, possibly passed on by parents and grandparents over several generations. Epsom Downs. Horses. Derby Day. It means a flutter. A bottle of stout. A bottle of bubbly. Slap and tickle. A handsome spread. A little of what you fancy does you good and the people love a lord, oh yes we do, God bless you, sir.

It's like Brighton, the whole town not just the races, must have been when Graham Greene imagined Pinkie, plotting the downfall of Colleoni's gang, while eating a fish-and-chip tea on the Palace Pier. For anyone who's ever despaired of catching a final departing glimpse of that England in all its gothic horror and garish vitality, bottled beer and jam tarts, whelks and mussels, princes and showgirls, forelock-tugging *politesse* and cut-throat razor menace, then Derby Day is the place to see it.

Epsom has always been a villains' course anyway. It was one warm Saturday back before the war when the police finally caught up with Dodger Mullins (a grim, thirties psychopath, who was one of the childhood heroes of the Kray twins) and settled their scores with him with knuckledusters outside Epsom Downs station. Derby Sabini's racecourse gang used to make their biggest profit of the year at Epsom and the Krays themselves were employed as minders to guard Jack Spot's bookmaking pitches at the spring meeting in 1955. In the minds of many of the professionals and serious enthusiasts turning up at the Derby in 1988 the modern racecourse villains carry briefcases and calculators instead of razors and knives. They are of course the Big Four (soon to become the Big Three) High Street bookmaking firms.

When Harold Macmillan's Conservative government licensed off-course betting shops in 1960, it all seemed to be entirely consistent with the rest of their HP, buy a car and a washing machine, 'You never had it so good', commercial television, consumer boom. Nearly thirty years later, many people feel that they and racing's rulers missed a golden opportunity. Up until that point, British attitudes to gambling had been confused and contradictory. As race-meetings proliferated around the country throughout the eighteenth and nineteenth centuries nobody ever seriously questioned the idea that bookmakers, provided they paid the entrance fee, should be allowed on to the course to make a book. The suggestion that they might be expected to return a portion of their profits to racing, as it was from racing that they were making their money in the first place, was practically unheard of. Right on through the first half of the twentieth century, betting in cash on a race-track was the accepted, if not applauded, form of gambling for most people. A gent or a big spender could have an account with a credit-layer or turf accountant but as these transactions were supposedly a thing of honour the debts were not legally enforceable. Off-course cash betting was completely illegal and totally rampant. Every working-class district in every major town had its local man who, according to convention, had to look like either Alistair Sim or Harry Fowler and operated from an alley or a street corner or a room over a pub. And half the time not just the local hoods but also the local police were pocketing a share of the take to permit the bookie to stay in business.

The 1960 Betting Shop Act was supposed to put an end to this hypocrisy by legally licensing certain operators to open shops for cash betting by the general public. Only society's, or at least the Conservative Party's, attitude to punting was still somewhat ambiguous. To counter the accusation that betting was a vice that should not be encouraged, it was considered inappropriate for all of these shops to be run by a nationalised tote which could've ploughed the profits back into racing itself. That would've meant outraging church and moral groups by sanctioning gambling with the establishment's blessing. Consequently the first betting offices tended to be out of sight of the main thoroughfares. Tucked away down side streets behind the station and next to the sort of barbers' shops that stocked *Titbits* and Gentlemen's Protection. They had to be as uncomfortable as possible as for years it was considered immoral to give the shiftless workers too much incentive to loaf away the day inside a bookie's. It wasn't until 1986 that they were even allowed to have television sets and serve tea and coffee. Yet by far the greatest flaw in the government's approach was that, when they rejected an off-course tote monopoly, they none the less allowed the shops they did license to rapidly fall under the control of a monopoly of a very different kind.

Every experienced punter is familiar with the difference between the friendly local betting office, which may be one of two or three run by a small family concern, and the super-sharp sell of the big combines. Yet by the start of the 1988 flat racing season, the local operator was becoming an endangered species, with no less than 56 per cent of all off-course cash betting turnover controlled by Ladbrokes, Mecca, Corals and Hills. The big firms are meant to make a direct contribution to the industry they live off via the betting levy which is a payment made up from the put-upon punters' betting slips and which goes to the Betting Levy Board who can use that revenue to boost prize money and improve facilities. If the bookmakers and the Levy Board cannot agree on what the accepted levy should be, then it is up to the Home Secretary to set a figure. Yet in 1988 the Big Four were in a terrible state at being asked by the Levy Board for a total levy of around £30 million or 0.088 per cent of turnover, even when the racing division of one company alone, Ladbrokes, had just announced a yearly profit of some £62 million.

It is staggering to realise that nearly ten million pounds is bet off-course every day and yet in many God-forsaken areas of the racing calendar, far away from the Derby, especially in jump racing where there are no Maktoums or Emperors of the Blue Grass playing poker at the big boys' table, horses are frequently competing for less than £1,500 prize money. Considering the owner's training fees and ever-increasing costs, it's virtually impossible for the small players to make ends meet from this kind of percentage. In France or America where there is a complete or virtual tote monopoly, even the smallest claiming race is usually worth at least £4,000 to the winner at even the humblest tracks.

In 1987 the Tote had a turnover of £146 million and an operating surplus of £7.1 million of which £3.1 million or some 2 per cent of turnover was ploughed back into racing. Yet here were the big betting shop proprietors protesting at less than 0.089 per cent of their own turnover going back to the sport that they leech off. It has taken long enough to get them even to accept just the principle that if they wish to make their living in a way that depends on other people being willing to pay to own and race horses, then they might like to see it as prudent self-interest to make a contribution to help to guarantee a secure future for that activity.

The bookies for their part insist that no one is forced to own horses or to strike a bet and that they have no moral obligation to subsidise what they see as the luxury pastime of wealthy men. In 1988 they insisted that their off-course profits were not 10–12 per cent but only as much as 2–3 per cent even before corporation tax and interest payments. They also avowed that the £31.7 million they were offering racing, would also mean £3.86 million for the government in corporation tax and £10 million in VAT.

Even so, racing professionals still get incensed by the sight of the Big Four pleading poverty. Are not Mecca owned by Grand Metropolitan, they say? And Corals by Bass Charrington, and Hills by Sears Ltd? And do these companies not regard racing as a valuable cash-flow facility giving them funds to invest in the other sides of their businesses such as hotels and catering, holiday and leisure industries, casinos and department stores and so on. Certainly other modern racing countries look on the situation in Britain with some incredulity. The Americans decided to do away with bookmakers around 1907 and now you can't wager with a bookie outside of Nevada and Atlantic City, unless you're prepared to risk getting more than your credit cut off if you don't pay your bills on time. The most envied model of all is Australia. A land consumed with a passion for racing and gambling where the whole racing industry is constantly expanding and looking ahead. They have all the crack and atmosphere of cash bookmakers on course, as well as the Tote windows, but all of the nation's numerous off-course betting offices are run by the state-owned Tote or TAB. Entry is actually free to some tracks. Ownership and prize money is rising all the time and betting turnover is enormous. In the words of one top Aussie trainer, Bart Cummings, speaking about the difference between British and Australian racing. 'We may have started three hundred years after you, but now we're about three hundred years out in front.'

In 1987 betting offices in Britain began receiving live satellite transmissions from race-meetings not covered by ordinary TV. This service is run by a company called SIS who have to pay the Racecourse Association for being allowed to set up in business. In 1988 an estimated £10 million was expected to come racing's way from this extra revenue. Acceptable enough until you learn that no less than 48 per cent of SIS shares are owned by the Big Four and that of the 40 per cent stock in the company still unlocated, there is no guarantee that they won't get their hands on that too. Why the racing authorities didn't insist that the satellite franchise went to an outside party to safeguard the integrity of the service and to maximise revenues for the good of the industry as a whole is still a mystery. Even now it is constantly bemoaned that the Jockey Club are not adopting a more aggressive and commercial policy and getting involved themselves.

This depressing sense of the dark and declining side of a great sport is never more aptly illustrated than by the state of the grand-stand at Epsom. The Derby may be Britain's foremost classic race but the accommodation for the paying customers, built in the twenties and scarcely renovated since, is unbelievably cramped, old-fashioned and inadequate. As you walk in through the Members' entrance you look up at the peeling paint and plasterwork and at the large damp stains above the heating pipes. It's reminiscent of the drearier partitioned outposts of the BBC in provincial cities or of an old-fashioned department store, before the Debenhams buy-out, in Tunbridge Wells or Hove.

The 1988 Derby was being sponsored for the fifth year running, with an agreement to continue until 1991, by Ever Ready batteries and its parent company, Hanson Trust, thus necessitating the wretched obligation that goes with all sponsorship deals to refer to this historic race as the Ever Ready Derby and to its companion event three days later as the Gold Seal Oaks. With £228,000 to the winning owner, some £92,000 to the runner-up and a further £44,000 to the third, the Derby may seem to be quite lavishly endowed, especially to sceptical observers of racing's priorities, viewing them from a harsher social context. Yet even if the race can still currently just about sustain its position in international racing on the basis of its accumulated prestige and its effect on the breeding industry alone, you can't duck away from the fact that in terms of hard cash it can now barely scrape into a list of the fifty most valuable races in the world. The Kentucky Derby on 7 May had been worth approxi-mately £327,000 to the winner while the Irish Derby sponsored by Budweiser would give almost the same sum to its winning owners on 26 June. Paltry stuff though compared to the half a million on offer for carrying off the Arc in Paris in October or the £725,000 for the Breeders Cup Classic and the £740,000 for Australia's Fosters-sponsored Melbourne Cup in November. And what about the Derby's supporting races? None of the other events on 1 June was worth more than £14,300 and all five of them posted a collective value of just £47,000 which is in stark contrast to the Breeders Cup pro-gramme, or the Arc day card at Longchamp, which under CIGA's new sponsorship, due to begin in October 1988, would now have four other group races as well as the Arc, three of them worth £50,000 apiece.

The other classic race at Epsom, the Oaks, which is for three-year-old fillies, is run over the same trip as the Derby on the Saturday after the big race. The Coronation Cup, Thursday's highlight, is another Group One, one-and-a-half mile contest, but for older horses only. Otherwise Thursday's supporting card would sink to an all-time low with five supporting races worth just £28,000 between them, including such enticing items as the HP Sauce Maiden Auction Stakes for two-year-olds over five furlongs. Derby week is Epsom's only major meeting of the year and they only race there on two other occasions each season. Neither of the other two meetings stage a Group race and there are no major two-year-old races run there at all. Similarly, Epsom the training centre, once the home of famous Derby-winning heroes like Walter Nightingale and Tommy Walls, has sent out no classic winners since John Sutcliffe's Right Tack won the 2,000 Guineas in 1969. Good trainers are still based there like Sutcliffe himself and the former jockey Geoff Lewis, but in Derby week these days they are more likely to be scratching around in the supporting handicaps than having a runner in the Blue Riband itself.

Few of these somewhat oppressive statistics were likely to be bothering the vast majority of serious and non-serious punters turning up to enjoy themselves at Epsom Downs on 1 June 1988. Yet unless the projected grandstand rebuilding scheme is a success, and the finance has been a long time coming, it's not hard to see Epsom ending up looking almost as run-down and dilapidated as Aintree became before it was rescued by Seagrams. And unless the supporting programmes can be made more attractive, Epsom may find itself emulating Aintree in another respect too by being left with just one showcase meeting a year at which the pick of the races at the existing three fixtures will be staged over a four-day period. With maybe even temporary grandstands, as at the National and the Open Golf tournament, replacing the need for expensive and permanent new structures. And then to round it all off, some new-generation racing impresario or marketeer will probably want to redesign the actual race-track too.

The extraordinary nature of the Epsom course certainly entitles it to a unique if not always revered place among the major racing venues of the world. The runners are faced with a stiff, uphill climb through the first half-mile and then with a steep descent to Tattenham Corner and its sharp left-handed turn into the home straight. If that isn't bad enough, they then find that for the last two furlongs the camber of the track tilts markedly towards the inside rail. That has been enough to unbalance many a potential Derby winner as he began his final run towards the line. Every few years some expert comes along and proposes that the whole thing should be scrapped, and the race itself transferred to a more 'sensible' course like Sandown or Ascot. How can we be serious, Americans ask, risking the most valuable bloodstock in the world around a switchback in the middle of a fairground?

Undoubtedly there have been great racehorses who were unlucky losers in the Derby just as the race has not always been won by the best horse of its generation. Only in 1986 a good horse, Shahrastani, rather fortuitously triumphed over an outstanding one, Dancing Brave. At the same time the Derby has also been won by some of the best and most famous horses in racing history. A long line of illustrious names stretching from Diomed to Ormonde and from Hyperion to Nijinsky. What is more, many of the winners have not only been top-class racehorses, they have also succeeded as *chefs de sire* and been able to pass on their qualities to their offspring. You have to believe that it is precisely because the Derby does ask such searching questions of a horse's temperament, agility, speed and stamina that it continues to find out annually just about the best three-year-old colt in England and Europe and, in exceptional years, like those of Sea Bird and Nijinsky, the best three-year-old racehorse in the world.

Derby Day, as opposed to just the Derby race, is also one of those annual occasions that sports editors for the serious newspapers consider to be too important to be left to the ordinary racing journalists alone. Famous names and famous bylines must be drafted in – 'great writers', generally more familiar with the rougher, tougher people's sports such as soccer and boxing. As well as throwing in the few necessary comments about the bizarre nature of the course, the famous reporters can also be relied upon to come out with the standard line about the great mass of common humanity being brought together on the downs, etc.

A few hours before the racing side of the 1988 ritual begins in earnest, a couple of celebrated members of the famous reporter school are sensibly observing the great mass of common humanity from the comfort of the Members' bar on the top floor of the grandstand. Like all of those with a press badge, they are not obliged to wear morning-dress. Many of the racing regulars wear it anyway, the more conservative amongst them because they like to and a lot of the others because they don't want to look like the peasant in a lounge suit at a black-tie do. The famous reporters are not wearing tails. Presumably out of respect to their closer links with Hampden Park and White Hart Lane. But just so as to keep one foot in both camps as it were, they are conducting a little first-hand research into the racing life-style by literally embracing the élitist pleasures of iced bubbly and Barrie Cope's seafood platter.

Next door to the bar, one of the premier stiffs of the social season is under way. The Jockey Club's annual Derby Day luncheon. This is being presided over by Ailwyn, Lord Fairhaven, who has the sort of preternatural doomed look associated with that member of the Baskerville family who gets eaten by the Hound in Chapter One. Amongst the assembled guests are a smattering of Conservative politicians including Douglas Hurd who, as Home Secretary, is the government minister nominally in charge of the racing and bookmaking industry. Hurd is wearing a very tall, very black top-hat which makes him look like a cross between Isambard Kingdom Brunel and a humourless Victorian undertaker. One of his predecessors, Lord Whitelaw, cuts an altogether more urbane and stylish figure. Very much Wilfred Hyde-White from *My Fair Lady* as he discusses his favourite casinos with Lord Howard de Walden.

Lord Whitelaw has arrived by motor from Tattenham Corner after hitching a lift in the Royal train. The flasher top-hatted nobs, not to mention the serious horse-owning classes, are even at this moment still whirling in from the heavens in scenes reminiscent of the helicopter attack in *Apocalypse Now*. And at the forefront of the aerial arrivals is a very special party containing the man who must be grovelled to for the day. Chairman of Hanson Industries and big-race sponsor, Sir Gordon White. Sir Gordon is one of those archetypal, self-made millionaires who were born in a shoebox but who worked their way up from the gutter to get knighted by Mrs Thatcher and be made the hero of an enterprise culture musical written by Andrew Lloyd Webber. He's also a serious candidate for the role of the oldest swinger in town. For year's he's been boasting to doubtful gossip-columnists (peering for signs of his toupee and his prostate operation) about all the glamorous women he's supposed to have 'escorted' the previous week. Hanson's Derby sponsorship has given Sir Gordon a whole new opportunity to bribe some of these dames, be they Joan Collins or Dyan Cannon, to pose on his arm for the afternoon. They get a free day out, lots of champers and tabloid pics and Sir Gordon gets to swank about it all to the *Sun*, the *Mail* and the *Express*, not to mention the cameras of Channel 4 television. 'We'll be right back with more of Sir Gordon and his lovely ladies right after this break,' chortles Bruffscot.

Two regular members of Sir Gordon's party are Judith Chalmers and that lightweight modern romancer 'Bungalow Bill' Wiggins. Wiggie's style is to sidle around looking about as charismatic as Patrick Mower opening a new Burton's shop in Maidstone. Meanwhile Judith provides the necessary TV back-up. '"We want Wiggie,"' the girls are shouting. 'They know their Wiggie. They love him. He's their man.' Sangster's there of course. Along with Susan, number two. And Michael Medwin. And George Hamilton. And Fatty Benson, naturally. Fatty's going to be signing copies of his new book down in the foyer after the big one and he looks as if he's contemplating a great deal of serious lunch to prepare him for this strenuous task.

Sir Gordon and pals have their own little private pavilion out there on the lawn. And down beyond the winning-post and behind the paddock (which at Epsom is a somewhat exhausting half-mile walk away from the enclosures) is the ubiquitous tented village of chalets and marquees packed with assorted advertising men, garage-owners, the odd porn merchant and, perhaps a little surprisingly, the entourage from Dubai. The fact that the sheikhs are down amongst the vulgar section amuses one trainer's wife no end. 'Hamdan's got a tent, you know. Down by the paddock.' 'Sounds awful.' 'Poor John (Leat). Fancy having to come back all the way from Dubai to watch the Derby on television. In a tent.' 'Sounds simply bloody.'

TV, tent or no, it has not escaped the notice of the serious racing observers that while the Maktoum family are collectively represented in the big race by Unfuwain (Hamdan) and Kefaah (Ahmed) there is not a single colt carrying the colours of Sheikh Mohammed which, considering the enormous financial investment laid out by the quarterback in the sales ring at Keeneland two years before, must be regarded as something of a commercial disaster. It's also a timely reminder once again not only that money cannot guarantee success on the track but that Sangster may still have been right six years before when he decided that the Arabs' people would never be a match for his. In fact there is to be no Vincent O'Brien-trained runner either in this 109th Derby but his record is still there for all to see whereas a whole posse of advisers from the original Colonels to Pasty Face Stroud have yet to be as lucky as to come up with a horse good enough to finish in the first three.

The Derby may be partly associated with top-hats, tails and the grandest of fashion, but the Members' Enclosure at Epsom is not like the Royal Enclosure at Ascot and is considerably more colourful as a result. At Ascot, entrance is by voucher only and they can only be obtained via a referee who's attended for at least six years and then there's still technically the possibility of being blackballed by Her Majesty's Representative for being quite the wrong sort. At Epsom, anyone can go into the Members' on Derby Day if they purchase an annual member's badge in advance and these are still on sale only days before the race. 'Formal wear' is then obligatory for all badge-holders but where you got your togs from, not to mention the lolly to buy or hire them, is less of a delicate issue than it can be at Ascot. Of course there are plenty of toffs in the smartest black silk hats as well as a sizeable gathering of young City men and Marks, Willies and Toms tagging along behind Hamish, Alistair and Rory in the hope that they and Henrietta might even see Pasty Face Stroud or the Honourable Acton and get invited into Hamdan's tent. There are one or two stunningly attractive and very hard-looking upper-class ladies in simple, elegant clothes and an astonishingly large number of brasses of all backgrounds, stumbling around on ankle-breaking heels and desperately trying to jam their unsuitably large-brimmed hats to their skulls. There are also a few very grand senior toffs, slipping unobtrusively on to the Downs with the pretty young thing that they can't be seen with officially and who thought that when they mentioned Derby Day they were talking about tail-coats, strawberries on the terrace and perhaps even an invitation to the Royal Box. But the best and most splendid thing of all about the Epsom Members' enclosure on 1 June is the remarkable concentration of Del Boys and Spivs, as resplendently morning-suited and fitted out as any member of the Jockey Club. Lots of big-frame glasses and Arthur Daley language; plus one or two heavier-looking boys with Marbella tans – men familiar with the used car trade and the cut of the plastic surgeon's knife, many of them accompanied by ladies so completely given over to the image of the brassy moll, to the flashing stocking-top and the gaping cleavage, that any serious feminist present might wonder why they don't tie a ball and chain to their leg and have done with it. The most engaging couple of all are a cute and handsome lad in a small top-hat – who's parked his Merc at the nearby RAC club and is now discussing credit card fraud in a confident voice – and a very ritzy dame in a Bruce Oldfield number, who's a Sabrina or Tamara if she's anything and who's got her bit of rough and is just loving it!

The most unfortunate women are the ones who are crammed into the hell-hole of Tatts enclosure next door. They're all dressed up in their best hats too but are being so ignored by the nobs that eventually one or two of them give up the pretence of being smart and begin to gently mock their social betters as they hurry into the ring to place a bet. 'Excuse me. Are you posh?' they ask a panic-stricken baronet in a black silk hat as he scuttles towards the Heathorns representative.

It's this truly daft mishmash of people and backgrounds and

images and styles that has always made a race-track such a natural haven for any confirmed devotee of irresponsible behaviour and easy money, of bad company and a wicked smile. And what matter that the prices in the Members' Bar are suicidally steep? The chaps from the Smitham and Reedham Express dive into the vintage Bollinger at £32 a time, knowing that one of the greatest joys of horse-racing is when you start feeling as if you're about 22,000 feet up in an unpredictable light aircraft from which the pilot has recently bailed out. You've no real idea of your eventual destination or of how to get there and only the vaguest notion of how to take over the controls. Flying blind, you realise that what is really important is that you should drink as much champagne as you possibly can and then have three times more than you can afford on the very next race. And if it loses . . . well, never mind. You can have another drink, or maybe twelve, and then hope that Sir Gordon will toss you a fiver or a smoked salmon sandwich or even one of Goldie Hawn's ear-rings as he flies away home.

Such a fate is unlikely ever to overtake the chairmen of the Big Four bookmaking firms – not on Derby Day. Ladbrokes were expecting to take in excess of £7 million on the race with around two million of that coming from small cash-wagers in their 716 nationwide betting offices. Corals' spokesman, Wally Pyrah, whose firm is going 6-4 the Dick Hern stable and 50-1 the Major's trio of Unfuwain, Minster Son and Charmer coming first, second and third, predicts that total turnover on the race could be a record with well over thirty million pounds being staked. All the big layers have taken much more ante-post than usual, probably because the race has seemed so open for so long. Hills are already counting the £70,000 losses to them alone on Sanquirico. Cecil's colt was supposed to have rehabilitated himself in the Dante Stakes at York. Instead he ran almost as badly as he did in the Craven at Newmarket and he's not been seen since.

With rain falling in the London area in the few days leading up to the race, all the big money in the final twenty-four hours has been for horses who have proven their ability to act on soft ground and who will definitely stay one and a half miles. Unfuwain, owned by Hamdan Al Maktoum, trained by Hern, but to be ridden by Cauthen rather than Willie Carson, has displaced Red Glow as Hills' favourite who make him a 100-30 shot as opposed to the 7-2 on offer with Corals and Mecca. Unfuwain is certainly bred to win a Derby, as he's a son of Northern Dancer out of a winning mare called Height of Fashion who was originally owned by the Queen. His record coming up to Epsom is of two wins in two starts, both of them on testing going and both of them over a mile and a half. Yet some good judges suspect that he may be too big and unbalanced to be suited by the Epsom track. Of his two stable-companions, Charmer, the 2,000 Guineas runner-up, has not run since Newmarket while Willie Carson's mount, Minster Son, has followed up his defeat of Red Glow with another game victory at Goodwood. Charmer and Minster Son are priced at 12-1 and 7-1 respectively.

According to the bookmakers, Unfuwain's biggest rival will be Red Glow who is to be ridden by Pat Eddery. This colt went on from the Newmarket Stakes to beat a high-class field in the Dante at York in which he demonstrated the kind of emphatic acceleration that is nearly always the hallmark of a top-class horse. Pat has compared him to Golden Fleece and, in his own words, described his final serious Newmarket gallop as like sitting at the wheel of a Rolls-Royce. Red Glow's trainer, Geoff Wragg, has been tempted to have a bet for the first time in years. Journalists have been too polite to speculate on Geoff's gambling record. Perhaps he's such a hopeless, lousy and incompetent punter that Mrs Wragg has been trying to drag him past betting shop doors for the entire length of their marriage.

Doyoun, the 2,000 Guineas winner, definitely runs and Michael Stoute and Walter Swinburn are sounding increasingly bullish about his chances. Even so, the doubts about his stamina, especially on rain-softened ground, have caused his price to drift from fives to 9-1.

There has been significant support for Robert Sangster's home-bred colt Glacial Storm, who is trained by Barry Hills at Manton and who will be ridden by Hills' son, Michael. Glacial Storm put in an eye-catching performance in the Dante where he was running on strongly in third place, behind Red Glow and Luca Cumani's Maktoum horse, Kefaah. The Dante was over a mile and a quarter and Glacial Storm seems sure to be suited by the extra two furlongs at Epsom although, like Unfuwain, there is a slight worry that he may be too big for the course. Ladbrokes have cut him from 20-1 to 12-1 after laying him to lose more than a quarter of a million.

Ladbrokes have also taken some hefty bets on the Aga Khan's other representative, Kahyasi, who, with Ray Cochrane riding, must be considered trainer Cumani's number one choice. Kahyasi, sure to stay the distance, is unbeaten in three races and has won the often influential Lingfield Trial which takes place on a track not dissimilar to Epsom. Kahyasi has been cut from 14-1 to 10-1 after being laid to take out roughly as much money as Glacial Storm.

For the ordinary public the Derby may be just the other day of the year when they go into a betting office. To the informed and serious punter, races like the Derby are particularly attractive as, in spite of the level of competition, they should still be slightly easier to call than the smaller races and handicaps. This is because the shrewdest gamblers can use their special understanding not just of form but also of breeding, of a horse's physical characteristics and of its trainer and jockey's record at the highest level, to assist them in making a selection.

The attention that the Derby receives and the spotlight it throws on the betting side of racing always encourages a rash of newspaper and magazine articles, some amusing, some pompous, some just averagely inaccurate, about this great vice . . . gambling. Gambling, it seems, is one of those subjects a bit like bringing up children, on which just about everyone feels qualified to have an opinion. Even if their acquaintance with the subject goes no further than two ten-bob each-way betting slips each year. The most widely accepted view is that gamblers suffer from a kind of incurable flaw or weakness which means that they can never walk away when they're up, but must always keep on playing until eventually they experience the really satisfying point of it all . . . they lose. By this version of it, gamblers are a species of masochist who actually enjoy pain and need to be hurt and humiliated. Well, both serious and light-hearted punters will admit that losing money is a regular aspect of the gambler's life. They also recognise those recidivists and even doomed and destructive characters who punt so hopelessly and powerlessly that they end up losing everything. Job. House. Family. Sanity. Life.

The idea though, that the larger proportion of the gambling fraternity are out there slitting their wrists on the race train home each night just doesn't stand up to serious examination. There are gamblers who chance everything on a single throw and win. Or who double up their stakes on the last race, the last bout, the final hand. And win. Then there are the punters who indulge their pleasure week in, week out, to sums neither great nor small. Sometimes they clear a bit. Sometimes they lose. Mostly they barely break even. But the pleasure and excitement that they get from gambling is enormous. However lousy, mistake-ridden, depressing or mundane a day or week has been, the all-embracing risk of a two-minute wager can wipe it all out in one simple, direct and visceral moment. And there's something eternally exciting about receiving those wads of well-fingered bookmakers' money. It connects with a feeling of illicit pleasure, of something prohibited and not quite approved of by conventional everyday society. Each new race, each new hand and spin of the wheel is a challenge to unpick in advance and to conduct endless post-mortems over afterwards.

There are some gamblers who think of themselves as professionals. It's a tough career. Many have tried it and few have lasted the course. It's sometimes akin to describing yourself as a professional idiot. For a short while the now warned-off North London commodity broker, Terry Ramsden, was built up by some sections of the press as a sort of King of the Big-time Punters. An invincible winner whose every move caused the bookies to quake in their slip-on shoes. The truth was that Ramsden was a disastrous gambler and known for many years as, literally, a Big Loser. The big layers always welcomed his bets and were quite happy to extend his credit because they knew that he'd always leave so much more cash in their satchels than he'd ever take out. Sadly the really professional gambler is only rarely a flamboyant character and more often a rather boring middle-aged fart who can't be bothered to do anything much other than go to the races, sip Britvic orange juice and then read the formbook all night. To this kind of punter the Breeders Cup and the Derby are no different from a six-furlong handicap – just another opportunity for investment. They can win just as much on a selling race as a classic and, if the pay-out's good, Pontefract can seem as romantic a setting as Paris. Eventually this kind of boring professional writes an autobiography in which he makes putting money on racehorses sound about as exciting an occupation as enrolling in a management training scheme with Lord Young.

Of course most armchair punters don't like to see it this way. To them a professional gambler, someone like themselves, say, if only they had the nerve, looks like Ryan O'Neal in *The Driver* or Steve McQueen in *The Cincinnati Kid*. He stays up most of the night making a killing at the gaming tables and then enjoys a few restful hours in the arms of Ann-Margret or Isabelle Adjani before driving off to Ascot in a red Ferrari where he accepts Ladbrokes' credit note for the cool half a million he's just won on the Cambridgeshire. He wears shades all summer and often all winter too. When he's in earshot of other, lesser punters, he's not really betting at all. He's just 'having an interest'. And he doesn't bet in cash. He has accounts with all the major firms. He may saunter down to the rails a half an hour before racing begins in order to discuss his requirements or he may move in purposefully a minute or two before the off. The most important thing is that he shows no emotion whether he wins or whether he loses. He mustn't be seen shouting his selection home as if he were a member of a social club outing in the next-door enclosure.

If he really is a big-time gambler, then the chances are that he makes just as much money from letting other punters bet with him, without tax, as he does from backing his own selections. He can lay odds on anything he feels confident about, from what will finish last in the 3.35 to the number of Rollers in the Members' car-park. What helps to give him the aura of seeming impregnability is his access to inside 'information', that magic word that bestows the illusion of superior wisdom on a select few. It's as if all horse-races and games of chance were a species of Chinese puzzle to which some men actually have the key in advance.

The very opposite of the professional gambler is the 'Go On My Son' kind of punter who does like to shout his selections home from the top of the grandstand. The various racecourse badges that he's collected over the years will be flapping around on his binoculars and he'll be punching the air with a rolled up copy of the *Sporting Life*. Unlike the professional, the 'Go On My Son' punter eschews information and follows his favourites. When he wins he likes to celebrate loudly and visibly. When he loses he bad-mouths everything and everyone in sight, especially the jockey, the trainer and the horse. 'Fucking Swinburn. Fucking cunt. There's no way he should've lost that race' etc. Of course, everyone can lose and lose badly. It's all relative. It's just that the smart money has appearances to maintain.

The 'Go On My Son' boys frequently slip out of their office or place of work to dash into a bookies to catch up on the progress of the bets they made that morning. The smart punter only rarely visits a betting shop. He's disdainful of exactly those aspects that tend to confuse and repel many ordinary non-racing outsiders: the smoke-filled airless room, the lack of windows, the uncomfortable stools, the floor carpet of discarded cigarette butts and losing betting slips; and the clientele, predominantly male, predominantly ignorant, and predominantly cheapies and losers. Neither Douglas Hurd's benevolent dispensation of TV or coffee machines or the SIS TV screens have done much to change this basic atmosphere. You don't look for popping champagne corks in the Ladbrokes office on the Fulham Palace Road. Even in this bright new technological age, the greyhound racing from Monmore always seems to be cutting in on the horse-race you really want to hear about. And even the classics are not exempt.

'Under orders, Newmarket. Off Newmarket. 3.47 (pause). And as they run through the first furlong. (Pause.) It's Tibullo from Lapierre.

And Charmer. Caerwent in behind. Dogs show, Hackney. (Pause.) They bet 2-1 Trap One, Ballylogue Kyra. 9-4, Trap Four, Parktown Darkie. Same price, 9-4, Trap Six, Night Time Lady. And 7-1, Trap Three, Raceway Dan. (Pause.) Back to Newmarket. (Pause.) Three furlongs still to run, Newmarket. And it's Doyoun. From Charmer. Charmer still making good headway. Doyoun. Charmer. Running on strongly, number seven, Bellefella. Result Hereford. (Pause.) First, number two. Mr Chris Chip. Second, number fourteen. The Goblin. Third, number five. Wide-boy Wallie. And Mr Chris Chip is Martin Pipe's 391st winner this season. Inside the final furlong now in the 2,000 Guineas. What a race it's been. As Doyoun. Goes on once more from Charmer. Aiglefin finishing well. Doyoun. Charmer. Doyoun. They go past together. (Pause.) S.P. Hereford . . .' etc.

The real road to disaster comes when the armchair punter or the Go On My Son enthusiast who has hitherto enjoyed his Channel 4 racing each Saturday, suddenly and rashly decides to throw over his normal life-style and join the ranks of the fantasy professionals. Perhaps he's just inherited a large sum of money or maybe his firm's gone public and thanks to a healthy share price he's suddenly more liquid than he thought. So one fatal morning he walks out of his job with its expense account and annual salary and begins to live out his cherished dream of reading the *Sporting Life* and the *Raceform Notebook* in the bath each morning and then enjoying the company of the regular on-course bookies as he shares their first-class compartment on the journey down to Salisbury. Within three months he's sold his car. Within six months he's sold his house. Within nine months he's being sued for bankruptcy. And on the stroke of a year those self-same bookies in the first-class carriage are having a quick whip round to see if they can help to get him out of that hostel he's living in near Vauxhall Bridge.

There is one unique and extraordinary exception to this woeful pattern. One man who *is* a professional gambler, who is anything but colourless or stupid and who has managed to win genuinely large amounts from punting on the racecourses of Britain and Ireland. He's a fifty-two-year-old Ulsterman and his name is Barney Curley. And whereas the Big Four bookmaking firms may have easily sidestepped the likes of the Betting Levy Board, the Monopolies and Mergers Commission and the Office of Fair Trading, Barney is one person that they genuinely fear. And that's a situation that both Curley himself and the thousands of ordinary punters who wish that they could be just like him, hope will never change.

In the bold, brash days of the sixties and early seventies it was the notorious Glaswegian, John Banks, who carried the mantle of the punters' friend, the rogue individual taking on the mighty corporations. To many close observers of the gambling milieu, the sight of those same big firms applauding loudly when Banks was warned off for three years in 1977, smacked of mendacious hypocrisy. There can be no doubt that many of those respectable bookmakers would gladly wish the same fate on Barney Curley. They're unlikely to get their request. For what makes Barney a lot more interesting than some caricature big-splash punter doing it all for the shampoo is his formidably ascetic background. He's a serious practising Catholic. He actually trained for the priesthood with the Jesuits and came close to taking holy orders. As a young man he nearly died of tuberculosis and the nine months he spent convalescing taught him a disciplined and philosophical sense of life's priorities that seems to have contributed to his rational, chess-player's assessment of the good and bad points about a racehorse.

When Barney wins, the money doesn't all go in a paperchase of sybaritic indulgence. Neither is it splashed out in drinks for all, around the champagne bars of Britain's racecourses. Barney, who is shaven-haired with a small toothbrush moustache, may seem to be a heavy, even sinister, man with his low-pitched and deliberate speech but although he enjoys a comfortable house and stateside vacations, he also invests a lot of his winnings in the kind of charitable activities that carry none of the 'East End businessman supports local boys club' tag associated with other less substantial racing characters. He has set up and personally bankrolled special appeals to take old-age pensioners to the races and to divert a chunk of racing's lolly to the Great Ormond Street Hospital Fund, although sometimes his concept of financial innovation has landed him in trouble too.

In 1975 he actually raffled his house, Middleton Curley in Southern Ireland, and did so very successfully for IR£375,000. Unfortunately the Eire government took a dim view of it all and decided that Curley had contravened various tax and fraud regulations. Barney was tried and fined IR£5,000. Still standing in the dock he took out his cheque-book and offered to double the fine immediately, with the balance going to charity.

His success as a race-track gambler is partly to do with his excellent memory and his sheer knowledge of horse-racing built up steadily over many years. It's also to do with the superior contacts he's made which include the very best informed people in Irish racing. Most of all though, it's simply because he's a hell of a lot shrewder than most of the other characters who've ever tried to make a living backing horses. He weighs things up as calmly and succinctly as an experienced civil servant summarising sixty pages of a complex ministerial brief in four short paragraphs. And Barney Curley never stops learning something from the racing results every day of the year.

Curley moved to England in 1985 and his current base is at Exning near Newmarket where he himself trains a string of some sixteen horses, most of them steeplechasers. At first the Jockey Club were extremely reluctant to grant him a licence and insisted that his horses be trained by neighbouring Dave Thom with whom Barney was sort of on parole. The Jockey Club were paranoid. It seemed they feared that this celebrated gambler might not always run all his horses on their merits, that he might start offering jockeys inducements for losing or for giving him information. Curley's the kind of serious gambler the bookmakers hate. The kind of man who sees an ante-post price of 12-1 offered about a horse for the Derby and wants twenty grand on at those odds and doesn't wish to be haggled with and offered ten thousand at eights, another five at tens and the rest at maybe 19-2. Mavericks like Curley must be frozen out and either they or their account closed down fast if they get out of order. Barney would argue that he simply wanted to back his judgement with his money at the moment that suited him best and that he expected the bookmakers to back theirs too.

He was eventually given his training licence, but within a short period of setting up in business he was shocked by what he felt was the irresponsible way in which racing's rulers were failing to protect the interests of the ordinary betting shop punter. He believed that the instances he saw of jockeys throwing races or making little effort on well-backed favourites should be properly investigated by the authorities. Instead he felt that the stewards were more often interested in looking the other way so that racing's public image wouldn't be harmed. And so that they could continue to pretend that, other than Barney Curley, there were no racetrack villains – except in Dick Francis novels.

In November 1987 Curley placed twelve thousand to win on a horse called Robin Goodfellow in a novice hurdle at Ascot. The horse was favourite and was ridden by the talented Yorkshire jockey, Graham Bradley. Robin Goodfellow lost the race to an animal called Teletrader whom he'd beaten in a similar race at Sandown previously. Barney thought that Robin Goodfellow's defeat was unsatisfactory and that the jockey may not have been riding to win. He tried, as he saw it, to alert the stewards to the situation but they'd have nothing of it. He kept on persistently bringing up the incident, talking about it to the racing press and generally refusing to be a good man and go away. Eventually he was summoned to a meeting of the Jockey Club's three-man Disciplinary Tribunal chaired by the smooth-faced Lord Vestey, the foxhunting butcher of Stowell Park, Gloucestershire. To Barney's anger and amazement the stewards proposed to do nothing about Bradley but informed the Irishman that they were withdrawing his licence for 'bringing racing into disrepute'. All because he'd supposedly intimidated Bradley in a telephone conversation in which he was meant to have demanded that the rider should contribute £12,000 to the Injured Jockeys Fund to 'atone' for his behaviour.

Curley was incensed that he'd been given no prior notice that he himself was to be the subject of an enquiry. In the circumstances he hadn't bothered to arrive with a solicitor. Jockey Club hearings may have changed a little since the terrifying days of the old Lord Rosebery, who would gladly have hanged a few trainers if he'd thought he could get away with it, but the proceedings still take place behind closed doors with no room for the press or public. A suspicion remains that some of the Clubmen involved secretly rather enjoyed those aspects of the whole summons to Portman Square that smack, as it were, of the disciplinary rituals of their public school youth. Miscreants are expected to take their punishment without complaining, to shake hands afterwards and admit that they were wrong. They're not supposed to disagree or make a fuss. Barney Curley did both of those things.

First of all he applied for and got a High Court injunction lifting the Jockey Club's ban and compelling them to arrange a second hearing at which he could be properly and legally represented. Barney arrived for this second case – presided over by three different stewards, including the new retired General Sir Cecil 'Monkey' Blacker – with a transcript of the relevant telephone call and with a very articulate and experienced brief, Mr Richard Du Cann, QC. The original case had been reported in the racing press in terms very favourable to the jockey who was always chummily referred to as 'Brad' while Barney was portrayed as a hideous, moustachioed Irishman – a malevolent force preying on all decent racing folk. Not after the second enquiry.

Du Cann's presentation was masterly. The approach of the Vestey panel was completely undermined and, against all the odds, Barney's suspension was overturned and he was given his licence back. It would be hard to exaggerate what an astonishing and unprecedented outcome this was. Mrs Thatcher may have remodelled the rest of the British establishment in her own image but the Jockey Club have remained obstinately unreconstructed and staunchly reactionary. Still drawn from an ever more ludicrously narrow class base of Eton and the Household Cavalry and, the Blacker tribunal notwithstanding, consistently lacking in any kind of style, imagination and professional expertise. Yet now the Bunter and Squiffy classes had just received their biggest sock in the puss since Florence Nagle took them to the High Court over the issue of women trainers in 1965. Barney preferred not to criticise the stewards in public. While reserving his judgement on Vestey and co., he claimed that in general the Jockey Club were still the best people to run racing. This might have been because he knew that he would still have to deal with them in the foreseeable future. On the other hand it might have been simply a brilliant and audacious joke.

In the autumn of 1987 Curley entered into a punt with the big bookmakers over whether he could train twelve winners between 1 October and the end of the year. The stakes were £126,000 to win £275,000. Public perception of Barney was still that he was 'just a gambler' and not a serious trainer of horses. The bookies reasoned that most of his string were simply selling hurdlers and broken-down rejects from the flat. If that were so, his success – he won his bet by 21 December – proved his real skill all the more conclusively. And the sight of the bookmakers snared so publicly and forced to pay out, firmly established Barney as the triumphant new punters' hero. It certainly did nothing to silence his criticism of the big firms who he still feels are throttling the racing industry both with their niggardly contribution to the betting levy and their constant attempts to double deal the punter by manipulating starting prices in their favour, say by backing on-course any horse that they've taken even a small amount of money for in their betting shops; so that in the event of that horse winning, they'll have shortened its odds up so much that their pay-out to their punters will be as minimal as possible. In a free market there's no law that prevents them from doing this but Barney feels that if they're not interested in taking a bet, they should clear out and give over their business to someone who is.

Barney was there by the rails on Derby Day. Not in a top-hat and tails but in his standard snap-brim trilby hat and camel-hair coat. He may be something of an outlaw in the eyes of the racing authorities but down in the ring with that hat, the moustache and the long coat, he looks more like one of those relentless old American railroad detectives of the late nineteenth century. Like Charlie Siringo or Joe

Lefors. Only Barney's Wild Bunch are the Big Four. And on those rare, exceptionally rare, occasions when Cyril Stein still puts in a personal appearance at the racecourse, he can count on looking over his shoulder just before the first and seeing Barney Curley standing there on the edges of the crowd. Watching. Waiting. And intent on doing serious damage to Cyril's wallet.

10 : Blue Riband

Barney Curley's Derby selection is Unfuwain. He thinks it's the only horse in the field with the potential to become a really outstanding middle-distance thoroughbred and he's already backed it to win him £250,000. Now he plans to top that up a little before the off. For the thousands of other punters, the mortal, regular losers and the happy once-a-year crowd, there are two other races first in which to essay a little wager.

In the opening event, the six-furlong Woodcote Stakes for two-year-olds, the 25-1 shot, Sno Serenade, ridden by the South African jockey 'Muis' or Michael Roberts, turns over the locally trained 5-4 favourite, Sylvan Tempest. Half an hour later, Roberts is in the winner's enclosure again after getting the 15-8 favourite, Waajib, up in the final one hundred yards to land the one-mile, Group Three, Diomed Stakes, which is one of the few really decent supporting races of the week. Two furlongs out, Waajib, a Try My Best colt, owned by Hamdan Al Maktoum and trained by new monitor Stewart, seems penned in on the rails with no chance of a clear run. But when the diminutive Roberts finally gets him out, he literally romps up the hill to the thrilled disbelief of the punters, including, it seems, the Queen, who is gripping the edges of the Royal Box with excitement. Waajib, laid to lose £125,000 in the ring, is cheered loudly on his return to the winner's circle and Roberts acknowledges the tributes with a little wave of the hand that will become his distinctive trademark before the season is out.

There is a full hour to go now between the Diomed and the Derby itself. The funfair crowds are getting larger and more abandoned and the sense of delicious and delayed anticipation seems to rise and reverberate with the amplified sound of the music. The on-course cash-only bookmakers are striving more passionately than ever to out-shout one another as they pitch in hard for the once-a-year punters. Channel 4, mindful of the approaching climax and purpose of it all, begins to change tone and gear. Temporarily at least there will be no more jokes about Oaksey's 'kit' (which is the noble lord's way of describing his morning-dress) or pictures of John McCririck shovelling highly sauced hot-dogs into the mouths of the great common mass of humanity from a burger van out there on the downs. It's time for a detailed appraisal – well, detailed waffle from old Eddie Fox in the grey top-hat and succinct comments from Francome and McGrath – of the form claims of the fourteen runners who will be going to post for this 209th running of the Blue Riband of the turf. For the top people this means the moment has arrived to head off to the saddling-up boxes to see the precious creatures they own or have shares in or have gone for a massive touch on with Heathorns and Hills. At Newmarket and Ascot this may be a cool player's determined but elegant stroll. At Epsom it's a serious gallop.

One of the most priceless sights of the racing year is the spectacle of the Royal party and their guests coming down from the Royal Box and making their way to the Epsom paddock to see the Derby runners before they come out on to the course for the parade. Ordinary paying spectators from the Members Enclosure have to undertake this journey along a narrow and congested walkway. It's by no means easy to negotiate either, especially in top-hat and tails. The Royals, naturally, are allowed exclusive use of the wider spaces of the race-track itself. The Queen, as always, is first out of the stalls at this particular event, and sets a very brisk pace through the first few furlongs. One or two of her party though, clearly hating the firm ground, are wearing that sulky and temperamental look so frequently displayed by the thoroughbred. It's also very noticeable that Mr Douglas Hurd isn't moving at all fluently, which suggests he must have sat in something nasty during lunch.

As the Royals arrive at the paddock so the big shots are coming back over from the pre-parade ring that adjoins it. Robert Sangster looks round nervously as the oh-so-confident John Francome, attired as the Artful Dodger on his way to the Mansion House ball, slips up and discreetly taps him on the shoulder and asks for a few final thoughts for the TV commentary. Mrs Sangster totters along behind, looking very pretty but also rather thin and fragile on her very high heels. In keeping with hundreds of other expensively dressed women, her right hand is jammed to her hat to make sure it stays firmly on her head and doesn't fly away in the sudden chill breeze. The Aga Khan, like Sangster, already a dual Derby-winning owner, rolls suavely through, looking like the Reverend Awdry's Fat Controller in dove-grey. And up ahead, the Maktoums, some immaculately turned out, some in a more motley assortment of tail-coats and hats, are already surveying the paddock and wondering perhaps if they might not buy up the whole place and relocate it next to the golf course in Dubai.

At last the horses themselves begin to make their entrance. First into the main arena are the Major's trio of Unfuwain, Charmer and Minster Son. Team Hern. They walk around quietly, proudly, arrogantly, the whole stage to themselves for almost five minutes. The Major's cards are on the table now and let's see if anyone can trump them. The Major himself scoots into the middle in his motorised wheelchair, sternly surveys his horses and then looks around briefly at the crowd, staring at them rather quizzically like a red-coat general regarding the undisciplined colonial forces at Bunker Hill. The Queen walks over beamingly to enquire after the Major's health and Hern reports to her on the condition of his troops.

You won't see many ugly or unkempt horses in a Derby field. Even the pacemaking outsiders, Al Muhalhal and Maksud, look svelte and expensive. But if any two runners stand out on looks alone, they have to be Sangster's Glacial Storm, who looks big and handsome and quite strong enough to be running over fences at Cheltenham, and the horse who has been backed down to favouritism once again, Pat Eddery's mount Red Glow. Contemplating this sleek bay colt, so keenly, so evidently, prepared to perfection by his trainer for this, the greatest test of his life, it's very hard to forget Pat's comments, delivered after that final gallop, about this horse being a veritable Rolls-Royce of a ride. The spectators have no TV presenters or live commentary to tell them what to think or look at. They have only the hushed, reverential voices as the favourite walks by; the sudden, rearing and whinnying of a horse, possibly beginning to get spooked by the huge crowd; the splash of brilliant colours right in front of their eyes; the nervous stares and laughter of the owners and trainers; the smell of expensive scent and horseshit and grass. It's a fluttering drug of tension, beauty and adrenalin that no amount of television cameras can ever fully bring to life.

As the jockeys, who are brought down from the weighing room by

Range Rover and mini-bus, arrive to mount up, it's time for the members to think seriously about their return journey to the stands. To get back up there in time to have a last bet if necessary and then to get a good position from which to watch the race is not an easy feat to achieve. Some are much better at it than others. Trainer Guy Harwood gets blocked in behind a wall of Sloanes and hats and grey-suited backs. But years of training on her private gallops seem to have equipped Her Majesty the Queen for the task quite wonderfully. And within a few yards of leaving the paddock the whole Royal field are strung out elegantly behind her.

'And they're inside the final two furlongs now and it's still the Queen with a commanding lead from Prince Philip and the Princess Royal. Prince Charles is beginning to lose ground as the Queen Mother looks for room on the inside rail. The Duchess of York is making some late headway but the Princess of Wales looks tailed off and completely disinterested and Mr Douglas Hurd has been pulled up. And we regret to announce that Princess Michael of Kent has shattered a hind leg and has had to be destroyed.'

Every precious inch of grass on the Members' Lawn is filling up now with chaps standing elbow to elbow and not always that bothered about how much Henrietta can see other than the brim of Charlie's top-hat in front of her. The portly little Turf Club member and Lloyds man Mr Gerald Cooper, a proper Mr Cheeryble with his stovepipe hat and lack of inches, is puffing away sagely about the wisdom of his selection. Cooper is completely dwarfed by his strapping and weary-eyed friend Mr Dan Abbot, whose bow-legged wife, Sue, President of the Racehorse Owners Association, is one of those smackingly hearty broads who, when all dressed up, look as if they've just fallen straight out of the saddle and into a powder-puff.

The terrace steps leading up to the restaurant are a prize viewing point and almost as worth scrambling for as the stairway beside Bruffscot's TV command bunker. The fourteen runners parade most calmly and elegantly and, in one or two instances, even languidly, in front of the enclosures. And then, with the noise and intensity of the betting ring still ringing in their ears, they turn and canter back past the winning-post, around the back of the paddock and down to the little holding area beyond the racecourse stables. Here they assemble again before crossing the road like a party of rich, prep school children on their way to a rounders game in the park. They still have to proceed in single file along the path over the downs that leads them finally to the mile-and-a-half start at the far side of the course. After they arrive there, the splendidly red-faced, sartorial and reliably choleric starter, Captain Michael Sayers, ticks off everybody's names, watches his assistants check their girths and then calls them round behind the stalls to begin the process of loading up.

These final moments before the Derby start are moments of tension, excitement and also of memories shared collectively by many thousands of the more than 250,000 racegoers present. The older ones amongst them will remember Sir Gordon Richards and Pinza, Charlie Smirke and 'What did I Tulyar?', Hyperion, maybe. Blue Peter. The servicemen's Derby when Airborne won at 50-1 in 1946. And possibly some of them were even present when Bahram and Mahmoud won in successive years for the old Aga Khan in 1935 and 1936. A slightly younger generation can recall Shergar in 1981. Henbit fracturing a cannon-bone in the last two furlongs but still winning in 1980. Troy in 1979. Grundy. Mill Reef. Scobie Breasley on Charlottown and Santa Claus. Psidium, the 66-1 shot ridden by the French jockey Roger Poinclet, going past Pardao and Dicta Drake in 1961. But perhaps inevitably, in these nervous, strung-out, always to be relished moments before the starting stalls crash open, a majority of the crowd will be thinking most particularly of the man associated with nine famous Derby winners, beginning, appropriately enough, with Never Say Die in 1954. They'll be thinking of Teenoso, Empery and The Minstrel. Of Crepello and St Paddy. Of Roberto and Sir Ivor. And surely of those half-a-dozen spellbinding seconds in 1970 when Nijinsky waited and waited and let both Stintino and Gyr have first run on him before finally his jockey let him down, let him go and away they both went into the history books. They'll be thinking of the man who even more than Fred Archer and Steve Donaghue completely symbolises racing and the Derby in the last one hundred years. The best jockey any of them have ever seen or are ever likely to see. The man who should be here today . . . but isn't. The Long Fellow. Old Stoneface. Lester.

And so they're off! The race is actually underway at 3.48, three minutes after the scheduled time. There are no last-minute disasters. No temperamental colt refuses to enter the stalls. No French jockey is thrown by his mount into an adjoining hamburger van. Captain Sayers requires only his normal amount of splenetic rage and then a huge cheer goes up from the crowd as Unfuwain's two pacemakers, Maksud and Al Muhalhal, move swiftly to the head of affairs. It's Maksud who actually leads through the first two uphill furlongs with Al Muhalhal second and Glacial Storm, Unfuwain, Doyoun, Kefaah and Project Manager all close up behind this leading pair. The runners are lost momentarily behind the tall marquees and tents, the coaches and the helicopters but then they reappear racing along the top of the downs with only the dull, grey sky behind them. Al Muhalhal takes them on until the mile gate where Maksud gets his head in front again and Al Muhalhal begins to lose ground. Glacial Storm is going well, going very well, in fact going quite superbly well just in behind the leaders while Cauthen has Unfuwain in exactly the right kind of forward position from which to make a bid for home when they turn into the straight. Doyoun is going sweetly on the inside rail. Walter Swinburn, balanced and relaxed and skilfully plotting precisely the kind of course that Piggott himself would've chosen. Kefaah is tracking Doyoun and Sheikh Hamdan's 'Big Spender' colt, Al Mufti, is making ground in the middle of the field. Kefaah's stable companion, Kahyasi, appears to be struggling to go the early pace and is already off the bridle.

But what makes the crowd gasp with a mixture of worry and admiration is the position of the favourite. Eddery has dropped him out at the rear of the field with not even one horse behind him and a good ten lengths between him and the leader. 'Pat must think that he's riding Nijinsky,' whispers a trembling and awestruck favourite-backer. And indeed for such an experienced jockey to be seemingly cruising so easily but so far off the pace, in the Derby for God's sake, does truly and stunningly suggest that all the hype might be true and that Pat really does think that he's riding not just a good but quite possibly a very good horse.

The field are lost briefly at the farthermost corner of the track but then you seen them once again, beginning the left-hand descent towards Tattenham Corner. With five and a half furlongs left to run, it's still Maksud from Unfuwain and Glacial Storm and Doyoun with Kefaah well there and also Al Mufti. They swing into the straight and almost immediately Unfuwain hits the front but if anyone thinks that this is going to be Shergar all over again or even a reprise of Unfuwain's Warren Stakes victory over the course and distance in April, then they're in for a bitter disappointment. Either the ground's too lively or he doesn't like the camber or he's just too slow but the massive Northern Dancer colt cannot go clear. With more than a quarter of a mile still to go it's Glacial Storm now who races past Unfuwain and into the lead. And so well is he travelling, so entirely full of running does he look, that a third Derby for Sangster and a first at last, at odds of 14-1, for Barry Hills seems entirely possible. Yet so much can happen inside the last few furlongs at Epsom as Sangster himself knows only too well.

As they race towards the furlong marker, Glacial Storm could still win it but so too could Doyoun who has been given a beautiful ride up the inner by Swinburn and who certainly isn't running out of stamina as yet. Kefaah has got a chance on the outside and now there are two other possibles who are running on strongly out of the pack up the home straight. One of them is the grey horse, Sheriff's Star, who is trained by the Duchess of Norfolk's daughter, Lady Herries. The other is the Aga Khan's second representative, Kahyasi, who, after labouring up the hill on the far side, has come round Tattenham Corner well and is starting to make his ground up rapidly. But then what the hell has happened to Red Glow? Pat seems to have delayed his move right the way down the hill and only after swinging into the straight has he picked his horse up. But instead of making his run on the outside, as he did in the Dante at York and on Golden Fleece in 1982, he's tried to dive in behind and come up the inside rail. And what's happened then? He's been stopped and checked and bumped and there are tiring horses and no room to go between them and all of a sudden this Derby favourite is getting no sort of clear run at all.

Inside the final furlong, Red Glow seems to burst through on to the heels of the leaders at last, but he's maybe a tired horse now. He's used up his speed and his stamina in those earlier frantic exchanges. And in the meantime the real Derby winner has been and gone. It's not Kefaah and it's not Doyoun either, who can find no more in the final half-furlong. Neither is it Glacial Storm who, heartbreakingly for Robert Sangster and Barry Hills, has been passed in the dying stages of the race by Luca Cumani's Kahyasi, who technically at least is only meant to be the Aga Khan's number-two choice. With jockey Ray Cochrane wearing the chocolate and green silks of the old Aga Khan, Kahyasi has powered his way courageously into the lead and he stays on right to the line which he passes one and a half lengths in front of Glacial Storm. Doyoun stays on almost as well to be another length and a half behind in third. Red Glow eventually finishes a further half-length away in fourth, a head in front of Kefaah. Sheriff's Star is sixth. Unfuwain is seventh, some seven lengths behind the winner, while the Major's other two runners, Minster Son and Charmer, who has never got into the race at all, finish a bitterly disappointing eighth and eleventh. Hamdan's Al Mufti is back in tenth position and the two Arab pacemakers, Maksud and Al Muhalhal, occupy the last two places.

The immediate and instinctive reaction of the crowd seems to be that they've seen a thrilling race and a brave winner but possibly not a great one. Yet such depressing diminution doesn't stand up to the official time for the 1988 Derby which at 2 minutes 33.84 seconds is the fastest electrically recorded time since electrical timing was introduced in 1984 and only 400ths of a second outside Mahmoud's hand-timed record in 1936.

As the horses pull up beyond the paddock and then as the principals slowly begin to canter and trot back towards the unsaddling enclosure, a thousand eyes are straining anxiously to see if comic tradition will be upheld and whether Channel 4 will once again supply the most uproarious moment of the racing year. This consists of allowing the smarmy Derek Thompson to try and interview the Derby-winning jockey with a hand-held microphone as the victorious combination jog back towards the winners circle. The best moments of these occasions are when Thommo, wearing his most oily grin, asks the winning jockey to take us through the race and tell us when he thought he was going to win. At this point the victorious horse usually breaks into a trot and Thommo, desperately trying to hang on to his hat, has to break into a run to keep up with him. It could be that the jockey is being less than garrulous. It could also be that the nervous trainer, watching anxiously as the microphone bumps up and down around this, by now, priceless multi-million-dollar equine head, unsubtly decides to elbow Thompson from the frame. Alas though, it seems that some traditions are not sacred. For 1988 Bruffscot and his producers have decided that dignity and a sense of occasion must at least briefly replace pantomime and burlesque. Kahyasi and Ray Cochrane are led into the hallowed place of champions, followed by Cumani and the Aga and Sir Gordon and the racing press ... but minus the grinning Thommo.

Being the spiritual leader of the Ismaili Moslems may not sound as if it should rank in financial terms with the position of the Dubai sheikhs but technically the Aga's subjects are meant to give him a tithe, as prescribed in the Koran, of up to 10 per cent of their personal earnings. This non-taxable income, which has been conservatively estimated at one hundred million dollars a year, is the Aga's alone to spend as he sees fit. In reality, a substantial amount of it is ploughed into all manner of charities, hospitals and educational, business and spiritual foundations in the Third World countries where most of the Aga's followers reside. No one would deny though that 'K' personally is a man of immense wealth as well as a sophisticated and cosmopolitan racehorse owner of considerable acumen. He was born in Switzerland, brought up in Kenya and educated at Harvard. He holds a British passport but his most famous home is his deluxe, purpose-built château at Aiglemont, a few miles from Chantilly racecourse in France. As well as being the head of the consortium that owns the Costa Smeralda complex on the northern coast of Sardinia, he is also the major shareholder in the Italian public company Fimpar, which makes him the controlling influence behind the luxury Italian hotel chain (and new Arc de Triomphe sponsors) CIGA.

The Aga's racing career hasn't always been a story of unruffled good fortune. As well as the Shergar kidnapping, he's had to endure several other controversial incidents. In 1981 his French trained colt, Vayrann, supposedly came up with a positive dope test after winning the Champion Stakes at Newmarket. After months of exhaustive investigation by his own team of forensic scientists the Aga was able to make a case that Vayrann had manufactured the 'illicit' substances naturally in his own bloodstream and his horse was allowed to keep the race. It was the same story in 1985 when another of his French-trained horses, Lashkari, was accused of having had a trace of the lethal narcotic, Etorphine, in his sample after running in the Breeders Cup Turf at Aqueduct race-track in New York. Once again the Aga spared neither effort nor expense to establish both his horse's and his trainer's innocence and the following year the accusations were dismissed.

The American bloodstock dealer, Wayne Murty, Professor Michael Moss and the English Jockey Club, and the New York State Racing Board have all discovered that it's unwise to embark in any litigious dispute with Karim, Aga Khan and expect to come out ahead. Only the real kidnappers of Shergar can ever say if they really got what they wanted or whether they were losers too. But few serious racing professionals would think twice if asked to suggest which current European Emperor Of The Blue Grass will still be getting most return on their money in, say, twenty years' time. Sangster? The sheikhs? Or the Aga Khan?

Of course Kahyasi's Derby is a triumph for Luca Cumani and Ray Cochrane as well as for his *soigné* owner. Cumani, in smart grey tails and black top-hat, is still tense but smiling too and generally has the look of a man who knew that this would rightfully happen to him before very long. As for the thirty-year-old jockey, every other rider and racing lover is openly and sincerely delighted for him. Back in 1977, this now highly successful flat-race pilot, third in the table behind Eddery and Cauthen, had actually turned to jump-racing because of increased worries about his weight. And riding in only his second Derby he'd been mightily nervous too and he reveals to the press boys that in fact he asked Susan Piggott to ring up Lester in jail and ask him for a bit of advice on how to ride a horse like

Kahyasi round Epsom. Lester's deceptively simple suggestion had been to let the horse flow up to the turn and then worry about a position from Tattenham Corner. For Ray this has not been that easy as Kahyasi had appeared to be so inconvenienced by the fast, early pace that it was only his considerable guts and courage that enabled him first to get back into the race and then to stay on and win. Cochrane suggests that Kahyasi might be the type for a race like the St Leger which is not the sort of comment to endear him to the Aga who has almost certainly got his eyes on much more prestigious prizes like the Irish Derby and the Arc. For all the other jockeys, owners and trainers, it is time for their post-mortems too.

Michael Hills says that Glacial Storm didn't really act on the course at all and that if it hadn't been for the camber in the last one and a half furlongs, he doesn't think that Kahyasi would have got to him. Hills senior and Sangster are both absolutely thrilled with their horse's performance and adamant that it will be the Irish Derby next. And you can sense a tremendous aura of hope and excitement about Sangster's party. A genuine feeling that with possibly softer going and the flatter, more galloping Curragh track in his favour, Glacial Storm may reverse the form with Kahyasi and bring Sangster back to the very centre, to the apex of the racing circus. If Michael Hills is pleased with the ride that his mount gave him, Walter Swinburn is being universally praised for the quite marvellous big-race ride that he gave Doyoun. He may not have won but who can seriously claim now that Doyoun doesn't stay a mile and a half or that he was only a substandard Guineas winner.

For Willie and the Major though, the 1988 Derby, the race that promised so much for them only a few weeks beforehand, has been a desperate anti-climax. And as for Unfuwain's owner, Hamdan Al Maktoum, well, he's done no better than any of his brothers have managed in previous years. But if Hern and the Arabs are losers, then Red Glow is the biggest loser of them all. Pat is insisting that his mount ran well but just didn't stay and that probably a mile and a quarter is his trip but poor Geoff Wragg, his betting vouchers all in tatters, looks desperately upset. Some old pro's are saying that the jockey must've been crazy to try and make his ground up the inside rail and that they cannot recall a worse ride by such an experienced horseman in recent Derby history. Well . . . not since Dancing Brave actually, when Greville Starkey misjudged his run and blew it and was replaced after the Eclipse Stakes by a truly cool world-class rider who wouldn't make the same kind of mistakes . . . called Pat Eddery.

If the Aga Khan is the big winner, the race is also a triumph for all owner-breeders, only recently depicted as a dying breed. The first four are all the result of breedings to commercial stallions of mares privately owned by the connections. Even so, those Emperors of the Blue Grass out in Kentucky and at Coolmore and Dalham Hall can only be gladdened by the result. For as Kahyasi's sire, Ile De Bourbon, is a son of Nijinsky, the race is yet another stunning homage to the continuing ascendancy of the Northern Dancer line in European racing. Glacial Storm too is out of a Nijinsky mare as is the fourth, Red Glow, while Doyoun's sire, Mill Reef, is from the other great bloodline started by Northern Dancer's grandsire, Nearco, via Nasrullah and Never Bend. With Northern Dancer's final full batch of yearlings, including one bred by Sangster's own Swettenham Stud, due to come up for sale at Keeneland in July, the Good Old Boys must be taking out advertising copy of Kahyasi's victory even now. Ironically, Ile De Bourbon had not hitherto been a great success as a stallion and had actually suffered the undignified devaluation of being 'exported' eighteen months before, to Japan.

So as the big boys depart to their private boxes to celebrate and count their winnings or the new value of their investments, the ordinary punters are left to try and get out on the remaining three races. Kahyasi's victory has been good for some of them but hardly a mass windfall and with nearly £300,000 going down on Red Glow in the ring alone it's hardly surprising that Hills are toasting profits on the race of about £2,500,000. Neither is it surprising that Ladbrokes are actually boasting of having laid the lowest morning price on Kahyasi of all the big firms. The last three races, all mediocre handicaps and all a dismal anti-climax, provide the punters with sparse consolation. Little Willie wins the first of them on an 8-1 shot and then local man, Geoff Lewis, scores a popular Derby Day victory when Rana Pratap, ridden by Paul Eddery and starting at 9-1, turns over the 4-1 favourite, Orient Line, on whom his brother seems to try and come from almost as far back as he did on Red Glow.

Well before the last race the glamorous jet-setters, the smart movers who don't rely on public transport, and the firm-jawed tycoons who are so important that they must be back at their City desks before 6 p.m. are making their exit by helicopter. Up in the Members' Bar the remaining toffs and spivs are plunging on the shampoo to try and console themselves over their losses. And as the men get more and more tight, so the tight hem-lines and buoyant cleavages of their brassy ladies start to beckon. Barry, a 'company director' from Sevenoaks, is sitting legs apart and conferring with Samantha, an air hostess from Heston. After each drink, Barry, now possibly incapable of standing, has his legs even further apart as Samantha's right knee, crossed daintily over the left, edges nearer to the zip on his trousers. Before the last race Barry and Samantha have wisely departed, presumably to complete their afternoon in the only way possible.

When the last race does come it's won by the 6-1 favourite, Bel Byou, who hardly compensates for Red Glow but who does take about eighty-six grand out of the bookies' satchels none the less. There can be no rush though to the car-parks. The funfair blares on. Bruffscot and company join the media party in their TV-land box and the sensible gypsies retire to their caravans to make a cup of tea and to watch it all again on the six o'clock news. Out on the downs some of the great common mass of humanity are already in their coaches. Stuck in the dust and fumes and settling in for the long jam home. Some of them, not surprisingly after nearly ten hours of the Great British Day Out, are looking, and no doubt feeling, a little rough around the edges. But as the mounted police begin to patrol across the downs and to trot up the straight where Kahyasi chased Glacial Storm to win the Derby of 1988, there are one or two arrests, and a disgusting eruption of abandoned litter, but no serious fights or aggravation.

The biggest crowd seems to be the one lumbering slowly back up to Tattenham Corner station where, Her Majesty long since gone, the British Rail staff have abandoned all pretence to civility and old-fashioned uniforms. The hordes of weary travellers are being treated in the manner they deserve – like a rabble of infected cattle. 'This is the fast to Waterloo via Purley?' ask the anxious chums in the grey morning-dress, their pockets lighter by almost everything they arrived with. 'That's it, sir. Hurry along now,' barks a pompous official as he bundles them into a carriage only three times more crowded than the one that they arrived in. 'And it is the first one out?' 'That's it, sir,' repeats the guard, simultaneously walking across the platform to the neighbouring train, blowing his whistle and waving his flag. And not only does the other train leave the station first, the chaps' conveyance is of course not the fast to Waterloo at all. It's the extremely slow to London Bridge via Whyteleafe, Smitham and Reedham Junction.

There are no adoring wives and children or glamorous lovers waiting to greet the fellows when they disembark at Purley. 'We're just a couple of prats/In a couple of hired top-hats,' they sing rather quietly, as they hide their hats by their ankles again for the return walk along the empty street, past the now closed supermarket and up to the multi-storey car-park where their Ford Sierra is waiting. 'I bet Robert Sangster doesn't go home like this,' mutters one of them. 'Or the Aga Khan.' Not half they don't, boys. Not half.

11 : Irish Eyes

Whatever the real or supposed strength of Robert Sangster's financial position there could be no doubt that the greying high-roller was greatly looking forward to the events at The Curragh on 25 and 26 June. On the Saturday afternoon Classic Thoroughbreds were due to have their very first runner when the two-year-old Kyra, a filly by Sadlers Wells out of a Riverman mare, would make her debut in a maiden race over five furlongs. The following day Caprifolia, a daughter of Lomond, would be the company's second runner in a similar contest over six furlongs. As Sadlers Wells had already won with his first runner in France – a filly called In The Wings had scored at Chantilly the week before – the omens were good. For Sangster personally though, the big moment this final weekend in June would come when his Epsom runner-up Glacial Storm clashed again with Kahyasi in the Irish Derby, sponsored for the third time by Budweiser and being run for the first time in its history on a Sunday.

Glacial Storm had worked well at Manton since the English race and in keeping with an agreement that Sangster had made with Michael Hills at the start of the season, Steve Cauthen, not required elsewhere by Henry Cecil, would take the ride. Glacial Storm was a top-priced 4-1 with the local bookies but Kahyasi, reckoned spot-on by the wily Cumani and just as well in himself as he had been before Epsom, was no better than 5-4 to become the Aga Khan's third Irish Derby winner and the third horse to do the classic double in eight years.

For the Irish Turf Club and the separate Irish Racing Board who actually have to try and promote horse-racing in the Republic, the Derby, with its massive – IR£500,000 – sponsorship, is easily the biggest event of their sporting year. For the ordinary punters it would mean a lot of commercial hard sell and an almost certainly exciting race but one that would not conceal the serious weaknesses in the whole structure of the Irish racing industry. And no one is more aware of those weaknesses than the Chairman of the Racing Board (and Robert Sangster's new partner in Classic Thoroughbreds), the fifty-three-year-old Michael Smurfit.

Smurfit and Sangster are the same age and the two men make an instructive contrast. They're both the sons of self-made men but Sangster ended up selling the family business, whereas Smurfit has transformed his inheritance, which was in the romantic area of cardboard box manufacture, into something bigger than Atlantic City. Devolving first into banking and insurance he proceeded to make the Smurfit Corporation not only Ireland's largest and richest multi-national but, in recent years, one of the financial world's very biggest of the big dogs. Between 1985 and 1987 the Group purchased 80 per cent of the Publishers Paper Company (now renamed the Smurfit Newsprint Corporation) from the *Los Angeles Times* and then 50 per cent of the Container Corporation of America from Mobil Oil. Not surprisingly the group's American subsidiary, the Jefferson Smurfit Corporation, now figures regularly in the pages of *Forbes Business Magazine* and in the *Fortune 500*.

Sangster's compulsive passion for horses has led him to great heights but also perilously close to some ominous depths. Smurfit has owned horses in partnership for a number of years. He has his own stud farm and he plans to become significantly involved in commercial breeding in Ireland in the next decade but he has never hurled his cap at the race-track or the sales ring. He's been in deals with Bert Firestone and he now shares a string with Fat Alligator Paulson at Dermot Weld's stable near The Curragh but he's yet to commit himself to anything like Sangster's level of investment. Both men are basically tax exiles, Sangster in the Isle of Man, Smurfit in Monte Carlo. And both men have attracted the gossip columnists, especially in Ireland. Like Sangster, Smurfit has a glamorous new wife but, whereas Robert is beginning to thicken a little with middle age, Michael still has the sort of craggy and windswept good looks that could genuinely sustain a leading role in a soap opera.

The Irish have more love and affection for horses and gambling and there is more beauty and poetry in their racing and breeding industry than in that of any comparable country in the world. Once upon a time it was axiomatic that one in three members of the population went off to the races at least once a week. Yet by the mid-1980s race-track attendances were falling. Irish-bred horses were being bought more and more by non-Irish interests to race elsewhere and maybe to breed from elsewhere when their careers were over. And Irish racing was suffering from a desperate lack of good prize money. The Irish Turf Club decided to set up a committee to do something about attracting commercial sponsors – not double-glazing barons but the Sir Gordons and General Accidents – to back the Irish sport. They asked Smurfit to chair it.

With a direct line to every major businessman in the country the hot-shot put them all in the picture and came up with an initial target of two million Irish punts to be invested each year for a three-year trial period. On the basis of this and also because of the transformation Smurfit had effected in the affairs of Irish Telecom, he was elected Chairman of the Irish Racing Board itself. But he quickly realised that introducing a commercial marketing approach to a centuries-old sport was not going to be immediately popular. Especially with some members of the predominantly conservative and reactionary Irish Turf Club who are still in charge of the rules, discipline and day-to-day administration of Irish racing.

Smurfit's main concern was that a vast majority of Ireland's racecourses were as run-down and dilapidated as some of the houses and finances of the more eccentric old ascendancy families in the pages of Molly Keane and Somerville and Ross. Fairyhouse, home of the Irish Grand National was, literally, tumbling brick by brick into the mud. How could you expect companies to sponsor new races and advertise their products when the actual race-tracks offered such dismal and inept facilities for catering and entertaining? And how could you launch a major advertising campaign to persuade the public to go racing when they too were going to be confronted by such inadequate accommodation?

Smurfit believed that the root of the problem lay in the fact that, unlike Britain, the Irish government kept every penny of the 10 per cent tax they levied on off-course betting, and didn't return a dime of it to the industry. With the Big Four all moving into the Irish betting shop market, he argued that Irish racing, like its British counterpart, had to get a fairer share of those profits. So he began a tough, high-profile, campaign – not yet successful but still incomplete – aimed at convincing the Haughey administration that two of the 10 per cent should go back to racing each year. Told that Ireland's finances were in such a poor state that the treasury just couldn't afford it, he retorted that in that case they should levy an extra 2 per cent on top of the 10 per cent and give that back to racing instead. This not surprisingly turned out to be thumpingly unpopular with the bookmakers.

Smurfit remains convinced that even though the Irish racing industry can never compete with the British model it can attract new owners if the prize money is improved, and the only way to do that is through sponsorship. Budweiser, whose deal over the Irish Derby was initially set in motion with Lord Hemphill, undoubtedly see Smurfit as a professional in their own image. But is Michael Smurfit's vision the whole picture? For many smaller Irish trainers, owners and breeders the massive boost for the Derby would do nothing to alleviate their problems but simply concentrate yet more money at the top in the hands of the same old people. These lower-tier players were substantially unmoved by the plea for better facilities for sponsors, their guests and the likes of Sangster, the Aga and the Maktoum family. What difference would it make to the bottom rung of the infrastructure? And yet ... how can you even begin to apply such a dreary, vogue word as 'infrastructure' to the elliptical, evocative world of the Irish provincial race-track?

Five days before the Budweiser Derby there was an ordinary run-of-the-mill evening meeting down at Clonmel in Vincent O'Brien country in Tipperary – except that you could never describe something but a few steps from heaven as run of the mill. To get to the race-track you first have to walk out through the town past the pink and blue and yellow wash walls and doors and old shop fronts of the newsagents, the tailors, the bakers, the bookmakers, the chip shops and the bars. Along the animated streets beside the river Suir, with the bunting strung up between the lampposts for the spring festival, and with the sun shining down between the dark trees. And out to the racecourse in Powerstown Park, home of the National Cup coursing festival each February. There's a tricolour flag flying over the stand and pictures of an old Anglo-Irish MFH circa 1932, in hunting pink with handlebar moustache, hanging on the wall behind the bar. The chairs scrape on the wooden floor littered with empty Smithwicks bottles and glasses of Guinness. The air is thick with the smoke of Carrolls Majors and alive with the talk of horses. Outside there's a big crowd with a priest or two and the local trainers gathering in a group by the rails and of course the bookies with their musical names. Hannafin, Milligan, Mulligan, McManus, O'Mahoney, O'Mara, O'Rourke.

There are mountains on three sides of the course and, as the grey clouds come and go, patches of intermittent sunlight filter down over the trees and on to the centre of the race-track. There aren't many Dublin or metropolitan faces among the punters. Most of them are wearing caps and smoking fags but there's one big red-faced man in shades and an even bigger man with white hair and a velvet-collar coat and a wide-brimmed hat who's still got an old roué's twinkle in his eye. This is not surprising as he's just had three hundred punts on the bumper winner at 7-1.

Kids beg for money and sweets and run in and out of the concrete snack bar selling ham sandwiches and tea. While down in the restaurant proper, which is just a room beneath the bar, kindly respectable people, entertaining parents and grandchildren, sit down at the tables with the little blue and white check tablecloths and tuck into the £8 supper of soup with salmon or steak.

After the racing is over, the crowd disperse quite peacefully. And the smell of turf smoke hangs over the town as the members of the Comeragh Bridge Club gather in the back room at Hearns Hotel. The chairman of the club is the old roué with the white hair and the two grand in readies. He tells you that the Comeragh Bridge Club is not named after a collection of card players but after a legendary local IRA unit who blew the shit out of some Black and Tans in 1921. The chairman expresses his admiration for Vincent O'Brien and Eamonn De Valera and for Charlie Haughey and Jimmy Fitzgerald and mentions that his brother Michael nearly bought Forgive 'N' Forget when he was an unbroken three-year-old down in Cork. And he adds that there's another very nice type who'll be running in a bumper in two weeks time and would you be interested in buying him now before that crafty Mulhern goes and gets in first?

Now, The Curragh is not quite like this. And certainly not on Irish Derby day. Some of the Coolmore management team, let alone the Budweiser Corporation or Breeders Cup Ltd would probably laugh out loud at the idea of anyone making a special trip to Clonmel races. But what were they selling instead this 25 and 26 June 1988?

The Curragh is as nearly the home and headquarters of top-drawer Irish thoroughbred racing as Newmarket is to England. Some twenty-five miles south-west of Dublin, and close to the towns of Newbridge, Naas and Kildare, it's literally a great plain of lush, green grass some twelve miles square. It's not quite as bare and lonely as Newmarket Heath. It has more beauty, but when it's deserted, on a grey day after the local horses have finished exercise, it also has something of the same melancholy bleakness.

On one side is the racecourse and many racing stables and several famous studs. Not all the premier Irish trainers are based at The Curragh but quite a few of them are. Weld, Oxx, Liam Browne, the Prendergasts and the once invincible Mick O'Toole. Only about a quarter of a mile beyond the winning-post is the front drive leading up to the Aga Khan's Ballymany Stud where Doyoun and Khayasi were born and from where Shergar was so infamously kidnapped. On the other side of the prairie are the headquarters of the Irish army and that means the same unlovely barrack buildings and military housing that you can see at Tidworth and on Salisbury Plain. You can't see the army depot from the racecourse as it's obscured by a line of trees way out beyond the far side of the track. What you can see are the blue hills of the Dublin mountains in the distance and in the opposite direction the lines of the old Great Southern railway, where the loop to Kilkenny and Waterford swings off from the main line to Cork and the south. Sheep graze quietly by the tracks and beyond around the Newbridge road. Where the trees and the railway line don't intervene, the gently rolling grass seems to stretch, like the Texas panhandle, uninterrupted and undiminished, as far as the eye can see.

There may be an almost straight mile like Newmarket but the Irish Derby is run on the round course which means that the horses start on the far side some half a mile away from the stands and then race in a horseshoe shape, swinging right-handed into the straight about three furlongs from home and providing the spectators with a genuine grandstand finish.

Leopardstown racecourse, which is in the suburb of Foxrock, five miles south of Dublin city centre, is one of the most modern in Europe – an Irish Sandown or Hollywood Park. But The Curragh's big long grandstand building is old and dilapidated, especially its great barren Tote Hall on the ground floor (which was due to be modernised before 1989). There's no decent restaurant to speak of. There's a self-service cafeteria where you queue up for bacon and cabbage and chicken and chips and there are a lot of gaunt old bars of the 1935-going-on-1953 era in which the throng of thirsty punters is always every bit as long, clamouring and impatient as at one of the big English tracks near London. When the weather's bad, as it often can be in spring and autumn, the wind seems to drive the rain across the course from Kildare and sweep it up on to the draughty old terraces of the reserved enclosure.

What with the rather ancient facilities and the relatively easy-paced approach of the old Turf Club stewards to the idea of marketing and promotion, the men from Budweiser decided that they didn't entirely get their money's worth from the first few runnings of 'their' race. And for the 1988 meeting the new Curragh management have unveiled various 'improvements' which range from a paint job on much of the buildings to new covered seating areas, a rash of new private boxes to cater for the nobs at the top of the stand and a large marquee and tented village beyond the paddock for the convenience of sponsors and their guests. There is also a special cheap section or 'infield' to be christened 'Budweiser Green' (oh, what marketing genius dreamed that one up?) and to be situated out in the middle but opposite the stands. The view of the racing may be limited but sideshows, stalls and live musical entertainment will provide wholesome distractions for the very young and for the less affluent and less serious racegoers. The whole idea of the race being staged on a Sunday as opposed to the old Saturday scheduling has also been mightily encouraged, partly so as to attract a bigger weekend crowd but also in order to assist the American TV companies to market the race back home. This is far from being the first experiment with Sunday racing in Ireland, and each new Sunday meeting – as it surely would in England if only absurd religious objections could be overcome – proves even more popular than the last.

The facilities may have been improved, well, somewhat, well, for the more privileged racegoers at least, but the punters have not only got to be lured through the gates, the whole population of metropolitan Dublin, indeed of the entire Republic, has got to be reminded of what the sponsors are really in Ireland to sell. This time no expense is to be spared and no punches are to be pulled to achieve this end. The boys from Anheuser Busch Inc., St Louis, Missouri have even imported some of their own, quote, 'shit-hot marketing people' to make sure that the local agency get the job done. And the result is a triumph for them all as they turn the 1988 Irish Derby into the biggest beer commercial ever seen this side of the Atlantic. It starts with the sponsors' messages pasted all over the luggage trolleys and duty-free bags at Dublin airport and it continues with banner adverts blazed across the hoardings on the Dublin-Newbridge dual carriageway. These claim that the Derby will be Europe's richest race, which is just a touch cheeky as, although the winner's prize of IR£336,000 is £70,000 more than at Epsom, the overall purse money, including for the placed horses, is slightly less. Untroubled by such minor distractions, the shit-hot promotional team extend their trail of logos, banners and fly stickers all the way from Grafton Street to the course, so that by the time the racing begins there's scarcely a blade of grass within six furlongs of the winning-post that hasn't been redecorated red, white and green or isn't urging the spectators to enjoy a cool brew with their sport. One or two seditious voices even suggest that the Turf Club itself is now a brewery and that the likes of Lord Hemphill and Gaisford St Lawrence actually have a sticker on the seat of their trousers saying, 'Brought to you by kind permission of the Anheuser Load of Old Bull and Busch Corporation'.

The Americans, at least, are entering into the spirit of it all. Several hundred excited Budweiser executives and their spouses, lovers, families, personal assistants and fax machines have flown over especially for the week of the race. Some of them with real Irish ancestry and a lot of the others desperately keen to try and claim a little bit for themselves if at all possible. On the Wednesday evening the happy wanderers partake of a special Irish pub night out at James Scott-Lennon's celebrated, cliché-ridden but still enjoyably boozy and atmospheric pub, the Abbey Tavern in Howth. Michael J. Roarty, the sun-tanned Walter Matthau figure who is the Executive Vice-President of Budweiser, and whose father John did actually emigrate to the States from Meenamara in County Donegal, entertains the party with an emotional rendition of 'Danny Boy'. The following night the acclaimed Irish folk singer, Colm Wilkinson, gives his version of the same song at a Budweiser reception in the old hospital at Kilmainham, not far from the grim prison where the British shot the leaders of the Easter Rising in 1916. This time the slightly more assured delivery of the classic ballad reduces the real homecoming Irish-Americans present to a state of tearful emotion not seen since the high point of Mayor Daley's annual St Patrick's Day parties in Chicago in the fifties and sixties. The festivities are rounded off by a pre-Derby Day banquet at medieval Luttrelstown Castle, which the corporation, disdaining the city centre hotels, have hired for the week for their guests. With a colourful *mélange* of Gaelic pipers, Elizabethan serving-wenches, and tuxedos, with buckets of claret and steaming slabs of beef on silver salvers, everyone's cup, stomach and liver is already overflowing long before the serious racing even begins.

The Saturday warm-up card, which plays to a small crowd in eighty degree heat, is a personal triumph for Vincent O'Brien. Kyra at 6-4 on (4-6) becomes Classic Thoroughbreds' first winner from their first runner, but the 2,500 shareholders, many of them present, are hoping that one or two of their subsequent victories will come a little easier. Losing three lengths at the start, Kyra battles her way up to the leaders at the furlong marker, but then runs alarmingly green and only just seems to get there by a head. The bookies make her no better than a 5-2 shot to triumph in the photograph and on top of that she has to survive a stewards' enquiry into possible interference suffered by the third-placed horse, Rainey. But triumph and survive she does and, against all expectations, her remarkable trainer *has* produced an early, if immature, two-year-old out of the hat just when the accountant needed it. And forty minutes later he completes a most satisfying double when Dark Lomond, also ridden by John Reid and wearing the Niarchos colours, takes the Group Two, ten-furlong, Pretty Polly Stakes in fine style with Sangster's Irish 1,000 Guineas runner-up, Dancing Goddess, back in fourth. Later in the season Dark Lomond will win the Irish St Leger over the same track to give O'Brien a second classic winner of 1988 to go with his victory in the Irish 2,000 Guineas in May with Prince of Birds, a Storm Bird colt owned by Sangster himself. The old firm weren't quite at the top again yet . . . but at least they were back on the leader board.

In the early hours of Sunday morning the weather breaks in Dublin for the first time in nearly a fortnight. Heavy rain between 1 and 5 a.m. means that come breakfast-time it's one of those particularly green and moist and misty days that seem to suit race-meetings in Ireland so perfectly. There are four race-specials from Heuston station, either running directly to The Curragh or making a special stop at the racecourse station on their way south. The station is in a deep cutting and as the punters scramble their way up the embankment path there are a wild gallery of faces staring down at them from the bridge up above. These are tinkers or travelling people, some sharp and suspicious, some dark and romantic, some bucolic and gentle – as rich an expression of contrast, life and colour as a canvas by Jack Butler Yeats. Two young boys in Clyde Barrow hats have fixed up a home-made roulette wheel by the exit from the trains. Further down the lane, away from the Garda and the railway officials, an older man with flared trousers and an ear-ring is trying to collect some stake money by offering a tin can variation on that old standby, the three-card trick. The crowd make their way along the narrow and muddy footpath that leads towards the back of the stands. Suddenly a helicopter descends from the sky into an adjoining field and out get, yes, Robert and Susan Sangster. The lady looks every bit as fragile and as attractive as at Epsom with another wide-

brimmed hat stuck firmly to her head. They pick their way out of
the wet field and around the piles of litter at the back of the stand,
she tottering on her high heels, he looking smart and relaxed in his
light grey suit, and then head in through the reserved enclosure
entrance.

Inside the racecourse, the Budweiser hustlers and huxters have
been rewarded by a crowd of up to thirty thousand, eight thousand
out in the infield of Budweiser Green. Several million other more
sedentary spectators will be watching the event on television, worldwide.

Whatever the significance of this Irish Derby day to the international racing community, it's without a doubt the grandest event of
the summer for every socially aspiring citizen of Dublin. All of them
it seems are longing to see their photographs next week in the
windows of *The Times*, *Press* and *Independent* with the caption,
'Seen at the races last Sunday. Eligible bachelor Mr Christy
McMahon, restaurant-owner from Mullingar and his attractive companion, Miss Cheryl O'Shaughnessy of Donnybrook' etc. The ladies'
fashions are not quite Paris or Milan and they're not quite the
Melbourne Cup either but they're not a lot worse than the worst of
Royal Ascot. Generally speaking it's hat city at The Curragh – from
the loud to the dull, the dated to the ordinary and from the stylish to
the merely bizarre. One lady, the busty Yvonne Costello, appears in
a blue dress and a blue hat covered with balloons and cans of
Budweiser beer. The old Duke of Norfolk would've loved it.

The champagne bar, a sort of prefabricated hut beside the paddock,
is filled at one end with Anglo-Irish Sloane Rangers who may be
natives of Kildare and Meath but look as if they've been transplanted
for the day from Newmarket and Ascot. At the other end of the bar
are young Irish yuppies – junior brokers with bold Dublin accents all
discussing the likely destiny of Classic Thoroughbreds' share price in
the wake of Kyra's victory. The VIP tent is beyond the champagne
bar and mingling busily in there are such serious men as Justice
Minister, Michael Noonan, Garda Commissioner, Eamonn Docherty
– who was the last guest to leave the Luttrelstown banquet the
previous night – and Finance Minister, Ray MacSharry, who may be
contemplating putting Smurfit's 2 per cent on Kahyasi in the big
one.

Next door, but out of reach of the politicians' marquee, is an even
more select pavilion: The VVIP tent. 'Who's in there, then?' a
wolfish reporter asks a slinky PR. 'God,' replies the foxy lady.
'Who's God?' 'Mike Roarty, of course.' Mr Roarty's companions

include the truly jet-set racing personalities like Sangster and Smurfit as well as the American celebrities who have been brought over especially for the occasion. The top-most attraction is old silver-haired Blake Carrington, the self-same John Forsythe, racing lover and thoroughbred breeder, who co-hosted the Breeders Cup banquet in LA the previous year. Forsythe does ads for Budweiser in the States and he's doing a few plugs live from The Curragh for American TV. At close quarters, the now seventy-two-year-old Blake looks rather too cosy and venerable for much boardroom skulduggery, let alone serious bedroom antics. But, undeterred by his age, Blake is not only thoroughly enjoying an intimate conversation with Vincent O'Brien, he is also understandably enthralled by the dazzling conformation of Jerry Hall's legs. The presence of the famous model is regarded as a tremendous coup by both Budweiser and the diary writers and photographers of the Irish and English press who are hanging around the marquee exit drooling with expectations. The fact that the luscious glamour-puss is here at all is due to the fortunate coincidence of the Derby taking place the day after Ireland's other big social event of the year – the wedding of John Boorman's daughter Katrine to Tom Conran in the film director's adopted village of Laragh in County Wicklow. For Derby Day, Jerry is wearing a caramel coloured Jasper Conran suit with a short jacket and a short, tight skirt. The press, thwarted of a glimpse of Michael Smurfit's new Scandinavian bride, Birgitta, are beside themselves at the thought of the new Mrs Sangster coming face to face with Robert's passing fling. But any such unseemly embarrassment is carefully avoided by Budweiser's 'shit-hot' handlers although 'the mettlesome Texan filly', as one Monty-like scribe will describe her, does teasingly admit that she just has to have a flutter on Glacial Storm in the big race.

As the party in the tent gets further into its stride so the dividing line between soap opera fantasy and normal reality becomes more and more blurred, seemingly to the contented delight of everybody present. At one point Forsythe is cheering on a race on the TV monitor. 'Go on Glacial Storm,' he shouts, apparently thinking that he's watching the afternoon's premier event until an unkind Adam Carrington-type, with a sneering mouth, informs him that it's actually a film rerun of the English Derby which took place three weeks before.

When the racing finally begins it's immediately dramatic and compulsive. The opening contest, the Anna Livia Plurabelle Millennium Maiden, goes to a filly of Jim Bolger's called Smaoineamh,

who touches off the favourite Missing Money by half a length.
Classic Thoroughbreds' Caprifolia finishes fourth. Half an hour later
we are on to the John J. Long Memorial, this one named after
another Budweiser executive with Irish roots, in this case in County
Kerry. And it goes to an 8-1 shot, Causa Sua, who gets home by a
short head in a four-sided finish with two horses, one of them
Sangster's Welsh Charm, dead-heating for third. Then it's Roarty's
turn for his race, in honour of that old pop of his from Meenamara.
Hakari, trained by John Oxx and ridden by New South Wales
champion, Ron Quinton, romps this by four lengths with the
favourite down the field. Three successive reversals for the punters.
But as Mike and Mrs Roarty chat with Hakari's connections
afterwards, the professionals, the insiders and the keenest devotees
of tension and theatre are making their way to The Curragh pre-
parade ring beyond the paddock. The 1988 Irish Derby is now only
forty-five minutes away and we have reached that moment once
again; the saddling-up boxes; the ritual of the pre-race manoeuvres
as the big players quietly come forth from their dressing-rooms,
watched by a thousand intense and curious eyes. This is the time
when the adrenalin, the juice, the sexual nervous excitement is
starting to pump and flow. This is when they raise the net, push
back the ropes and triple the stakes beyond our mortal reach. 'Ladies
and gentlemen. Will you please stand back. This is a restricted
heavyweight contest over two and half minutes for multi-millionaires
only. And I'm going to open the bidding at three hundred thousand.'

At The Curragh, only owners, trainers and staff are allowed
through into the stabling area. Slowly, one by one and then in pairs,
the horses come out to walk around the preliminary ring. A public
address announcement rambles on in the background. A gaggle of
young girls stump past looking for the Radio Liffey trailer and going
in the wrong direction. And there now, walking quietly and placidly
around is a small bay colt. And yes . . . this is him. Number seven.
Kahyasi. The Derby winner. Six feet away. In the flesh. Ten million
pounds worth of classic racehorse. And all of that valuation will
shortly be on the line. Here in Kildare on this grey June Sunday
afternoon.

For this one race the organisers have decided that the paddock
formalities will be moved out into the centre of the course to give as
many of the crowd as possible a chance to get a good view of the
action. Glacial Storm walks through looking so strong and well that
once again you think that he wouldn't look out of place challenging
over the last at the National Hunt Festival in March, only you dare

not insult him by mentioning such a heinous idea in front of his trainer and owner. Kahyasi follows Glacial Storm – small and hard like his trainer, Cumani, who today is more openly and visibly nervous than he was at Epsom. Behind Cumani comes the Aga, purring and smiling away in a dark blue suit and tie. And it has to be said that, so far from looking slimmer, His Highness actually appears to have put on weight since Newmarket and Epsom and, that this summer at least, he is clearly a stranger to the Aiglemont tennis court.

Kahyasi is difficult to back now at anything better than odds-on. But Glacial Storm at threes is still the professional tip. The slightly rain-softened ground should suit him ideally and hope has turned first into optimism and then confidence. Although as Robert and Sue walk over to the crisp, trilby-hatted and cigar-smoking Barry Hills who is standing next to the relaxed and smiling Steve Cauthen, Sangster too looks appreciably more nervous than he seemed when he first arrived at the course a few hours before. Not that this is entirely a two-horse race in spite of the betting. Amongst the other nine runners are two from France and one of them is Hours After, the winner of the Prix du Jockey Club or French Derby at Chantilly.

France is a marvellous country to go racing in as long as you're not that interested in racing. At tracks like Longchamp, Deauville and Chantilly – where Condé's stables and the neighbouring château combine to make a ravishingly beautiful setting – you can enjoy a calm, elegant and unhurried afternoon. But one without any of the passion, noise and colour of Epsom and The Curragh. The food in the restaurant may be superb but it's also superbly expensive (550 francs for a three-course lunch without wine) and for all that the admission prices are ridiculously cheap there is, in the end, something rather anticlimactic about standing on a racecourse without those fluent and villainous bookmakers to do battle with.

Nobody is taking Hours After's chance too seriously at The Curragh. The form of his Chantilly win looks suspect as about half a dozen horses all finished on top of one another. Further to that, his jockey that day, Pat Eddery, has been claimed to ride for Khalid Abdulla at Longchamp so it's the Frenchman, Gerard Mossé, who takes the ride instead. And as Irish punters are every bit as prejudiced about French jockeys riding outside of their own country as their compadres are in England, Hours After is a generously priced 14-1 to get to the finishing line first.

Sheikh Mohammed has two representatives, both of them trained in Ireland. One, Baltic Fox, is a Danzig colt from David O'Brien's yard, but his seemingly second-division form rates him no better than a 66-1 shot. Then there's Curio. There's a bit of a move for Curio – each way money mainly. He's by the American stallion, Majestic Light, and he's trained not far from the racecourse by John Oxx. As a winner last time out, and possibly still on the upgrade, Curio is definitely the dark horse of the race, but even so it's another dismal result for the Sheikh, after all that expenditure, to have nothing better than these two – and nothing at all from Cecil and Stoute – to represent him in one of the three most important races for three-year-olds of the whole season.

And that leaves Insan. Another American-bred who cost but $40,000 at Keeneland's September sale in 1986. Insan is owned by the Saudi Arabian, Fahd Salman, and trained at Whatcombe by Paul Cole, the same upright gentleman who sent Bint Pasha, unsuccessfully, to the Breeders Cup in 1987. Insan's jockey is to be the young Scotsman, Richard Quinn, who was on board for the Lingfield Derby Trial back in May when the combination gave Kahyasi five pounds and were only beaten two lengths. Having had to miss Epsom due to a minor setback, Insan is coming to The Curragh a possibly fresher horse than either Kahyasi or Glacial Storm and at 10-1 he looks a stand-out each-way bet.

The jockeys mount up and the runners all parade in front of the stand and then slowly, very slowly, they make their way across The Curragh to the mile-and-a-half start on the far side of the track. For the biggest punters and for the connections of the most fancied horses, these suspended, drawn-out seconds are the most nerve-tingling and yet the most delicious moments of all. For the Budweiser senior management they're a complete nightmare. Twelve months before, a sudden bomb scare (that turned out to be a hoax) delayed the start for more than an hour and resulted in people being evacuated chaotically in all directions by a comic-opera police team under the supervision of the inimitable Chief Superintendent Jim 'Shergar' Murphy. The top execs reckoned that it ruined the whole spectacle and they don't want a repeat. And fortunately for them and their security hot-dogs all of their fears prove groundless. There is no trouble or disturbance. 1988 is to be quite safe and without incident, at least of that kind. The runners go behind. Curio is momentarily difficult at the stalls but then that's it. They're all in. They're under starters orders. And they're off.

The early leader is the 300-1 outsider Wagon Load, trained by Liam Browne and ridden by John Reid. Insan goes immediately into second place with Glacial Storm dropping into third, Hours After handy in fourth and the other French runner, Port Lyautey, back in fifth. After six furlongs Kahyasi is going nowhere. It seems to be Epsom all over again and he just can't keep up with the pace at this stage of the race. About four furlongs from home Insan takes up the running. He's going strongly and he's looking very, very good. Glacial Storm is still right there in behind him and at long last Kahyasi is starting to make a little ground. Then approaching the turn into the straight, there appears to be a right barging match between Reid, Gerard Mossé and Ray Cochrane. Wagon Load and the French Derby winner suddenly drop out of contention altogether as Kahyasi begins to make his way on the outside. But as they hit the home straight and face up dramatically to the run towards the line, Insan is not stopping and Kahyasi still has an awful lot to do.

With a quarter of a mile left to run, Kahyasi goes past Glacial Storm who most disappointingly, not to say tragically for Sangster and his backers, just doesn't change gear at all. The duel is on now between Insan and the favourite and it's a titanic battle, a fight to the death, with both horses galloping at full power, their strength and stamina stretched to the very limit. You can hear the thunderous roar of their hoofs, the cracking of Cochrane's whip and, behind you and ringing in your ears, the deafening sound of the passionate Irish crowd – louder than anything in America, louder even than at Epsom. In one final climactic burst of noise and colour and sensation the two horses flash past the winning-post together. It looks as if Kahyasi may just have got up but it can't be by more than a short head if that. Officially, it's most definitely a photograph. But that's only one part of this pulsating Derby Day drama.

Kahyasi pulls up with blood pouring from a cut on his near fore. A breathless Cochrane, whose whole family from Gilford, Northern Ireland, have come down to see his big day, explains that he thinks his horse sustained the cut as he tried to get a run through the scrimmaging in the race towards the home turn. As Luca Cumani gazes nervously at the cut the result of the photograph is announced. Kahyasi has indeed completed the Epsom-Curragh double. But only by the minutest short head. Cumani literally jumps in the air for joy – a very neat, rather camp little leap with both legs together. And then he sprints across The Curragh towards his jockey who is already on his way towards the weighing room. Meanwhile anyone about to commiserate Richard Quinn and Insan's connections, as they watch the TV replay, is aghast to see that Quinn actually dropped his whip in the final fifty yards and was unable to give his mount the kind of red-blooded assistance that Cochrane supplied to Kahyasi in those final crucial seconds. Quinn is mortified, although he insists that his horse would not have given any more for a beating. Cole stands loyally by him and many outside observers are inclined to take the same view. But, sadly for Richard Quinn, they do not include Insan's owner. Fahd Salman will insist that Quinn be replaced on the horse before its next appearance.

Luca Cumani confirms that Kahyasi is bleeding quite profusely just below the knee, that the cut is about an inch deep and that hopefully it hasn't gone down into the champion's tendon. The Aga is being interviewed about his horse's future. Will the colt run again? is the immediate question. Now that it's won twice, two classics, two Derbys, will its injury lead to premature commercial retirement? The Aga insists that the future of both Kahyasi and Doyoun will not be decided by mercenary considerations but by what best suits the athletic requirements of the two horses. Some people remain unconvinced but both Cumani and the Aga are patently disdainful of running their horse in the St Leger. Who would want to go for that lowly fourteen-furlong slog at Doncaster? Oh no, it's his own race that 'K' has his eyes on. The first ever CIGA-sponsored Arc de Triomphe to be run in Paris in October. If the colt recovers. But after this game, dramatic victory gained in spite of pain and injury when he was at least four to five lengths down, who can deny that if not a great Derby winner, Kahyasi is at least an exceedingly tough and courageous one.

The Aga Khan is the big winner. Kahyasi is a winner. But today, even with third place, Robert Sangster is a loser. Glacial Storm has actually finished further behind Kahyasi than he did at Epsom. And over the course that was supposed to suit him so perfectly. Hills surveys the horse, looking serious and tight-lipped. Cauthen tries to explain, to soften the blow, to make it seem easier. Finally he walks calmly and nonchalantly away back to the weighing room. Hills assures a journalist that there are no excuses, that he wasn't at all disappointed and that Glacial Storm may now be trained . . . for the St Leger. Sangster keeps standing there. Running his tongue up and down over his teeth. Looking at his horse and then across at where they're setting up the podium to present the winner's prize and then back at his horse again. He looks frankly devastated, like the man who has had his final twenty grand on the getting-out stakes, the final race of the meeting at Cheltenham or Royal Ascot, and then seen it all go down. All the big Derbys are over now for another season. Where can he find himself a three-year-old good enough to aim at the rich autumn prizes? Must he already start thinking of next year?

Around the podium the band of the Kildare Civil Defence League have suddenly launched into a spirited rendition of the theme tune from 'Neighbours'. Is this a secret favourite of His Highness? Can he possibly be familiar with the goings-on in Ramsey Street? And does he catch up with them every lunchtime by satellite at Aiglemont? It couldn't be a more appropriate tune really as all of the racing soap opera characters have been assembled now for the presentation. Margaret Heckler, American Ambassador to Ireland is there. Roarty is there. Blake is there. Smurfit is there. Jerry Hall is close by. Mrs Ambassador hands the trophy over to the grinning Aga who says a few words about it being a great day for Ireland. And an even better one for you, mutters an irreverent local writer.

Sangster gazes at it all over the heads of the onlookers. Smiling faintly and doing his best to lose in the most appropriate and dignified style. The press and cameramen move in. Their shutters click. And then again. And again. They push forward to get a close-up picture of Cumani, Cochrane and the Aga. It's at this point that Sangster, now relegated to the back of the crowd, reaches out instinctively for his wife. And that's how it is as, hand in hand, they walk quietly and unobtrusively away.

12 : Emperors of the Turf

Kahyasi never won another race after his Irish victory. His injury kept him off the course until September when he ran second in the Prix Niel at Longchamp. The following month he finished sixth in the Prix d l'Arc de Triomphe and was subsequently retired to the Aga's Ballymany Stud at The Curragh where he was joined by Doyoun.

Glacial Storm didn't run in the St Leger. He finished unplaced in the King George VI and Queen Elizabeth Diamond Stakes and in the Arc and at the end of the season he was sold.

Of the two one-time Derby favourites, Red Glow flopped in the Grand Prix de Paris and was retired for the year. Unfuwain restored his reputation – and the morale of his trainer, who underwent serious heart surgery in the summer – by finishing second in the King George and fourth in the Arc and in September his stable companion, Minster Son, won the Leger at Doncaster. The following spring though, the racing community were stunned to hear that the Queen's advisers had decided not to renew Major Hern's lease at West Illsley after the end of the 1989 flat-racing year.

Henry Cecil became champion trainer for the eighth time in thirteen years. He topped the table with earnings of £1,186,000 – more than the £370,000 clear of his nearest pursuer, Luca Cumani. Pat Eddery won his sixth jockeys championship with 183 winners – 53 ahead of the runner-up, Willie Carson. Steve Cauthen, who had to miss the last ten weeks of the season due to an injury sustained in a horrific-looking fall at Goodwood, finished fifth. The Kid's accident occurred on the last Saturday in August. On the first Saturday of that month a man died after a drunken brawl involving more than forty racegoers in the car-park of the July course at Newmarket.

Sheikh Mohammed was leading owner for the fourth successive year with prize money totally £1,143,343. He was the only owner to top the million-pound mark and his 122 winners put him twelve clear of his brother Hamdan in the category of races won. Sheikh Ahmed and Sheikh Maktoum finished fifth and eighth in the table. Sangster was in sixth place with winnings of £445,559.

The Maktoum family's most successful horses of 1988 were Indian Skimmer, Diminuendo and Mtoto. Indian Skimmer won Group One races in both Ireland and England in September and October and was then sent on to Kentucky for the Breeders Cup Turf. Diminuendo pulled off a magnificent treble in the Oaks, the Irish Oaks and the Yorkshire Oaks. She finished second to Minster Son in the St Leger and tenth in the Arc. At the end of the year she was retired to join Sheikh Mohammed's ever-more dazzling band of brood-mares at Dalham Hall. Dabaweyaa, Diminuendo's conqueror in the 1,000 Guineas, finished down the field in the Oaks and never quite recaptured her early season form.

Mtoto collected a second Eclipse Stakes as well as the King George for new monitor Stewart but was beaten in the Arc by the Italian five-year-old, Tony Bin, ridden by John Reid. 'Tony' was originally bought for just 3,000 guineas as a foal in Ireland and was intended to be the lead horse for a now forgotten animal called Alex Nureyev. His owner was Veronica Del Bono Gaucci, whose husband, Luciano, is the Vice-President of Roma football club. 'Tony' was apparently named after an Italian painter, one Antonio Bin. As a son of the frankly plebeian stallion, Kampala, now standing in New Zealand, it was hard to believe that Tony's thrilling victory was the prelude to an illustrious career as a commercial sire. And after his subsequent flop in the Japan Cup in Tokyo, it seemed likely that his owners might experience similar problems in trying to get him started at stud to those that befell To Agori Mou's connections after his not quite blue-blooded enough successes in 1981.

Mtoto was not the first English-trained horse to be a narrow and possibly unlucky loser at Longchamp. The Arc is the one day when French racing really comes to life but in modern times only Dancing Brave, Mill Reef, Ballymoss and Ribot have managed to win both the King George VI and the Arc in the same season. Nobody who was there will ever forget the drama and emotion surrounding the

1970 running of the French race in which the immortal Nijinsky, ridden by Lester Piggott, finally met his Waterloo at the hands of the Prix du Jockey Club winner, Sassafras, ridden by the French champion, Yves St Martin.

In 1988 the English horses didn't do that well in the other four Group races on the card either, although Robert Sangster's Handsome Sailor, trained by Barry Hills at Manton, did collect the five-furlong Prix de l'Abbaye after the disqualification of the first past the post, Cadeaux Généreux, ridden by Pat Eddery. Not that these reversals were enough to dampen the excitement and enjoyment of the massive crowd of British racegoers who made the journey across the Channel.

Longchamp is a large, modern race-track. Its carefully designed stands and stairways which can cope with even the biggest crush can best be described as elegant but in a functional sort of way. Fortunately the horse chestnut trees in the middle of the paddock and in the surrounding Bois de Boulogne are as old as the famous paintings of French racing by Degas, Dufy and René Princeteau. And they provide exactly the kind of atmospheric backdrop that any great racing spectacle needs. You can't imagine Europe's end-of-season championship taking place at, say, Kempton Park. Everywhere you look at Longchamp there is a sense of space and scale. The home straight must be the widest of any turf racecourse in the world. The last three and a half furlongs of the Arc all take place in full view of the massive grandstand and this ensures that the race always builds towards an epic climax of passion and excitement.

Even on Arc day the main entrance fee to the Pesage at Longchamp is only about thirty-five francs. This is an absolute snip compared to the fifteen quid that you are required to shell out to enter the Members' Enclosure at Ascot to see the King George. At Longchamp you have unlimited access to almost all parts of the course except for the reserved seating and a special hallowed area behind the paddock which is *privé* unless you're a steward, an owner, a trainer, a jockey, a journalist or a 'connection' of any of these parties. In practice any reasonably well-dressed English racegoer with a quick wit and a fifty-franc note can usually gain access to this inner sanctum. You can then enjoy the distinctive pleasures of a little watering hole at the far side of the enclosure which has been known for years as the Bar des Anglais. Here you can get a deliciously dry bottle of Pol Roger or vintage Bollinger. Unfortunately it's also deliciously expensive. This is horse-racing after all and while it may be cheap to get in, the French still try to weed out the toffs from the *hoi polloi* by making the food and drink prices decidedly on the larcenous side.

Horse-racing occupies a rather ambiguous position in French society. Just as in England it's much appreciated by the aristocracy, many of whom attend on Arc day in their capacity as members of the Société d'Encouragement or French Jockey Club. Société members wear rather natty grey suits and curly-brimmed grey bowler hats that would be considered positively effeminate by the firmer jaws at Newmarket or Ascot. As well as the aristos, the other main racing constituency in France are the hardened turfistes of the Paris metropolitan area.

The French middle classes tend to look down on racing and gambling as somewhat degenerate activities unsuitable for technocratic lawyers and civil servants. By contrast the English middle and upper-middle classes have had the Arc etched into their social diaries now for the best part of twenty-five years and no Arc Sunday would be complete without the serried ranks of brown trilby hats and Hermès scarves. Several hours before the first race you can hear the clunk of a thousand Volvo and BMW car boots opening up in the Pelouse or infield car-parks. Out come the Harrods bags, the baskets and the corkscrews and, with a splash of Volnay and a hunk of *pâté de campagne*, Dick and Sarah, Billy and Anne, Charles and Amanda *et al.* begin yet another pre-race Arc day picnic.

Of even more amusement to the locals are the antics taking place in a strange old building some two furlongs from the winning-post which looks like a cross between a Crimean barracks and the Versailles stable block in the days of Marie Antoinette. On Arc day this pre-war relic of the old Longchamp grandstand is hired out by a Sussex businessman, Ian Fry. He uses it as a private pavilion to entertain the more than 2,000 English racegoers that his company Horse Racing Abroad bring over to Paris each year. Fry's package doesn't exactly offer a quintessentially French experience. It seems designed for the kind of English person who wishes to make sure that there is some corner of a foreign field that will be forever Sandown. Clients get a roast beef lunch, a cream tea and unlimited supplies of gin and tonic. It is rumoured that there is even English lavatory paper for the sensitive. Needless to say the French find this highly entertaining. 'Ce n'est pas Longchamp. C'est Longfield!' proclaimed *Paris Turf* in 1982.

From 1982 to 1987 the Arc was sponsored by Trusthouse Forte but the THF image and style was never really to the taste or palate of most Société members and there was no disguising their delight when they announced their spanking new deal with the Aga. For 1988, CIGA decked out Longchamp surprisingly tastefully with numerous lavish banners advertising the delights of their most desirable joints like the Gritti Palace in Venice, the Excelsior in Rome and the Meurice in Paris. Any one of those could've been the next stop-over for those sensible English punters who backed Tony Bin ante-post in Britain at almost double the 14-1 price he was returned at on the Pari Mutuel. And amongst their number were those two heroic fellows from the Epsom, Smitham and Reedham Express. One of them was so overcome as his horse passed the winning-post in first place that he almost died of a heart attack. Fortunately his wife was able to nurse him back to health before the evening so that he could spend a large part of his winnings on a slap-up dinner, complete with dancing girls and *fin de siècle* romance. Much better that than waste it on embarrassing funeral expenses at Père Lachaise cemetery.

Ravinella was in action on Arc day but she could only finish fourth in the one-mile Prix du Rond Point. She had successfully emulated Miesque by completing the English-French 1,000 Guineas double in the spring but after a defeat at Royal Ascot in June she was rested through the summer. She came back to form with a victory in a $250,000 race at Laurel Park, Maryland in October and from there travelled on to Louisville for the Breeders Cup. There was tragedy for her owners though. In August, Comte Roland de Chambure died of a heart attack on the golf course at Deauville. That meant that a majority of the Société Aland interests had to be dispersed at the end of the year and, at Newmarket's November sales, Ravinella was sold for 1.4 million guineas. Her new owner was Fat Alligator Paulson who had been in-flight on his way from Georgia to Washington, DC at the time of the purchase.

Ravinella's rider, Gary Moore, lost his job as Criquette Head's stable-jockey at the end of 1988. Back in May, he'd appeared in court in Hong Kong, having agreed to give evidence for the prosecution in the trial of the so-called 'Shanghai Syndicate' of gamblers and jockeys who were accused of fixing races for betting purposes. Moore admitted that he had gambled secretly on horses he rode and said he was aware of other jockeys 'pulling their horses' to stop them from winning. He said he'd never done that because he was already making 'a good enough living without it'.

The brilliant Miesque ran three times in France in 1988, winning twice and finishing second on the other occasion. In the Prix Jacques Le Marois at Deauville in August she defeated Warning, who Guy Harwood had brought back triumphantly to win the Sussex Stakes at Goodwood in July. Warning also won the Queen Elizabeth II Stakes at Ascot in September and was then booked for a return match with Miesque in Kentucky.

A few months before the Breeders Cup, Lester Piggott was released from prison on parole. The following April he began a new career offering his daily tips on a British Telecom phone line. The previous month the Big Three bookmaking firms, as they now were – Mecca having taken over Hills – had managed to persuade Douglas Hurd that the new betting levy should be just 0.086 per cent which was even less than the miserable 0.089 per cent that the Jockey Club had been asking for.

Lester's old partner, Vincent O'Brien, didn't have a runner in the 1988 Breeders Cup. But at Keeneland in July he bought four yearlings for Classic Thoroughbreds for a total of $4,300,000. The Maktoums between them purchased thirty-eight yearlings for a gross outlay of $29,285,000 including Swettenham Stud's Northern Dancer colt out of Detroit for £2,450,000. Yet it was Vincent O'Brien who came away with the sales-topper. He was a son of Nijinsky out of a mare called Crimson Saint and O'Brien went to $3,500,000 to secure what he described as 'the best-looking horse I've seen for years with a pedigree to match'. When they got him back to Ballydoyle they named the yearling Royal Academy. With so much speed on his dam's side, his natural target will probably be the 1990 2,000 Guineas and then maybe the Derby. The only worrying thing about Royal Academy is that he's a full brother to Laa Etaab who cost the sheikhs $7 million in 1985. And he never made it to the races.

In September 1988 Classic Thoroughbreds enjoyed their first Group One victory when another Nijinsky colt called Classic Fame won the National Stakes at The Curragh. Later that month Vincent was in action on the company's behalf again at the Tattersalls Highflyer Sale in Newmarket. The atmosphere at the Highflyer in September is vastly different from Keeneland in July. For the English 'vendue' all the domestic owners, trainers and bloodstock agents turn up in regulation flat tweed cap and Husky and everyone tries to pretend that there's nothing very exciting happening at all. Tattersalls Chairman Michael Watt, whose family still run the company, is a very arch fellow with a remarkable resemblance to the late Richard Wattiss, who used to play silly-ass Men from the Ministry in the St Trinian's films. His senior staff also have the aura of the sort of upstairs English character-actors who used to play frightfully snooty butlers with names like Boats or Snooks in pre-war Hollywood comedies. In spite of this off-putting ambience, or lack of it, the Highflyer catalogue still generally offers the best collection of yearlings to come up for sale on the open market in Europe each year. The catalogue is drawn up in much the same way as the Keeneland brochure and many of the most traditional stud farms and respected private breeders are annually represented.

At the 1988 Highflyer, Vincent O'Brien went to 2,400,000 guineas – a Tattersalls yearling record – to secure a son of Northern Dancer sent up by his own Lyonstown Stud and partly owned by Sangster. He also bought a 1,000,000-guinea son of Nijinsky but the Arabs were still dominant. The Maktoums made forty-seven purchases at the four-day sale and their total outlay was more than 8.5 million guineas.

Back at Newmarket racecourse in October another Classic Thoroughbred two-year-old called Saratogan, who was a son of El Gran Senor, finished a close third, on only his second run, in the Dewhurst Stakes. By March 1989, he was ante-post favourite for the 2,000 Guineas.

The growing influence of the Breeders Cup idea could be seen in many aspects of the European racing programme in 1988. Ascot's second 'Festival of British Racing' in September posted total prize money of almost half a million pounds. There was more than fourteen million francs at stake during CIGA's superbly organised Arc weekend and at Phoenix Park racecourse in Dublin, on the day before the Arc, the first ever Cartier Million took place. The Million was the ingenious invention of Jonathan Irwin, the racing impresario who is both managing director of the Park and also boss of the Irish sales company, Goffs. The Million race, for two-year-olds only, was eligible only to horses who had been bought as yearlings at Goffs' sale the previous autumn. There was half a million pounds in prize money to the winning owner and generous prizes right down to tenth place. There was also a million-pound pay-out waiting for any inspired punter who could correctly forecast the first three horses home in the last six races. Nobody collected the first Million bet but the first running of the Million race went to the 7-1 shot Corwyn Bay, a son of the Coolmore stallion Caerleon. Corwyn Bay was trained and bred by Tommy Stack, one of the shrewdest men in Ireland, a former lieutenant to Vincent O'Brien and one of the Coolmore team's top stud-managers. The jubilant post-race scenes in the unsaddling enclosure were reminiscent of an Irish victory at Cheltenham and if racing were a normal industry Jonathan Irwin would've been invited to take over the running of the Jockey Club from the following Monday.

The whole point of the Million was to encourage more people to get involved in racehorse ownership and at the second Goffs Million Sale, the week after the race, there were many new faces as well as a 10 per cent increase in the average sales price to IR86,160 guineas. As Robert Sangster went to IR£1.3 million to get his hands on what would almost certainly be the last Northern Dancer yearling ever to be sold at auction in Europe, Irwin declared, 'I have not seen a buzz like this place all year. We have totally bucked the northern hemisphere trend.'

'Increased owner-participation and investment diversification' was also meant to be one of the main purposes of the Breeders Cup, yet at Keeneland in July it had been the same old faces who had dominated the action. The combined purchases of the Maktoums, O'Brien, Sangster, Lukas and Paulson had accounted for some $46,955,000 or 48 per cent of the gross and the absence of serious new buyers had left the Good Old Boys more worried than ever about just what might happen if the 'A' team players should ever decide to stay at home.

The city of Louisville and the race-track at Churchill Downs, venue of Breeders Cup Five, are roughly a hundred miles up the interstate from Lexington. Of course Louisville had already been host to one major racing occasion in 1988. Out in Kentucky the locals call the Breeders Cup the 'Run for the Riches'. The Kentucky Derby which takes place in May they call the 'Run for the Roses'.

When D. Wayne Lukas first revealed his intention to try and win the 1988 Kentucky Derby, his jinx race run in a state where they seemed to love to see him fail, with a filly and not a colt, the Lukashaters couldn't believe their good fortune. Golden Boy had finally flipped. He was completely wacko. The record books showed that in the 113-year history of the Derby only two fillies had ever managed to beat the colts. To think that he could succeed where twenty-five others had failed was just another example of Lukas's absurd arrogance and disregard for tradition. The old-time trainers from Kentucky and New York like Woody Stephens would kick his butt all over Churchill Downs. Naturally enough D. Wayne didn't quite share their conviction.

The filly he had decided was special enough to merit a crack at the 1988 Derby was called Winning Colours and she was a daughter of the French multiple Group One winner Caro, now standing as a stallion at Spendthrift Farm in the Blue Grass. The filly was owned by Gene Klein and Lukas had paid $575,000 for her at the 1986 Keeneland Select Yearling Sale. What had impressed him about her was that she was a big, strong animal with a fluid and chiselled look that boded well for her race-track career.

Nobody was more scornful of Winning Colours than the grizzled old veteran Woody Stephens, who made no secret of his belief that the Derby was no place for fillies. His candidate for the 1988 classic was Forty Niner, a magnificent-looking chestnut son of Mr Prospector, who was owned by the Hancock family of Claiborne Farm, archetypal representatives of the traditional heart and power base of American racing. Come the great day though, both Winning Colours and Forty Niner were displaced from favouritism before the off by another Kentucky-bred, the unbeaten colt Private Terms, who had posted impressive times in winning two traditional Derby prep races at Aqueduct in New York.

Winning Colours' jockey, Gary Stevens, took his filly into the lead immediately the stalls opened and as they went around the clubhouse turn she was already three and a half lengths up on her field. At the three-quarter-mile marker she'd increased the lead to four lengths and that was still the margin, with the filly seemingly still full of running, as they turned into the home stretch. At this point Forty Niner was back in fourth position. His jockey, Pat Day, who had ridden Theatrical in the Breeders Cup in Hollywood, now went into overdrive. Hurling himself at the leader and going after his mount like Piggott after Roberto at Epsom in 1972. He was recorded to administer no fewer than twenty-one cracks of the whip to Forty Niner as he slowly closed the gap to three lengths, two lengths, one length . . . but it was just too late. Winning Colours crossed the line inches in front. The winning margin was a nose. Risen Star, who had enjoyed little luck in running and who was fourteen lengths back at the four-furlong pole, ran on strongly up the stretch to be only three and a a quarter lengths away in third.

For Lukas and Klein this Derby victory was the sweetest, the most jubilant, the most vindicating moment of their racing lives. Woody Stephens could barely stomach it. 'Now come after my five Belmonts' – meaning his five victories in the Belmont Stakes – he growled, in the unsaddling enclosure. Lukas would do that. First though he was heading for round two of the Triple Crown. The Preakness Stakes, over nine and a half furlongs at Pimlico racecourse near Baltimore a fortnight later. The week leading up to the Preakness was completely dominated by the obsessive determination of Stephens to get even with his younger rival. Every interview, every question by his barn in the days prior to 21 May, ended in the same statement. 'We're going after the filly.' Just how far he was prepared to go was quickly demonstrated when the race itself got underway.

Pat Day on Forty Niner seemed to set out quite deliberately not so much to try and win the race himself but to ensure the downfall of the favourite. Through the first six furlongs his main tactic seemed to be to herd Winning Colours away from the rail and to push her further and further towards the outside. At the top of the stretch Eddie Delahoussaye, riding Risen Star, suddenly found himself presented with an unusually wide opening along the inside rail and took full advantage of it. He kicked Risen Star through the gap and all the way to the line which they reached with one and a quarter lengths to spare over Winning Colours who had finally shaken off the unwelcome attentions of Forty Niner, who himself completely capitulated in the stretch to finish a tired seventh of fourteen.

This time Lukas's post-race mood was grim-faced and silent. Many onlookers were convinced that Stephens had ordered Day to stitch the filly up and *Daily Racing Form*, the American *Sporting Life*, went so far as to print a front-page editorial two days later openly accusing Woody of malevolent and unsportsmanlike behaviour. The sizzling afterglow of the incident was still in the air when the two Preakness principals met again three weeks later in New York in the Belmont Stakes over a mile and a half.

At Belmont Park, one thing was quickly apparent. The exhausting battles of Churchill Downs and Pimlico had completely worn out Winning Colours. At Belmont she was beaten all of $41\frac{3}{4}$ lengths into last place in a field of six. The sight to relish this time was the performance of the winner, Risen Star, who galloped his five rivals into the ground, coming home $14\frac{2}{3}$ lengths clear in a time of 2 minutes 25.4 seconds, the second-fastest Belmont time in history. The fastest having been set, appropriately enough, by the Star's sire, Secretariat, a decade and a half before.

Risen Star was now arguably the pre-eminent three-year-old colt on the North American continent, the Kahyasi of the 1988 season in the USA. For winning two legs of the Triple Crown, his owners, Ronnie Lamarque and Louis Roussel jun., picked up a million-dollar bonus from the Chrysler Corporation. Not that they needed the money. Even by American standards of wealth, Louis Roussel is a rich man. He's into banking, he's into insurance and he also owns a controlling share in the Fair Grounds race-track in his home city of New Orleans. Down in the Big Easy they refer to Roussel as 'King Louie'. He's very religious, naturally. He will proudly display the chair in his den that Pope John Paul sat on during a visit to the city in 1987. At the same time his black moustache and his slim, dark looks give him the aura of a rather sinister character in a Revenge

Tragedy. It's not that he probably isn't a terrific guy. It's just that he's, well, kind of disconcerting. As for Louie's partner, Lamarque, he's a used-car dealer, but an extremely prosperous one, also in the state of Louisiana. Apparently he believes that he's something of a red-hot crooner too. After each of the Star's big victories, Ronnie would appear in the unsaddling enclosure with a new, hastily written ballad about the horse's exploits which he would proceed to sing to his captive audience of pressmen. He thinks he's Mel Tormé, Tony Bennett, even. One or two of his friends, not to mention his enemies, say that it stinks.

After the Belmont, Roussel and Lamarque might've been contemplating a rest and then a trip to Saratoga in August followed by a fall campaign culminating in the Breeders Cup. Sadly for them though, the Belmont was to be Risen Star's last race. An old suspensory ligament injury had been aggravated and through late June into early July the colt was confined to his stall at Belmont Park. While statements declared that no decision would be taken on the horse's future until after another ultrasound examination on 24 July, Louis Roussel moved fast. A 50 per cent share in the Star was sold to Walmac Warnerton for $7 million giving him an overall syndication value of fourteen million bucks. King Louie had made sure that for the 1989 covering season his baby would be joining Alleged and Nureyev at one of the most élite farms in the Blue Grass.

Roussel and Lamarque were in town all the same for the Breeders Cup. As were D. Wayne Lukas and Winning Colours. The grey filly was returning to the sight of her most famous victory to compete in the nine-furlong Breeders Cup Distaff. And her most formidable rival was set to be another great filly, the almost legendary Personal Ensign, a four-year-old daughter of Private Account, trained by Shug McGaughey and owned by the old-money blue-blood, Ogden Phipps of New York. The Distaff was to be Personal Ensign's final appearance and she was bidding to retire undefeated after a thirteen-race career.

The press encouraged Lukas and McGaughey to talk a good race even before their horses had walked out on to the track. D. Wayne, in shades and windbreaker, was typically crisp and positive, reminding the handicappers that Winning Colours was exceptionally tough to pass but that she might not be at her best over an 'off' (wet or sloppy) track. Shug McGaughey was confident that if Personal Ensign ran her usual race, the others would simply be chasing the place money. He described how the Phipps family grandchildren got so excited the night before her races that they could never sleep. So they sat up all night long reading clippings and articles about her famous victories. 'And on Sunday morning,' he added with a smile, 'they should have much more to read about.'

Gary Stevens' tactics in the Distaff were exactly the same as those he employed in the Kentucky Derby. He took his filly to the front from the moment that the stalls opened and as they raced down the back stretch he'd already built up an incredible ten-length lead over his nearest rival. Coming out of the far turn, Personal Ensign was still eight lengths adrift. But then as they swung into the home stretch and faced up to the run towards the line she began slowly, slowly, slowly to claw the advantage back. Roared on by the emotional and partisan 71,237-strong crowd, beside themselves with excitement at seeing this great popular heroine duelling all the way up the stretch with a Kentucky Derby winner, Stevens and Personal Ensign finally, narrowly, closed the gap. They went past the wire together but the photograph gave it to Personal Ensign by a nose. And so it was that she bowed out from the racecourse as America's first undefeated champion in eighty years.

The defeat of Winning Colours, which was hardly a defeat anyway, was Wayne Lukas's only setback at Breeders Cup Five. With his selected riders all wearing aero-dynamic Flo-Jo silks, he sent out the winners of three of the other seven races – the Sprint and the Colts and Fillies Juvenile – as well as two other second places, besides Winning Colours, and a third. His total haul of prize money was a staggering $2,190,000. And in the brief five-year history of the series he had now sent out nine winners. The top sports-photographers of America captured some inimitable pictures of Lukas in his moment of triumph. Especially the sight of him out there on the track by the winning-post, kitted out in his hat and his Beverly Hills rainwear, and defiantly embracing his principal jockey, the forty-six-year-old Angel Cordero jun., the man, the boss, the irreplaceable Roberto Duran of the weighing room.

Yet little more than four months after the Breeders Cup, Lukas was to face sensational allegations that one of his horses, Crown Collection, had twice tested positive for cocaine after competing in races at Del Mar race-track in Southern California in the August and September of 1988. Lukas vigorously rebutted all the charges against himself and his staff and the case was due to be heard in the early summer of 1989.

Back at Churchill Downs, at 3.25 on the afternoon of Saturday 5 November, Louisville's mayor, Jerry Abramson, presented the Distaff trophy to Ogden Phipps. Personal Ensign was clapped and cheered away and this was the cue for the twelve contestants in the Breeders Cup Mile on turf to make their way down from the training barns. The general consensus of the large gallery of English, French and Irish professionals who had gathered in Kentucky was that in Indian Skimmer, Warning and Miesque, European racing was being represented by three of the best horses ever to cross the Atlantic. Once again though, for two of them at least ... the Breeders Cup would be a race too far.

The first thing that the Europeans discovered on arriving in Kentucky was that Louisville in early November was, oh boy, oh my, a far far cry from luscious, sunny and glamorous LA. To start with the weather was supposed to be crisp and autumnal. Instead it was first grey and humid and then grey and wet and extremely cold. Louisville, which is situated on the banks of the Ohio river, a fence-sitter between North and South, may be a wild address in Derby week but nothing much seems to happen there for the rest of the year. It certainly has a very different atmosphere from Lexington, down in the Blue Grass. It's quite an industrial centre and, amongst other things, manufactures half of the world's bourbon output, but for all its modern downtown shopping malls and riverfront plaza it still feels like a large, provincial Mid-western town trying to be a city. For Cup week, Breeders Cup Ltd were holed up in a hotel called the Galt House which from the outside looked like a fifty-storey concrete blancmange, and on the inside was filled with miles of plush red carpet and a great many imitation Versailles antiques.

All the high and low-life character of Louisville is provided by the racing fraternity. The race-track itself is about six miles out of town in a somewhat dilapidated and run-down area of single-storey white, weatherboard, low-rent housing. Across the highway from the training barns is Larry's Souvenirs Shop, which was selling a tasty line in Bush and Quayle stickers, and an adult movie theatre, which was playing *Backside to the Future*. The surroundings may not be exactly majestic or elegantly beautiful but the racecourse itself is a grand old structure with its huge wooden stand and its famous twin spires. There was a time when Churchill Downs threatened to slide downhill, like Epsom, but an extensive refurbishment programme, especially designed for the Cup, had brought it numerous bright new bars and refreshment areas and two whole new tiers of covered seating at the top of the clubhouse section. The delicious ground-floor Eclipse Restaurant and the Sky Terrace on level four, echoed to the clink of ice and the slurp of Scotch Soda and on Cup day they were awash with vast helpings of turkey, lobster and beef. And the sheer professionalism and quality of the service was, naturally, an entire culture away from Letheby and Christopher. (Professionalism was also the key word for the way in which the more than seventy thousand people and automobiles who attended the Cup were directed in and out of the racecourse with scarcely a traffic jam and certainly never a glimpse of a BR official or the Smitham and Reedham Express.)

The Downs press-box with its pictures of famous reporters, like Red Smith, and its photographs of past Kentucky Derby winners, including Northern Dancer, is right up at the top of the building. Sheafs of update notes on the training progress of the various Breeders Cup aspirants were pinned to the walls. 'Champion English trainer Henry Cecil says the going is like dead fish' proclaimed one of them. This was not entirely true. What Henry really said was that the going was sort of 'deadish' but, understandably, the local reporters were not used to his mumbled, English, upper-class vowels.

The mile-long dirt course – a left-handed oval as always in the States – and the brand-new seven-furlong Matt Winn turf course which is on its inside, looked tight and sharp, not at all sympathetic to European horses. But the start and finish of all of the races would take place in full view of the grandstand and that's what helps to give these spectacular American occasions an intimacy and a theatricality that is rarely present at Newmarket.

Some of the outside stairways at the back of the stand had, like the West Pier at Brighton, been roped off as unsafe for large gatherings. Yet the continuing presence of the old, white wood and the wrought-iron railings, supplied the setting with a tangibly atmospheric aura, redolent of the era of Man O'War and Gallant Fox, of white fedoras and prohibition whiskey. What was not redolent of prohibition was the 'Hospitality Village' which seemed to have been exported intact from Sandown, complete with hostess girls and white picket-fences.

The night of 3 November was hot and oppressive, but early the following morning the city awoke to a tumultuous thunderstorm with bolts of lightning shooting dramatically across the sky. It was wet and grey and muddy down by the training barns at 7 a.m. that Friday morning. You longed for some California blue sky, for Sunset Boulevard and the Ray-bans. The European runners had gone through quarantine in a converted warehouse across the street. Now they were in isolation behind a high wire-fence in Barn 45. They were due to work on the turf course after the American horses had finished on the dirt.

Up pulled a black stretch-limo and out got an Arab in an Alain Delon trenchcoat. He was followed by Henry and Julie Cecil and by Michael Roberts who, in the enforced absence of Steve Cauthen, would be riding Indian Skimmer. Gucci Shoes, fag in hand, was wearing a suede jacket, a polo-necked jersey, jeans and cowboy boots. Julie, sucking a sweet as always, was in a waterproof mack and cap. She looked just like an upper-crust English tourist about to take a walk around Florence on a wet afternoon. By comparison with the other two, the pinched-faced Michael Roberts looked about two foot six inches tall.

The English racing press were all there to greet them. Most of them, taken by surprise by the inclement weather, looked cold, wet and bedraggled – like the ill-equipped family that you don't want to get stuck with on a ten-day package to Majorca. There was Tim Richards of the *Post*, Jim Stanford of the *Mail*, genial Chris Poole from the *Evening Standard*, Geoff Lester of the *Sporting Life* with his moonboot walk and his pen and paper, Geoff's mate, Mike Dillon of Ladbrokes, very dapper in his blazer and Breeders Cup hat and even the three boys from the Newmarket gallops. Bruffscot was there of course. Seconded to NBC for the week and looking quite superb in his trenchcoat, baseball cap and trainers. He kept scurrying around in that frightfully important way of his as if he'd already jogged three times around the course before anybody else had even got out of bed.

Roberts and Indian Skimmer came out on to the course followed by Henry in riding cap and blue-fringed chaps and mounted up on a decidedly frisky little pony. 'Good morning, everybody,' he called, cheerfully. 'Morning, boys. Everybody all right?' The Skimmer did a gentle three-quarter-mile spin and Cecil seemed satisfied that the ground wouldn't be too firm for her. The story was that, worried about her recurrent neck and shoulder problems, he had wanted to give her a shot of Bute before the race but had been prevented from doing so by the (much-resented) interference of the Senior Steward of the Jockey Club.

François Boutin would administer 'un petit peu' of Bute to Miesque. He thought she was entitled to it as most of her American rivals in the Mile would be using it. To some eyes Miesque looked quite devastatingly strong and well as she almost danced out on to the track. A majority of the English press though were agin her. They had convinced themselves that Warning couldn't lose and in any case Jim Stanford, for one, kept prattling on about the fact that she'd grown her 'winter woolly'. M. Boutin quietly insisted, through the translating services of Patricia, that while the going was a little soft, Miesque had been trained for this race all year. So who were you going to believe? Lamorlaye's silver fox? Or Jolly Jim?

Guy Harwood marched ferociously past in the background. He was wearing his flat cap and Barbour and he looked as if he was about to saddle one in the Adjacent Hunts race at the Southdown point-to-point. After the Dancing Brave disaster the whole event appeared to be something of a strain for the clean-limbed Guy. When Warning came out of the barn though, he too looked in superb condition. Dark and fit and immensely powerful. Pat Eddery was positively oozing confidence. It was Pat the press-boys' friend today, not the Pat the poor deaf-mute.

As Eddery held court outside the barn gates, Freddie Head, sporting a dashing new neckerchief, swaggered past towards the car-park. Somebody threw him a question. 'Do you think you'll beat Warning?' Freddie paused and stared at them for a moment with his best 'Le Pissed Off' look. 'Who knows?' He shrugged his shoulders. 'If she like ze course . . . and if it's not too wet . . . I zink she win.' And with that, contemptuous little Freddie joined Papa and Criquette in the back of their mahogany-coloured Chevrolet station-wagon and the Head family roared off hungrily for breakfast.

On Friday afternoon there was another apocalyptic thunderstorm with black skies and a tornado warning. 'If you hear the sirens, duck under the table and keep the hell away from the God-damned windows.' On Friday evening, the thirsty attendant press corps attended an upbeat Breeders Cup cocktail party held in their honour in a nightclub on a riverboat called the *Belle of Ohio*. The hospitality was truly lavish and if journalists were subject to similar rules as English racehorses and forbidden to write under the influence of alcohol then quite a few of those present would've been quite unable to file their copy the following day.

The rain came down throughout the party and it was still raining at dawn on the great day itself. By 3.40 p.m. though, as the runners came out on to the track for the 1983 Breeders Cup Mile, the conditions had changed to a persistent drizzle, but it was also grey and bitterly cold. The twelve horses, accompanied by their ponies, paraded up and down in front of the crowd and then were led back down the wet dirt stretch, which had turned to slop and mud with all the water running off the top, and then across to the inside turf-course starting stalls.

The turf course, which has a sand base, was expected to ride on the soft side of good. The latest *pari mutuel* odds were 2-1 Miesque and Warning, 6-1 Woody Stephens' runner Bet Twice and 18-1 the

almost unconsidered Ravinella. 'This is it,' said the announcer
generously. 'The Mile championship of Europe. Warning for England
... against Miesque for France!' Pause. 'And they're running!' And
oh my. Oh dear, oh dear. What an unmitigated disaster it turned out
to be ... if you'd backed Warning.

Pat Eddery would insist afterwards that his colt could never
handle the course and that he was never going on what he says was a
soft and slippery surface. Looking at it another way you could say
that Warning's chance was gone from the moment that he missed the
break. And then Pat, incomprehensibly on such a sharp track,
seemed to deliberately try and settle him in at the rear of the field as
if they were riding round Goodwood. Going down the back stretch
Warning was already way off the pace and he was a beaten horse well
before he even got to the turn into the straight. And Miesque? She
was simply breathtaking. Freddie jumped her out fast and had her in
about fifth place, right on the heels of the pacemakers, all the way
down the far side. Coming off the final bend he collected her and
gathered her up and when he asked her to go she did it, she did it
again, with all of that superlative speed that you'd seen so many
times before in her magnificent career. She had four lengths in hand
at the wire. The Americans were on their feet. Freddie kept punching
the air in triumph as he cantered back to receive his winner's
bouquet of flowers which was fetchingly spread across his minute
saddle. Niarchos was there in person to collect his prize. 'It's a lovely
race,' he said. 'We're going to come every year.' Bruffscot endeav-
oured to get out on to the track and interview Pat but the proceedings
were suddenly cut short by the appearance of the thunderous
Harwood. Miesque's racing days were over. The following spring she
would be on her way to Claiborne Farm. To be covered by Mr
Prospector. Warning would stay in training as a four-year-old.

At half-past four the Maktoum entourage entered the paddock:
Sheikh Mohammed, John Leat, Bill Smith, Alec Notman, the
Honourable Acton, Pasty Face Stroud, and Henry – no hat, blue
suit, light blue shirt and dark blue tie, brown suede shoes and
cigarette. While the Governor of Kentucky was presenting the Colts
Juvenile trophy to Gene Klein, Henry was saddling up Indian
Skimmer in stall number one. The filly's American groom was
wearing a purple satin Breeders Cup jacket. Henry seemed to like
the look of it. Bruffscot dashed over in his green plimsolls. Henry
didn't like the look of them at all. The Sheikh kept looking around
and smiling in a rather bemused but enthusiastic way. Three stalls
away from the Skimmer they were saddling up America's champion

turf horse of 1988, Sunshine Forever. The two camps looked one
another in the eye. A separate TV camera followed each of them as
they made their way out through the tunnel and on to the track.
Sunshine Forever's jockey, Angel Cordero, with two wins behind
him already, looked harder and meaner than ever. You almost feared
for Michael Roberts in this company.

You could feel another ripple of tension and excitement spreading
through the crowd as the bugler led the field of ten out into the
middle. Up above them a small bi-plane flew across the sky trailing
an election ad. 'At the wire . . . it's Duke and Lloyd.' Bet on that
one and you'd be bankrolling your bookmaker's Florida holiday for
the next ten years.

Alas though, if you'd taken the 6-5 about Indian Skimmer, you
wouldn't be collecting on that one either. For once, an almost
unheard of occurrence in America, the race was run at a moderate
pace and the grey daughter of Storm Bird seemed to pull too hard
and never really settled for 'Muis' Roberts. She was not disgraced
though. She actually hit the front for a few brief strides at the head
of the straight but then her stamina gave out on the rain-softened
ground. The race went to the 12-1 chance Great Communicator, a
five-year-old gelding who had been jacked up with both Bute and
Lasix and who made virtually every yard of the running. Sunshine
Forever was half a length second and the Skimmer finished another
three-quarters of a length away, in third.

Cecil, the Arabs, Geoff Lester, Bruffscot and the gang all charged
out on to the slop to ruin their shoes and greet the beaten favourite.
Henry was adamant that she'd run a fantastic race and that he was
very proud of her. And she would stay in training as a five-year-old.
Cecil and the Sheikh stayed out on the track in deep and close
consultation as another presentation ceremony began away to their
left. And then finally, as their filly was led back up to the concrete
training barns they took one last yearning look at it all . . . and
walked away.

And so there we were. Six races down . . . and just one left to go.
It may have been all over for the British and the French but at
5.12 p.m. as the runners arrived from the barns for the final contest
of the afternoon, the three-million-dollar Breeders Cup Classic, the
climax was still to come. Out back behind the stands the garbage
bins were filling up with abandoned paper cups and Budweiser cans,
half-eaten hot-dogs and torn-up pages of the *Daily Racing Form*. In
the Eclipse Restaurant, the Gin Ritz ladies and their well-heeled,
well-groomed Eastern and Old Southern companions were replete

with food and drink, with power and excitement. And up in the Sky
Terrace on level four, as you looked down the row of the most
expensive tables by the window, you could easily have been looking
at a curtain call for almost every character in the show. 'Ladies and
gentlemen. Will you please put your hands together for Mr Woody
Stephens. Mr Peter Brant. Gene Klein. Fat Alligator Paulson and his
US cavalryman's fur-collar overcoat. Michael Smurfit. Timmy Hyde.
Khalid Abdulla. Jeremy Tree. François Boutin. Louis Romanet.
John Magnier. David Nagle. And Mr Charles 'Fatty' Benson. Yes,
he's here too. Let's hear it, please, ladies and gentlemen.'

Outside now the sky was darkening and all over the racecourse the
lights were coming on: in the restaurants and bars; in the weighing
rooms and museum and in all the training barns across the other side
of the track. The tractor moved the stalls back over on to the dirt
course. And finally at 5.23 the bugle sounded and the nine runners
for the Classic, the biggest prize of them all, made their way out on
to the course. And just as at Hollywood Park the previous year,
Breeders Cup Ltd had been rewarded with a glittering field. Ferdinand may have been retired after all to Claiborne Farm but the
Hancock family's controversial three-year-old Forty Niner was there.
Ogden Phipps's Seeking The Gold and Personal Flag were there.
Plus the speed-horse, Waquoit. The six-times winner, Cutlass Reality.
And at the head of them all, the four-year-old son of Alydar that they
were calling . . . America's Horse. The 1987 Kentucky Derby winner.
The colt so narrowly touched off by Ferdinand in the 1987 Classic
and the winner of seven of his nine races in 1988, the last four of
them without Lasix. Alysheba.

Due to the demands of West Coast television it was almost 5.35
before the runners were finally ready to be loaded up into the stalls.
And if they hadn't started then, it was going to be virtual darkness
anyway. In the final few moments before the race began, the course
commentator, NBC's Don Durkin, set the scene up perfectly:
'Breeders Cup day is a day to crown champions and this *is* the jewel
in the crown. The $3 million Breeders Cup Classic . . . the richest
horse-race in the world.'

Waquoit, the horse who had won Belmont Park's Jockey Club
Gold Cup in the slop, was the early leader. Alysheba, breaking from
the number five draw, settled in fourth in the run to the first turn.
Racing down the back stretch it was still Waquoit and Slew City
Slew with Cutlass Reality in third and Alysheba holding his position.
As they reached the turn into the home straight there were literally
six horses fanned out across the track and the crowd were almost

hysterical with excitement. Alysheba passed Cutlass Reality and then took the lead off Waquoit at the furlong pole. Only now though, racing on the outside and making ground up rapidly in the diminishing light, Seeking The Gold and Pat Day were coming with a thrilling late charge. Waquoit was trying to hang in there. And Forty Niner, who had lost ground at the far turn, was beginning to run on again through the middle. But Alysheba would not give in. With less than fifty yards to go he dug down deep into his reserves of courage and class and stuck out his neck and battled and battled his way to the wire. The NBC amplified commentary said it all: 'It's Seeking The Gold and Alysheba. (Louder) Seeking The Gold. (Louder) Alysheba ... and oh yes ... America's Horse has done it!'

The great gaggle of connections and press and photographers streamed out on to the track. If it hadn't been for the lights it would have been completely dark. The ecstatic crowd were still rocking with tumultuous emotion. Alysheba had now won $6,679,242 in his racing career, making him the biggest single money-winner in racing history. And that career was over too. He would now be retired as a stallion to Lanes End Farm.

Trainer Jack Van Berg was in tears. The atmosphere everywhere was wild and crazy. The press office produced flags and banners bearing the names of the most famous and successful stallions: Mr Prospector, Northern Dancer, Nijinsky, Nureyev, Danzig, Alydar, Seattle Slew. Over the public address system they were playing the title music from *Rocky*. Everything was so totally and joyously over the top that you felt as if the huge illuminated grandstand, looming up out of the darkness, could suddenly take off and fly away into the night. Like some enormous intoxicated space ship at the climax of a Spielberg movie. 'What an end,' people were saying, 'What a climax! "I got vision and the rest of the world is wearing bifocals."''

The 1989 Breeders Cup is already scheduled to take place at Gulfstream Park, Miami. And in 1990 it moves on to Belmont Park, New York. But beyond that? Well, out in Louisville they have little doubt about that. After the drama of 5 November 1988, it would surely be only appropriate if the single most exciting event in flat-racing should in future permanently reside at Churchill Downs, Kentucky. The very heart and home of the Emperors of the Blue Grass.

Postscript

On 4 May 1989, Michael Stoute finally broke his duck in the 1,000 Guineas by saddling the first two fillies home. The winner, Musical Bliss, sired by The Minstrel, was ridden by Walter Swinburn. The runner-up, Kerrera, sired by Diesis, was ridden by Pat Eddery. They were both owned by Sheikh Mohammed.

Two days later, the 1989 2,000 Guineas was won by a chestnut son of Blushing Groom called Nashwan. He was ridden by Willie Carson, trained by Dick Hern and owned by Sheikh Hamdan Al Maktoum. His first English classic winner at last.

Major Hern, who was there in his wheel chair to greet his champion in the unsaddling enclosure, was accorded a prolonged and emotional ovation by the Newmarket crowd.

Saratogan finished ninth.

Four and a half weeks later at Epsom Downs, Nashwan won the Derby by five lengths. Classic Thoroughbreds' Classic Fame finished seventh. By 4 July the Company's share price had fallen to 19p.

The 1989 Oaks was won by the Aga Khan's filly Aliysa, trained by Michael Stoute. It was subsequently revealed that she had failed her post-race dope test.

In the same week as the Derby and the Oaks, the California State Racing Board announced that they were dropping all charges against the D. Wayne Lukas stable on the grounds of insufficient evidence.

Index